Published Titles

Stated Preference Methods Using R, *Hideo Aizaki, Tomoaki Nakatani, and Kazuo Sato*

Using R for Numerical Analysis in Science and Engineering, *Victor A. Bloomfield*

Event History Analysis with R, *Göran Broström*

Computational Actuarial Science with R, *Arthur Charpentier*

Statistical Computing in C++ and R, *Randall L. Eubank and Ana Kupresanin*

Reproducible Research with R and RStudio, Second Edition, *Christopher Gandrud*

Introduction to Scientific Programming and Simulation Using R, Second Edition, *Owen Jones, Robert Maillardet, and Andrew Robinson*

Nonparametric Statistical Methods Using R, *John Kloke and Joseph McKean*

Displaying Time Series, Spatial, and Space-Time Data with R, *Oscar Perpiñán Lamigueiro*

Programming Graphical User Interfaces with R, *Michael F. Lawrence and John Verzani*

Analyzing Sensory Data with R, *Sébastien Lê and Theirry Worch*

Parallel Computing for Data Science: With Examples in R, C++ and CUDA, *Norman Matloff*

Analyzing Baseball Data with R, *Max Marchi and Jim Albert*

Growth Curve Analysis and Visualization Using R, *Daniel Mirman*

R Graphics, Second Edition, *Paul Murrell*

Data Science in R: A Case Studies Approach to Computational Reasoning and Problem Solving, *Deborah Nolan and Duncan Temple Lang*

Multiple Factor Analysis by Example Using R, *Jérôme Pagès*

Customer and Business Analytics: Applied Data Mining for Business Decision Making Using R, *Daniel S. Putler and Robert E. Krider*

Implementing Reproducible Research, *Victoria Stodden, Friedrich Leisch, and Roger D. Peng*

Graphical Data Analysis with R, *Antony Unwin*

Using R for Introductory Statistics, Second Edition, *John Verzani*

Advanced R, *Hadley Wickham*

Dynamic Documents with R and knitr, Second Edition, *Yihui Xie*

Reproducible Research with R and RStudio

Second Edition

Christopher Gandrud

Hertie School of Governance

Berlin, Germany

CRC Press
Taylor & Francis Group
Boca Raton London New York

CRC Press is an imprint of the
Taylor & Francis Group, an **informa** business
A CHAPMAN & HALL BOOK

Reprint 2019

CRC Press
Taylor & Francis Group
6000 Broken Sound Parkway NW, Suite 300
Boca Raton, FL 33487-2742

ISBN: 978-0-367-24124-7 (hbk)

Digitally Printed at Replika Press Pvt. Ltd.

Visit the Taylor & Francis Web site at
http://www.taylorandfrancis.com

and the CRC Press Web site at
http://www.crcpress.com

For sale in India, Pakistan, Nepal, Bhutan, Bangladesh and Sri Lanka only.

Contents

Preface

This book has its genesis in my PhD research at the London School of Economics. I started the degree with questions about the 2008/09 financial crisis and planned to spend most of my time researching capital adequacy requirements. But I quickly realized that I would actually spend a large proportion of my time learning the day-to-day tasks of data gathering, analysis, and results presentation. After plodding through for a while with Word, Excel, and Stata, my breaking point came while reentering results into a regression table after I had tweaked one of my statistical models, yet again. Surely there was a better way to *do* research that would allow me to spend more time answering my research questions. Making research reproducible for others also means making it better organized and efficient for yourself. My search for a better way led me straight to the tools for reproducible computational research.

The reproducible research community is very active, knowledgeable, and helpful. Nonetheless, I often encountered holes in this collective knowledge, or at least had no resource organize it all together as a whole. That is my intention for this book: to bring together the skills I have picked up for actually doing and presenting computational research. Hopefully, the book, along with making reproducible research more widely used, will save researchers hours of googling, so they can spend more time addressing their research questions.

Changes to the Second Edition

The tools of reproducible research have developed rapidly since the first edition of this book was published just two years ago. The second edition has been updated to incorporate the most important of these advancements, including discussions of:

- The *rmarkdown* package, which allows you to create reproducible research documents in PDF, HTML, and Microsoft Word formats using the simple and intuitive Markdown syntax.
- Improvements and changes to RStudio's interface and capabilities, such as its new tools for handling R Markdown documents.
- Expanded *knitr* R code chunk capabilities.
- The `kable` function in the *knitr* package and the *texreg* package for dynamically creating tables to present your data and statistical results.

- An improved discussion of file organization allowing you to take full advantage of relative file paths so that your documents are more easily reproducible across computers and systems.

- The *dplyr*, *magrittr*, and *tidyr* packages for fast data manipulation.

- Numerous changes to R syntax in user-created packages.

- Changes to GitHub's and Dropbox's interfaces.

Acknowledgements

I would not have been able to write this book without many people's advice and support. Foremost is John Kimmel, acquisitions editor at Chapman and Hall. He approached me in Spring 2012 with the general idea and opportunity for this book. Other editors at Chapman and Hall and Taylor and Francis have greatly contributed to this project, including Marcus Fontaine. I would also like to thank all of the book's reviewers whose helpful comments have greatly improved it. The first edition's reviewers include:

- Jeromy Anglim, Deakin University

- Karl Broman, University of Wisconsin, Madison

- Jake Bowers, University of Illinois, Urbana-Champaign

- Corey Chivers, McGill University

- Mark M. Fredrickson, University of Illinois, Urbana-Champaign

- Benjamin Lauderdale, London School of Economics

- Ramnath Vaidyanathan, McGill University

The developer and blogging community has also been incredibly important for making this book possible. Foremost among these people is Yihui Xie. He is the main developer behind the *knitr* package, co-developer of *rmarkdown*, and also an avid blog writer and commenter. Without him the ability to do reproducible research would be much harder and the blogging community that spreads knowledge about how to do these things would be poorer. Other great contributors to the reproducible research community include Carl Boettiger, Karl Broman, Markus Gesmann (who developed *googleVis*), Rob Hyndman, and Hadley Wickham (who has developed numerous very useful R packages). Thank you also to Victoria Stodden and Michael Malecki for helpful suggestions. And, of course, thank you to everyone at RStudio (especially JJ Allaire) for creating an increasingly useful program for reproducible research.

The second edition has benefited immensely from first edition readers' comments and suggestions. For a list of their valuable contributions, please see the book's GitHub Issues page `https://GitHub.com/christophergandrud/Rep-Res-Book/issues` and the first edition's Errata page `http://christophergandrud.GitHub.io/RepResR-RStudio/errata.htm`.

My students at Yonsei University were an important part of making the first edition. One of the reasons that I got interested in using many of the tools covered in this book, like using *knitr* in slideshows, was to improve a course I taught there: Introduction to Social Science Data Analysis. I tested many of the explanations and examples in this book on my students. Their feedback has been very helpful for making the book clearer and more useful. Their experience with using these tools on Microsoft Windows computers was also important for improving the book's Windows documentation. Similarly, my students at the Hertie School of Governance inspired and tested key sections of the second edition.

The vibrant community at Stack Overflow `http://stackoverflow.com/` and Stack Exchange `http://stackexchange.com/` are always very helpful for finding answers to problems that plague any computational researcher. Importantly, the sites make it easy for others to find the answers to questions that have already been asked.

My wife, Kristina Gandrud, has been immensely supportive and patient with me throughout the writing of this book (and pretty much my entire academic career). Certainly this is not the proper forum for musing about marital relations, but I'll do a musing anyways. Having a person who supports your interests, even if they don't completely share them, is immensely helpful for a researcher. It keeps you going.

Stylistic Conventions

I use the following conventions throughout this book:

- **Abstract variables**: Abstract variables, i.e. variables that do not represent specific objects in an example, are in `ALL CAPS TYPEWRITER TEXT`.
- **Clickable buttons**: Clickable Buttons are in `typewriter text`.
- **Code**: All code is in `typewriter text`.
- **Filenames and directories**: Filenames and directories more generally are printed in *italics*. I use CamelBack for file and directory names.
- **File extensions**: Like filenames, file extensions are *italicized*.
- **Individual variable values**: Individual variable values mentioned in the text are in *italics*.
- **Objects**: Objects are printed in *italics*. I use CamelBack for object names.
- **Object columns**: Data frame object columns are printed in *italics*.
- **Packages**: **R** packages are printed in *italics*.
- **Windows and RStudio panes**: Open windows and RStudio panes are written in *italics*.
- **Variable names**: Variable names are printed in **bold**. I use CamelBack for individual variable names.

Required R Packages

In this book I discuss how to use a number of user-written R packages for reproducible research. Many of these packages are not included in the default R installation. They need to be installed separately.

Note: in general you should aim to minimize the number of packages that your research depends on. Doing so will lessen the possibility that your code will "break" when a package is updated. This book depends on relatively many packages because of its special and unusual purpose of illustrating a variety of tools that you can use for reproducible research.

To install key user-written packages discussed in this book, copy the following code and paste it into your R console:

```
install.packages(c("brew", "countrycode",
                   "devtools", "dplyr",
                   "ggplot2", "googleVis",
                   "knitr", "MCMCpack",
                   "repmis", "RCurl",
                   "rmarkdown", "texreg",
                   "tidyr", "WDI",
                   "xtable", "Zelig"))
```

Once you enter this code, you may be asked to select a CRAN "mirror" to download the packages from.[1] Simply select the mirror closest to you.

In Chapter 9 we use the *Zelig* package (Owen et al., 2013) to create a simple Bayesian normal linear regression. For this to work properly you will need to install an additional package called *ZeligBayesian* (Owen, 2011). To do this, type the following code into your R console:

```
install.packages("ZeligBayesian",
                  repos = "http://r.iq.harvard.edu/",
                  type  = "source")
```

[1]CRAN stands for the Comprehensive R Archive Network.

Special issues for Windows and Linux Users

If you are using Windows, you will also need to install *Rtools* (Ripley and Murdoch, 2012). You can download *Rtools* from: `http://cran.r-project.org/bin/windows/Rtools/`. Please use the recommended installation to ensure that your system PATH is set up correctly. Otherwise your computer will not know where the tools are.

On Linux you will need to install the *RCurl* (Temple Lang, 2015) and *XML* (Temple Lang, 2013) packages separately. Use your Terminal to install these packages with the following code:

```
sudo apt-get update

sudo apt-get install libcurl4-gnutls-dev
sudo apt-get install libxml2-dev
sudo apt-get install r-cran-xml
sudo apt-get install r-cran-rjava
```

Additional Resources

Additional resources that supplement the examples in this book can be freely downloaded and experimented with. These resources include longer examples discussed in individual chapters and a complete short reproducible research project.

Chapter Examples

Longer examples discussed in individual chapters, including files to dynamically download data, code for creating figures, and markup files for creating presentation documents, can be accessed at: `https://GitHub.com/christophergandrud/Rep-Res-Examples`. Please see Chapter 5 for more information on downloading files from GitHub, where the examples are stored.

Short Example Project

To download a full (though very short) example of a reproducible research project created using the tools covered in this book go to: `https://GitHub.com/christophergandrud/Rep-Res-ExampleProject1`. Please follow the replication instructions in the main *README.md* file to fully replicate the project. It is probably a good idea to hold off looking at this complete example in detail until after you have become acquainted with the individual tools it uses. Become acquainted with the tools by reading through this book and working with the individual chapter examples.

The following two figures give you a sense of how the example's files are organized. Figure 1 shows how the files are organized in the file system. Figure 2 illustrates how the main files are dynamically tied together. In the *Data* directory we have files to gather raw data from the World Bank (2015) on fertilizer consumption and from Pemstein et al. (2010) on countries' levels of democracy. They are tied to the data through the `WDI` and `download.file` commands. A *Makefile* can run *Gather1.R* and *Gather2.R* to gather and clean the data. It runs *MergeData.R* to merge the data into one data file called *MainData.csv*. It also automatically generates a variable description file and a *README.md* recording the session info.

The *Analysis* folder contains two files that create figures presenting this data. They are tied to *MainData.csv* with the `read.csv` command. These files are run by the presentation documents when they are knitted. The presentation documents tie to the analysis documents with *knitr* and the `source` command.

Though a simple example, hopefully these files will give you a complete sense of how a reproducible research project can be organized. Please feel free to experiment with different ways of organizing the files and tying them together to make your research really reproducible.

FIGURE 1
Short Example Project File Tree

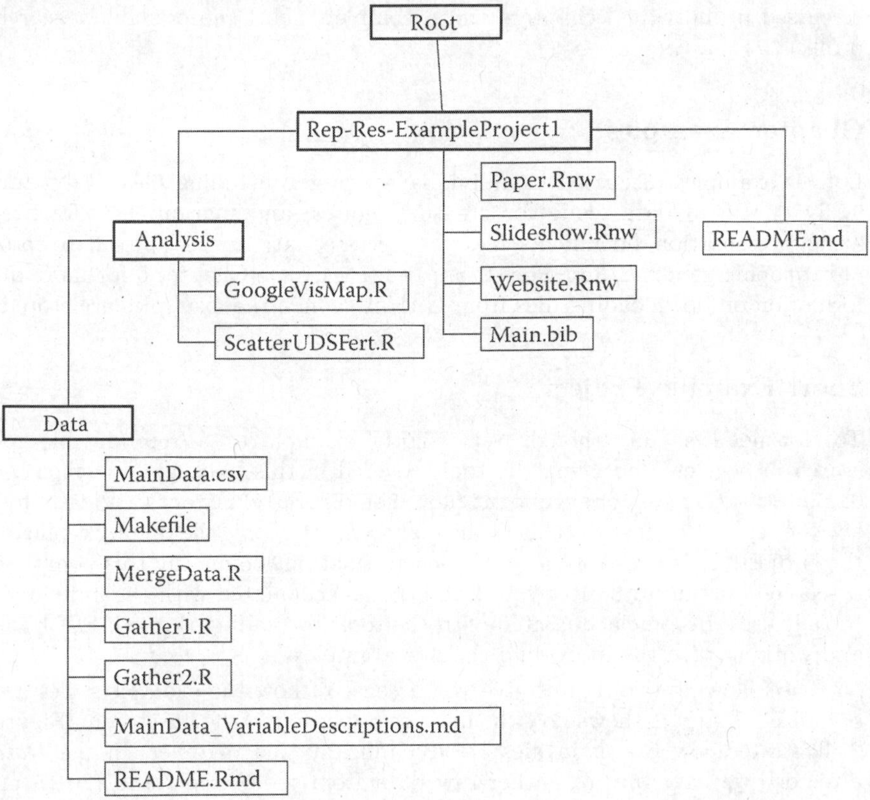

FIGURE 2
Short Example Main File Ties

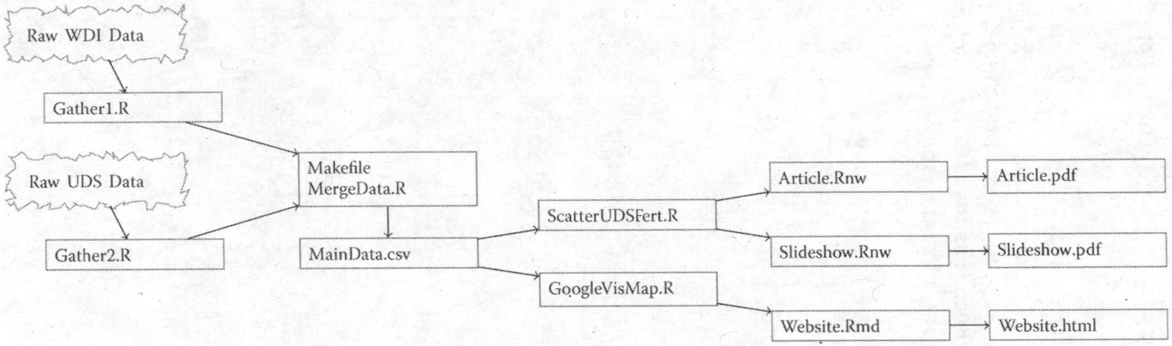

`download.file`
`Make`
`merge`
`WDI`

`read.csv`

`knitr`
`source`

Updates

Many of the reproducible research tools discussed in this book are improving rapidly. Because of this I will regularly post updates to the content covered in the book at: `https://GitHub.com/christophergandrud/Rep-Res-Book`.

Corrections

If you notice any corrections that should be made to fix typos, broken URLs, and so on, you can report them at: `https://GitHub.com/christophergandrud/Rep-Res-Book/issues`. I'll post notifications of changes to an Errata page at: `http://christophergandrud.GitHub.io/RepResR-RStudio/errata.htm`.

List of Figures

List of Tables

Part I

Getting Started

1

Introducing Reproducible Research

Research is often presented in very selective containers: slideshows, journal articles, books, or maybe even websites. These presentation documents announce a project's findings and try to convince us that the results are correct (Mesirov, 2010). It's important to remember that these documents are not the research. Especially in the computational and statistical sciences, these documents are the "advertising". The research is the "full software environment, code, and data that produced the results" (Buckheit and Donoho, 1995; Donoho, 2010, 385). When we separate the research from its advertisement we are making it difficult for others to verify the findings by reproducing them.

This book gives you the tools to dynamically combine your research with the presentation of your findings. The first tool is a workflow for reproducible research that weaves the principles of reproducibility throughout your entire research project, from data gathering to the statistical analysis, and the presentation of results. You will also learn how to use a number of computer tools that make this workflow possible. These tools include:

- the **R** statistical language that will allow you to gather data and analyze it;
- the **LaTeX** and **Markdown** markup languages that you can use to create documents–slideshows, articles, books, and webpages–for presenting your findings;
- the *knitr* and *rmarkdown* **packages** for R and other tools, including **command-line shell programs** like GNU Make and Git version control, for dynamically tying your data gathering, analysis, and presentation documents together so that they can be easily reproduced;
- **RStudio**, a program that brings all of these tools together in one place.

1.1 What Is Reproducible Research?

Though there is some debate over what are the necessary and sufficient conditions for a replication (Makel and Plucker, 2014, 2), research results are generally considered *replicable* if there is sufficient information available for independent researchers to make the same findings using the same procedures with new data.[1] For research that relies on experiments, this can mean a researcher not involved in the original research being able to rerun the experiment, including sampling, and validate that the new results are comparable to the original ones. In computational and quantitative empirical sciences, results are replicable if independent researchers can recreate findings by following the procedures originally used to gather the data and run the computer code. Of course, it is sometimes difficult to replicate the original data set because of issues such as limited resources to gather new data or because the original study already sampled the full universe of cases. So as a next-best standard we can aim for "*really reproducible research*" (Peng, 2011, 1226).[2] In computational sciences[3] this means:

> the data and code used to make a finding are available and they are sufficient for an independent researcher to recreate the finding.

In practice, research needs to be *easy* for independent researchers to reproduce (Ball and Medeiros, 2011). If a study is difficult to reproduce it's more likely that no one will reproduce it. If someone does attempt to reproduce this research, it will be difficult for them to tell if any errors they find were in the original research or problems they introduced during the reproduction. In this book you will learn how to avoid these problems.

In particular you will learn tools for dynamically "*knitting*"[4] the data and the source code together with your presentation documents. Combined with well-organized source files and clearly and completely commented code, independent researchers will be able to understand how you obtained your results. This will make your computational research easily reproducible.

---

[1] This is close to what Lykken (1968) calls "operational replication".

[2] The idea of really reproducible computational research was originally thought of and implemented by Jon Claerbout and the Stanford Exploration Project beginning in the 1980s and early 1990s (Fomel and Claerbout, 2009; Donoho et al., 2009). Further seminal advances were made by Jonathan B. Buckheit and David L. Donoho who created the Wavelab library of MATLAB routines for their research on wavelets in the mid-1990s (Buckheit and Donoho, 1995).

[3] Reproducibility is important for both quantitative and qualitative research (King et al., 1994). Nonetheless, we will focus mainly on on methods for reproducibility in quantitative computational research.

[4] Much of the reproducible computational research and literate programming literatures have traditionally used the term "weave" to describe the process of combining source code and presentation documents (see Knuth, 1992, 101). In the R community weave is usually used to describe the combination of source code and LaTeX documents. The term "knit" reflects the vocabulary of the *knitr* R package (knit + R). It is used more generally to describe weaving with a variety of markup languages. The term is used by RStudio if you are using the *rmarkdown* package, which is similar to *knitr*. We also cover the *rmarkdown* package in this book. Because of this, I use the term knit rather than weave in this book.

1.2 Why Should Research Be Reproducible?

Reproducible research is one of the main components of science. If that's not enough reason for you to make your research reproducible, consider that the tools of reproducible research also have direct benefits for you as a researcher.

1.2.1 For science

Replicability has been a key part of scientific inquiry from perhaps the 1200s (Bacon, 1859; Nosek et al., 2012). It has even been called the "demarcation between science and non-science" (Braude, 1979, 2). Why is replication so important for scientific inquiry?

Standard to judge scientific claims

Replication opens claims to scrutiny, allowing us to keep what works and discard what doesn't. Science, according to the American Physical Society, "is the systematic enterprise of gathering knowledge ... organizing and condensing that knowledge into testable laws and theories". The "ultimate standard" for evaluating scientific claims is whether or not the claims can be replicated (Peng, 2011; Kelly, 2006). Research findings cannot even really be considered "genuine contribution[s] to human knowledge" until they have been verified through replication (Stodden, 2009b, 38). Replication "requires the complete and open exchange of data, procedures, and materials". Scientific conclusions that are not replicable should be abandoned or modified "when confronted with more complete or reliable ... evidence".[5]

Reproducibility enhances replicability. If other researchers are able to clearly understand how a finding was originally made, then they will be better able to conduct comparable research in meaningful attempts to replicate the original findings. Sometimes strict replicability is not feasible, for example, when it is only possible to gather one data set on a population of interest. In these cases reproducibility is a "minimum standard" for judging scientific claims (Peng, 2011).

It is important to note that though reproducibility is a minimum standard for judging scientific claims, "a study can be reproducible and still be wrong" (Peng, 2014). For example, a statistically significant finding in one study may remain statistically significant when reproduced using the original data/code, but when researchers try to replicate it using new data and even methods, they are unable to find a similar result. The original finding could simply have been noise, even though it is fully reproducible.

---

[5]See the American Physical Society's website at `http://www.aps.org/policy/statements/99_6.cfm`. See also Fomel and Claerbout (2009).

Avoiding effort duplication & encouraging cumulative knowledge development

Not only is reproducibility important for evaluating scientific claims, it can also contribute to the cumulative growth of scientific knowledge (Kelly, 2006; King, 1995). Reproducible research cuts down on the amount of time scientists have to spend gathering data or developing procedures that have already been collected or figured out. Because researchers do not have to discover on their own things that have already been done, they can more quickly build on established findings and develop new knowledge.

1.2.2 For you

Working to make your research reproducible does require extra upfront effort. For example, you need to put effort into learning the tools of reproducible research by doing things such as reading this book. But beyond the clear benefits for science, why should you make this effort? Using reproducible research tools can make your research process more effective and (hopefully) ultimately easier.

Better work habits

Making a project reproducible from the start encourages you to use better work habits. It can spur you to more effectively plan and organize your research. It should push you to bring your data and source code up to a higher level of quality than you might if you "thought 'no one was looking' " (Donoho, 2010, 386). This forces you to root out errors–a ubiquitous part of computational research–earlier in the research process (Donoho, 2010, 385). Clear documentation also makes it easier to find errors.[6]

Reproducible research needs to be stored so that other researchers can actually access the data and source code. By taking steps to make your research accessible for others you are also making it easier for yourself to find your data and methods when you revise your work or begin new a project. You are avoiding personal effort duplication, allowing you to cumulatively build on your own work more effectively.

Better teamwork

The steps you take to make sure an independent researcher can figure out what you have done also make it easier for your collaborators to understand your work and build on it. This applies not only to current collaborators, but also future collaborators. Bringing new members of a research team up to speed on a cumulatively growing research project is faster if they can easily understand what has been done already (Donoho, 2010, 386).

[6]Of course, it's important to keep in mind that reproducibility is "neither necessary nor sufficient to prevent mistakes" (Stodden, 2009a).

Changes are easier

A third person may or may not actually reproduce your research even if you make it easy for them to do so. But, *you will almost certainly reproduce parts or even all of your own research.* No actual research process is completely linear. You almost never gather data, run analyses, and present your results without going backwards to add variables, make changes to your statistical models, create new graphs, alter results tables in light of new findings, and so on. You will probably try to make these changes long after you last worked on the project and long since you remembered the details of how you did it. Whether your changes are because of journal reviewers' and conference participants' comments or you discover that new and better data has been made available since beginning the project, designing your research to be reproducible from the start makes it much easier to change things later on.

Dynamic reproducible documents in particular can make changing things much easier. Changes made to one part of a research project have a way of cascading through the other parts. For example, adding a new variable to a largely completed analysis requires gathering new data and merging it with existing data sets. If you used data imputation or matching methods you may need to rerun these models. You then have to update your main statistical analyses, and recreate the tables and graphs you used to present the results. Adding a new variable essentially forces you to reproduce large portions of your research. If when you started the project you used tools that make it easier for others to reproduce your research, you also made it easier to reproduce the work yourself. You will have taken steps to have a "better relationship with [your] future [self]" (Bowers, 2011, 2).

Higher research impact

Reproducible research is more likely to be useful for other researchers than non-reproducible research. Useful research is cited more frequently (Donoho, 2002; Piwowar et al., 2007; Vandewalle, 2012). Research that is fully reproducible contains more information, i.e. more reasons to use and cite it, than presentation documents merely showing findings. Independent researchers may use the reproducible data or code to look at other, often unanticipated, questions. When they use your work for a new purpose they will (should) cite your work. Because of this, Vandewalle et al. even argue that "the goal of reproducible research is to have more impact with our research" (2007, 1253).

A reason researchers often avoid making their research fully reproducible is that they are afraid other people will use their data and code to compete with them. I'll let Donoho et al. address this one:

> *True. But competition means that strangers will read your papers, try to learn from them, cite them, and try to do even better. If you prefer obscurity, why are you publishing?* (2009, 16)

1.3 Who Should Read This Book?

This book is intended primarily for researchers who want to use a systematic workflow that encourages reproducibility as well as practical state-of-the-art computational tools to put this workflow into practice. These people include professional researchers, upper-level undergraduate, and graduate students working on computational data-driven projects. Hopefully, editors at academic publishers will also find the book useful for improving their ability to evaluate and edit reproducible research.

The more researchers that use the tools of reproducibility the better. So I include enough information in the book for people who have very limited experience with these tools, including limited experience with R, LaTeX, and Markdown. They will be able to start incorporating reproducible research tools into their workflow right away. The book will also be helpful for people who already have general experience using technologies such as R and LaTeX, but would like to know how to tie them together for reproducible research.

1.3.1 Academic researchers

Hopefully so far in this chapter I've convinced you that reproducible research has benefits for you as a member of the scientific community and personally as a computational researcher. This book is intended to be a practical guide for how to actually make your research reproducible. Even if you already use tools such as R and LaTeX you may not be leveraging their full potential. This book will teach you useful ways to get the most out of them as part of a reproducible research workflow.

1.3.2 Students

Upper-level undergraduate and graduate students conducting original computational research should make their research reproducible for the same reasons that professional researchers should. Forcing yourself to clearly document the steps you took will also encourage you to think more clearly about what you are doing and reinforce what you are learning. It will hopefully give you a greater appreciation of research accountability and integrity early in your career (Barr, 2012; Ball and Medeiros, 2011, 183).

Even if you don't have extensive experience with computer languages, this book will teach you specific habits and tools that you can use throughout your student research and hopefully your careers. Learning these things earlier will save you considerable time and effort later.

1.3.3 Instructors

When instructors incorporate the tools of reproducible research into their assignments they not only build students' understanding of research best practice, but are also better able to evaluate and provide meaningful feedback on students' work (Ball and Medeiros, 2011, 183). This book provides a resource that you can use with students to put reproducibility into practice.

If you are teaching computational courses, you may also benefit from making your lecture material dynamically reproducible. Your slides will be easier to update for the same reasons that it is easier to update research. Making the methods you used to create the material available to students will give them more information. Clearly documenting how you created lecture material can also pass information on to future instructors.

1.3.4 Editors

Beyond a lack of reproducible research skills among researchers, an impediment to actually creating reproducible research is a lack of infrastructure to publish it (Peng, 2011). Hopefully, this book will be useful for editors at academic publishers who want to be better at evaluating reproducible research, editing it, and developing systems to make it more widely available. The journal *Biostatistics* is a good example of a publication that is encouraging (actually requiring) reproducible research. From 2009 the journal has had an editor for reproducibility that ensures replication files are available and that results can be replicated using these files (Peng, 2009). The more editors there are with the skills to work with reproducible research the more likely it is that researchers will do it.

1.3.5 Private sector researchers

Researchers in the private sector may or may not want to make their work easily reproducible outside of their organization. However, that does not mean that significant benefits cannot be gained from using the methods of reproducible research. First, even if public reproducibility is ruled out to guard proprietary information,[7] making your research reproducible to members of your organization can spread valuable information about how analyses were done and data was collected. This will help build your organization's knowledge and avoid effort duplication. Just as a lack of reproducibility hinders the spread of information in the scientific community, it can hinder it inside of a private organization. Using the sort of dynamic automated processes run with clearly documented source code we will learn in this book can also help create robust data analysis methods that help your organization avoid errors that may come from cutting-and-pasting data across spreadsheets.[8]

[7]There are ways to enable some public reproducibility without revealing confidential information. See Vandewalle et al. (2007) for a discussion of one approach.

[8]See this post by David Smith about how the J.P. Morgan "London Whale" problem may have been prevented with the type of processes covered in this book: `http://blog.revolutionanalytics.com/2013/02/did-an-excel-error-bring-down-the-london-whale.html` (posted 11 February 2013).

Also, the tools of reproducible research covered in this book enable you to create professional standardized reports that can be easily updated or changed when new information is available. In particular, you will learn how to create batch reports based on quantitative data.

1.4 The Tools of Reproducible Research

This book will teach you the tools you need to make your research highly reproducible. Reproducible research involves two broad sets of tools. The first is a **reproducible research environment** that includes the statistical tools you need to run your analyses as well as "the ability to automatically track the provenance of data, analyses, and results and to package them (or pointers to persistent versions of them) for redistribution". The second set of tools is a **reproducible research publisher**, which prepares dynamic documents for presenting results and is easily linked to the reproducible research environment (Mesirov, 2010, 415).

In this book we will focus on learning how to use the widely available and highly flexible reproducible research environment–R/RStudio (R Core Team, 2014; RStudio, Inc., 2015).[9] R/RStudio can be linked to numerous reproducible research publishers such as LaTeX and Markdown with Yihui Xie's *knitr* package (2015b) or the related *rmarkdown* package (Allaire et al., 2015a). The main tools covered in this book include:

- **R**: a programming language primarily for statistics and graphics. It can also be useful for data gathering and creating presentation documents.

- ***knitr* and *rmarkdown***: related R packages for literate programming. They allow you to combine your statistical analysis and the presentation of the results into one document. They work with R and a number of other languages such as Bash, Python, and Ruby.

- **Markup languages**: instructions for how to format a presentation document. In this book we cover LaTeX, Markdown, and a little HTML.

- **RStudio**: an integrated developer environment (IDE) for R that tightly combines R, *knitr*, *rmarkdown*, and markup languages.

- **Cloud storage & versioning**: Services such as Dropbox and Git/GitHub that can store data, code, and presentation files, save previous versions of these files, and make this information widely available.

- **Unix-like shell programs**: These tools are useful for working with large

[9] The book was created with R version 3.2.0 and developer builds of RStudio version 0.99.370.

research projects.[10] They also allow us to use command-line tools including GNU Make for compiling projects and Pandoc, a program useful for converting documents from one markup language to another.

1.5 Why Use R, *knitr*/*rmarkdown*, and RStudio for Reproducible Research?

Why R?

Why use a statistical programming language like R for reproducible research? R has a very active development community that is constantly expanding what it is capable of. As we will see in this book, R enables researchers across a wide range of disciplines to gather data and run statistical analyses. Using the *knitr* or *rmarkdown* package, you can connect your R-based analyses to presentation documents created with markup languages such as LaTeX and Markdown. This allows you to dynamically and reproducibly present results in articles, slideshows, and webpages.

The way you interact with R has benefits for reproducible research. In general you interact with R (or any other programming and markup language) by explicitly writing down your steps as source code. This promotes reproducibility more than your typical interactions with Graphical User Interface (GUI) programs like SPSS[11] and Microsoft Word. When you write R code and embed it in presentation documents created using markup languages, you are forced to explicitly state the steps you took to do your research. When you do research by clicking through drop-down menus in GUI programs, your steps are lost, or at least documenting them requires considerable extra effort. Also it is generally more difficult to dynamically embed your analysis in presentation documents created by GUI word processing programs in a way that will be accessible to other researchers both now and in the future. I'll come back to these points in Chapter 2.

Why knitr *and* rmarkdown*?*

Literate programming is a crucial part of reproducible quantitative research.[12] Being able to directly link your analyses, your results, and the code you used to produce the results makes tracing your steps much easier. There are many different literate programming tools for a number of different programming

[10] In this book I cover the Bash shell for Linux and Mac as well as Windows PowerShell.

[11] I know you can write scripts in statistical programs like SPSS, but doing so is not encouraged by the program's interface and you often have to learn multiple languages for writing scripts that run analyses, create graphics, and deal with matrices.

[12] Donald Knuth coined the term literate programming in the 1970s to refer to a source file that could be both run by a computer and "woven" with a formatted presentation document (Knuth, 1992).

languages.[13] Previously, one of the most common tools for researchers using R and the LaTeX markup language was *Sweave* (Leisch, 2002). The packages I am going to focus on in this book are newer and have more capabilities. They are called *knitr* and *rmarkdown*. Why are we going to use these tools in this book and not *Sweave* or some other tool?

The simple answer is that they are more capable than *Sweave*. Both *knitr* and *rmarkdown* can work with markup languages other than LaTeX including Markdown and HTML. *rmarkdown* can even output Microsoft Word documents. They can work with programming languages other than R. They highlight R code in presentation documents making it easier for your readers to follow.[14] They give you better control over the inclusion of graphics and can cache code chunks, i.e. save the output for later. *knitr* has the ability to understand *Sweave*-like syntax, so it will be easy to convert backwards to *Sweave* if you want to.[15] You also have the choice to use much simpler and more straightforward syntax with *knitr* and *rmarkdown*.

knitr and *rmarkdown* have broadly similar capabilities and syntax. They both are literate programming tools that can produce presentation documents from multiple markup languages. They have almost identical syntax when used in Markdown. Their main difference is that they take different approaches to creating presentation documents. *knitr* documents must be written using the markup language associated with the desired output. For example, with *knitr*, LaTeX must be used to create PDF output documents and Markdown or HTML must be used to create webpages. *rmarkdown* builds directly on *knitr*, the key difference being that it uses the straightforward Markdown markup language to generate PDF, HTML, and MS Word documents.[16]

Because you write with the simple Markdown syntax, *rmarkdown* is generally easier to use. It has the advantage of being able to take the same markup document and output multiple types of presentation documents. Nonetheless, for complex documents like books and long articles or work that requires custom formatting, *knitr* LaTeX is often preferable and extremely flexible, though the syntax is more complicated.

Why RStudio?

Why use the RStudio integrated development environment for reproducible research? R by itself has the capabilities necessary to gather data, analyze it, and, with a little help from *knitr*/*rmarkdown* and markup languages, present results in a way that is highly reproducible. RStudio allows you to do all of

[13] A very interesting tool that is worth taking a look at for the Python programming language is HTML Notebooks created with IPython. For more details see `http://ipython.org/ipython-doc/dev/notebook/index.html`.

[14] Syntax highlighting uses different colors and fonts to distinguish different types of text.

[15] Note that the Sweave-style syntax is not identical to actual *Sweave* syntax. See Yihui Xie's discussion of the differences between the two at: `http://yihui.name/knitr/demo/sweave/`. *knitr* has a function (`Sweave2knitr`) for converting *Sweave* to *knitr* syntax.

[16] It does this by relying on a tool called Pandoc (MacFarlane, 2014).

these things, but simplifies many of them and allows you to navigate through them more easily. It also is a happy medium between R's text-based interface and a pure GUI.

Not only does RStudio do many of the things that R can do but more easily, it is also a very good standalone editor for writing documents with LaTeX and Markdown. For LaTeX documents it can, for example, insert frequently used commands like `\section{}` for numbered sections (see Chapter 11).[17] There are many LaTeX editors available, both open source and paid. But RStudio is currently the best program for creating reproducible LaTeX and Markdown documents. It has full syntax highlighting. Its syntax highlighting can even distinguish between R code and markup commands in the same document. It can spell check LaTeX and Markdown documents. It handles *knitr*/*rmarkdown* code chunks beautifully (see Chapter 3).

Finally, RStudio not only has tight integration with various markup languages, it also has capabilities for using other tools such as C++, CSS, JavaScript, and a few other programming languages. It is closely integrated with the version control programs Git and SVN. Both of these programs allow you to keep track of the changes you make to your documents (see Chapter 5). This is important for reproducible research since version control programs can document many of your research steps. It also has a built-in ability to make HTML slideshows from *knitr*/*rmarkdown* documents. Basically, RStudio makes it easy to create and navigate through complex reproducible research documents.

1.5.1 Installing the main software

Before you read this book you should install the main software. All of the software programs covered in this book are open source and can be easily downloaded for free. They are available for Windows, Mac, and Linux operating systems. They should run well on most modern computers.

You should install R before installing RStudio. You can download the programs from the following websites:

- **R**: `http://www.r-project.org/`,
- **RStudio**: `http://www.rstudio.com/products/rstudio/download/`.

The download webpages for these programs have comprehensive information on how to install them, so please refer to those pages for more information.

After installing R and RStudio you will probably also want to install a number of user-written packages that are covered in this book. To install all of these user-written packages, please see page xix.

[17] If you are more comfortable with a what-you-see-is-what-you-get (WYSIWYG) word processor like Microsoft Word, you might be interested in exploring Lyx. It is a WYSIWYG-like LaTeX editor that works with *knitr*. It doesn't work with the other markup languages covered in this book. For more information see: `http://www.lyx.org/`. I give some brief information on using Lyx with *knitr* in Chapter 3's Appendix.

Installing markup languages

If you are planning to create LaTeX documents you need to install a TeX distribution.[18] They are available for Windows, Mac, and Linux systems. They can be found at: `http://www.latex-project.org/ftp.html`. Please refer to that site for more installation information.

If you want to create Markdown documents you can separately install the *markdown* package in R. You can do this the same way that you install any package in R, with the `install.packages` command.[19]

GNU Make

If you are using a Linux computer you already have GNU Make installed.[20] Mac users will need to install the command-line developer tools. There are two ways to do this. One is go to the App Store and download Xcode (it's free). Once Xcode is installed, install command-line tools, which you will find by opening Xcode then clicking on `Preference` → `Downloads`. However, Xcode is a very large download and you only need the command-line tools for Make. To install just the command-line tools, open the Terminal and try to run Make by typing `make` and hitting return. A box should appear asking you if you want to install the command-line developer tools. Click `Install`. Windows users will have Make installed if they have already installed Rtools (see page xx). Mac and Windows users will need to install this software not only so that GNU Make runs properly, but also so that other command-line tools work well.

Other Tools

We will discuss other tools such as Git that can be a useful part of a reproducible research workflow. Installation instructions for these tools will be discussed below.

1.6 Book Overview

The purpose of this book is to give you the tools that you will need to do reproducible research with R and RStudio. This book describes a workflow for reproducible research primarily using R and RStudio. It is designed to give you the necessary tools to use this workflow for your own research. It is not designed to be a complete reference for R, RStudio, *knitr*/*rmarkdown*, Git, or any other program that is a part of this workflow. Instead it shows you how

[18]LaTeX is is really a set of macros for the TeX typesetting system. It is included in all major TeX distributions.

[19]The exact command is: `install.packages("markdown")`.

[20]To verify this, open the Terminal and type: `make -version` (I used version 3.81 for this book). This should output details about the current version of Make installed on your computer.

these tools can fit together to make your research more reproducible. To get the most out of these individual programs I will along the way point you to other resources that cover these programs in more detail.

To that end, I can recommend a number of resources that cover more of the nitty-gritty:

- Michael J. Crawley's (2013) encyclopaedic R book, appropriately titled ***The R Book***, published by Wiley.

- Hadley Whickham (2014a) has a great new book out from Chapman and Hall on ***Advanced R***.

- Yihui Xie's (2013) book ***Dynamic Documents with R and knitr***, published by Chapman and Hall, provides a comprehensive look at how to create documents with *knitr*. It's a good complement to this book's generally more research project–level focus.

- Norman Matloff's (2011) tour through the programming language aspects of R called ***The Art of R Programming: A Tour of Statistical Design Software***, published by No Starch Press.

- Cathy O'Neil and Rachel Schutt (2013) give a great introduction the field of data science generally in ***Doing Data Science***, published by O'Reilly Media Inc.

- For an excellent introduction to the command-line in Linux and Mac, see William E. Shotts Jr.'s (2012) book ***The Linux Command-line: A Complete Introduction*** also published by No Starch Press. It is also helpful for Windows users running PowerShell (see Chapter 4).

- The RStudio website (`http://www.rstudio.com/ide/docs/`) has a number of useful tutorials on how to use *knitr* with LaTeX and Markdown. They also have very good documentation for *rmarkdown* at `http://rmarkdown.rstudio.com/`.

That being said, my goal is for this book to be *self-sufficient*. A reader without a detailed understanding of these programs will be able to understand and use the commands and procedures I cover in this book. While learning how to use R and the other programs I personally often encountered illustrative examples that included commands, variables, and other things that were not well explained in the texts that I was reading. This caused me to waste many hours trying to figure out, for example, what the `$` is used for (preview: it's the component selector, see Section 3.1.2). I hope to save you from this wasted time by either providing a brief explanation of possibly frustrating and mysterious things and/or pointing you in the direction of good explanations.

1.6.1 How to read this book

This book gives you a workflow. It has a beginning, middle, and end. So, unlike a reference book, it can and should be read linearly as it takes you through an empirical research processes from an empty folder to a completed set of documents that reproducibly showcase your findings.

That being said, readers with more experience using tools like R or LaTeX may want to skip over the nitty-gritty parts of the book that describe how to manipulate data frames or compile LaTeX documents into PDFs. Please feel free to skip these sections.

More-experienced R users

If you are an experienced R user you may want to skip over the first section of Chapter 3: Getting Started with R, RStudio, and *knitr/rmarkdown*. But don't skip over the whole chapter. The latter parts contain important information on the *knitr/rmarkdown* packages. If you are experienced with R data manipulation you may also want to skip all of Chapter 7.

More-experienced LaTeX users

If you are familiar with LaTeX you might want to skip the first part of Chapter 11. The second part may be useful as it includes information on how to dynamically create BibTeX bibliographies with *knitr* and how to include *knitr* output in a Beamer slideshow.

Less-experienced LaTeX/Markdown users

If you do not have experience with LaTeX or Markdown you may benefit from reading, or at least skimming, the introductory chapters on these top topics (chapters 11 and 13) before reading Part III.

1.6.2 Reproduce this book

This book practices what it preaches. It can be reproduced. I wrote the book using the programs and methods that I describe. Full documentation and source files can be found at the book's GitHub repository. Feel free to read and even use (within reason and with attribution, of course) the book's source code. You can find it at: `https://GitHub.com/christophergandrud/Rep-Res-Book`. This is especially useful if you want to know how to do something in the book that I don't directly cover in the text.

If you notice any errors or places where the book can be improved please report them on the book's GitHub Issues page: `https://GitHub.com/christophergandrud/Rep-Res-Book/issues`. Corrections will be posted at: `http://christophergandrud.GitHub.io/RepResR-RStudio/errata.htm`.

1.6.3 Contents overview

The book is broken into four parts. The first part (chapters 2, 3, and 4) gives an overview of the reproducible research workflow as well as the general computer skills that you'll need to use this workflow. Each of the next three parts of the book guides you through the specific skills you will need for each part of the reproducible research process. Part two (chapters 5, 6, and 7) covers the data gathering and file storage process. The third part (chapters 8, 9, and 10) teaches you how to dynamically incorporate your statistical analysis, results figures, and tables into your presentation documents. The final part (chapters 11, 12, and 13) covers how to create reproducible presentation documents including LaTeX articles, books, slideshows, and batch reports as well as Markdown webpages and slideshows.

2

Getting Started with Reproducible Research

Researchers often start thinking about making their work reproducible near the end of the research process when they write up their results or maybe even later when a journal requires their data and code be made available for publication. Or maybe even later when another researcher asks if they can use the data from a published article to reproduce the findings. By then there may be numerous versions of the data set and records of the analyses stored across multiple folders on the researcher's computers. It can be difficult and time consuming to sift through these files to create an accurate account of how the results were reached. Waiting until near the end of the research process to start thinking about reproducibility can lead to incomplete documentation that does not give an accurate account of how findings were made. Focusing on reproducibility from the beginning of the process and continuing to follow a few simple guidelines throughout your research can help you avoid these problems. Remember "reproducibility is not an afterthought–it is something that must be built-into the project from the beginning" (Donoho, 2010, 386).

This chapter first gives you a brief overview of the reproducible research process: a workflow for reproducible research. Then it covers some of the key guidelines that can help make your research more reproducible.

2.1 The Big Picture: A Workflow for Reproducible Research

The three basic stages of a typical computational empirical research project are:

- data gathering,
- data analysis,
- results presentation.

Each stage is part of the reproducible research workflow covered in this book. Tools for reproducibly gathering data are covered in Part II. Part III teaches tools for tying the data we gathered to our statistical analyses and presenting the results with tables and figures. Part IV discusses how to tie these findings into a variety of documents you can use to advertise your findings.

Instead of starting to use the individual tools of reproducible research as soon as you learn them, I recommend briefly stepping back and considering how the stages of reproducible research *tie* together overall. This will make your workflow more coherent from the beginning and save you a lot of backtracking later on. Figure 2.1 illustrates the workflow. Notice that most of the arrows connecting the workflow's parts point in both directions, indicating that you should always be thinking about how to make it easier to go backwards through your research, i.e. reproduce it, as well as forwards.

Around the edges of the figure are some of the commands you will learn to make it easier to go forwards and backwards through the process. These commands tie your research together. For example, you can use API-based R packages to gather data from the internet. You can use R's `merge` command to combine data gathered from different sources into one data set. The `getURL` function from R's *RCurl* package (Temple Lang, 2015) and the `read.table` function can be used to bring this data set into your statistical analyses. The *knitr* or *rmarkdown* package then ties your analyses into your presentation documents. This includes the code you used, the figures you created, and, with the help of tools such as the `kable` function in the *knitr* package, tables of results. You can even tie multiple presentation documents together. For example, you can access the same figure for use in a LaTeX article and a Markdown-created website with the `includegraphics` and `![]()` commands, respectively. This helps you maintain a consistent presentation of results across multiple document types. We'll cover these commands in detail throughout the book. See Table 2.1 for a brief but more complete overview of the main *tie commands*.

2.1.1 Reproducible theory

An important part of the research process that I do not discuss in this book is theoretical stage. Ideally, if you are using a deductive research design, the bulk of this work will precede and guide the data gathering and analysis stages. Just because I don't cover this stage of the research process doesn't mean that theory building can't and shouldn't be reproducible. It can in fact be "the easiest part to make reproducible" (Vandewalle et al., 2007, 1254). Quotes and paraphrases from previous works in the literature obviously need to be fully cited so that others can verify that they accurately reflect the source material. For mathematically based theory, clear and complete descriptions of the proofs should be given.

Though I don't actively cover theory replication in depth in this book, I do touch on some of the ways to incorporate proofs and citations into your presentation documents. These tools are covered in Part IV.

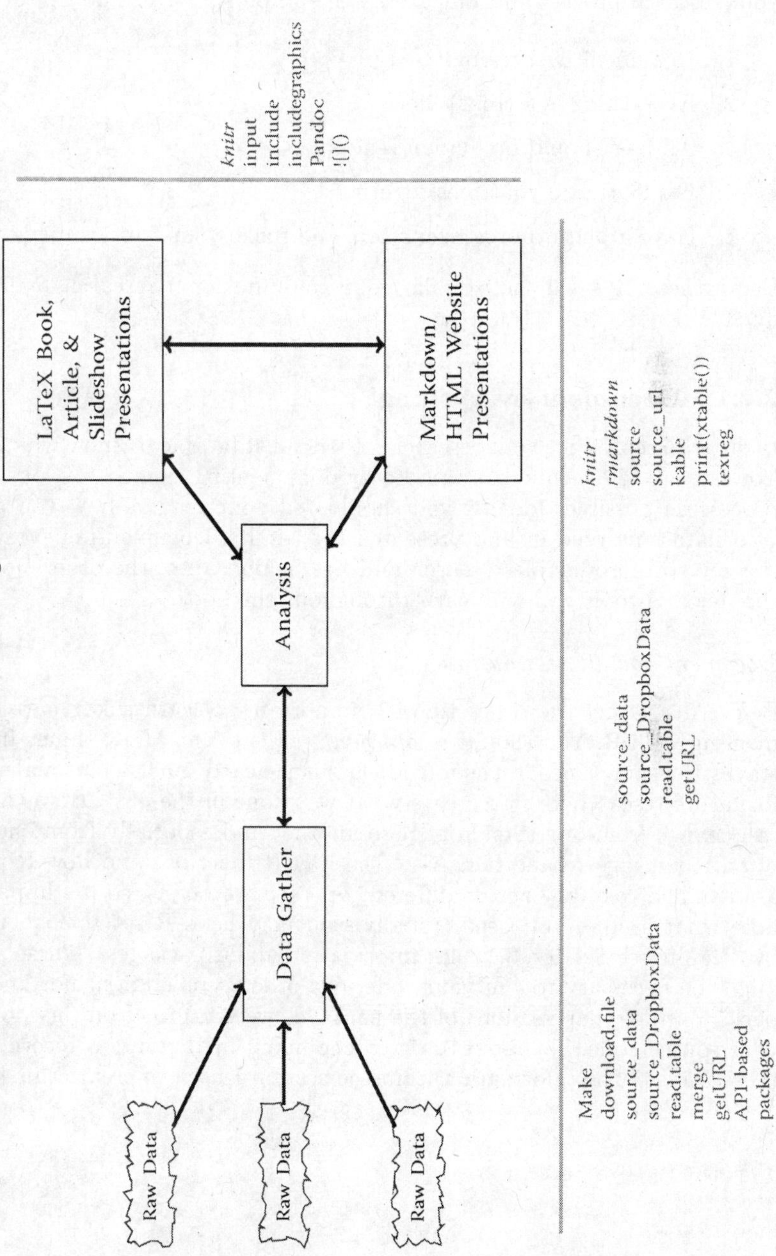

FIGURE 2.1
Example Workflow & a Selection of Commands to Tie It Together

2.2 Practical Tips for Reproducible Research

Before we start learning the details of the reproducible research workflow with R and RStudio, it's useful to cover a few broad tips that will help you organize your research process and put these skills in perspective. The tips are:

1. Document everything!
2. Everything is a (text) file.
3. All files should be human readable.
4. Explicitly tie your files together.
5. Have a plan to organize, store, and make your files available.

Using these tips will help make your computational research really reproducible.

2.2.1 Document everything!

In order to reproduce your research, others must be able to know what you did. You have to tell them what you did by documenting as much of your research process as possible. Ideally, you should tell your readers how you gathered your data, analyzed it, and presented the results. Documenting everything is the key to reproducible research and lies behind all of the other tips in this chapter and tools you will learn throughout the book.

Document your R session info

Before discussing the other tips it's important to learn a key part of documenting with R. You should *record your session info.* Many things in R have stayed the same since it was introduced in the early 1990s. This makes it easy for future researchers to recreate what was done in the past. However, things can change from one version of R to another and especially from one version of an R package to another. Also, the way R functions and how R packages are handled can vary across different operating systems, so it's important to note what system you used. Finally, you may have R set to load packages by default (see Section 3.1.8 for information about packages). These packages might be necessary to run your code, but other people might not know what packages and what versions of the packages were loaded from just looking at your source code. The `sessionInfo` command in R prints a record of all of these things. The information from the session I used to create this book is:

```
# Print R session info
sessionInfo()
```

```
## R version 3.2.0 (2015-04-16)
## Platform: x86_64-apple-darwin14.3.0 (64-bit)
## Running under: OS X 10.10.3 (Yosemite)
##
## locale:
## [1] en_GB.UTF-8/en_GB.UTF-8/en_GB.UTF-8/C/en_GB.UTF-8/en_GB.UTF-8
##
## attached base packages:
## [1] stats     graphics  grDevices utils     datasets  methods   base
##
## other attached packages:
##  [1] ZeligBayesian_0.1    MCMCpack_1.3-3     coda_0.17-1
##  [4] Zelig_4.2-1          sandwich_2.3-3     MASS_7.3-40
##  [7] boot_1.3-16          xtable_1.7-4       WDI_2.4
## [10] tidyr_0.2.0          texreg_1.35        survival_2.38-1
## [13] stargazer_5.1        shiny_0.11.1       rvest_0.2.0
## [16] RJSONIO_1.3-0        rmarkdown_0.5.1    repmis_0.4.2
## [19] RCurl_1.95-4.6       bitops_1.0-6       quantmod_0.4-4
## [22] TTR_0.22-0           xts_0.9-7          zoo_1.7-12
## [25] packrat_0.4.3        openair_1.5        maps_2.3-9
## [28] lazyeval_0.1.10      markdown_0.7.7     magrittr_1.5
## [31] knitcitations_1.0.5 httr_0.6.1          htmlwidgets_0.3.2
## [34] highlight_0.4.7      googleVis_0.5.8    ggplot2_1.0.1
## [37] formatR_1.2          extrafont_0.17     dplyr_0.4.1
## [40] digest_0.6.8         devtools_1.7.0     data.table_1.9.4
## [43] countrycode_0.18     brew_1.0-6         animation_2.3
## [46] knitr_1.10
##
## loaded via a namespace (and not attached):
##  [1] bit64_0.9-4          splines_3.2.0      R.utils_2.0.2
##  [4] assertthat_0.1       highr_0.5          latticeExtra_0.6-26
##  [7] twitteR_1.1.8        Rttf2pt1_1.3.3     lattice_0.20-31
## [10] extrafontdb_1.0      chron_2.3-45       RColorBrewer_1.1-2
## [13] RefManageR_0.8.45    colorspace_1.2-6   htmltools_0.2.6
## [16] httpuv_1.3.2         Matrix_1.2-0       R.oo_1.19.0
## [19] plyr_1.8.2           XML_3.98-1.1       bibtex_0.4.0
## [22] scales_0.2.4         mgcv_1.8-6         mapdata_2.2-3
## [25] hexbin_1.27.0        proto_0.3-10       mime_0.3
## [28] memoise_0.2.1        evaluate_0.7       R.methodsS3_1.7.0
## [31] R.cache_0.10.0       nlme_3.1-120       tools_3.2.0
## [34] RgoogleMaps_1.2.0.7 stringr_1.0.0       munsell_0.4.2
## [37] cluster_2.0.1        grid_3.2.0         rjson_0.2.15
## [40] labeling_0.3         gtable_0.1.2       DBI_0.3.1
## [43] reshape2_1.4.1       R6_2.0.1           lubridate_1.3.3
## [46] bit_1.1-12           stringi_0.4-1      parallel_3.2.0
## [49] Rcpp_0.11.6          mapproj_1.2-2      png_0.1-7
```

Chapter 4 gives specific details about how to create files with dynamically included session information. If you use non-R tools you should also record what versions of these tools you used.

2.2.2 Everything is a (text) file

Your documentation is stored in files that include data, analysis code, the write-up of results, and explanations of these files (e.g. data set codebooks, session info files, and so on). Ideally, you should use the simplest file format possible to store this information. Usually the simplest file format is the humble, but versatile, text file.[1]

Text files are extremely nimble. They can hold your data in, for example, comma-separated values (`.csv`) format. They can contain your analysis code in `.R` files. And they can be the basis for your presentations as markup documents like `.tex` or `.md`, for LaTeX and Markdown files, respectively. All of these files can be opened by any program that can read text files.

One reason reproducible research is best stored in text files is that this helps *future-proof* your research. Other file formats, like those used by Microsoft Word (`.docx`) or Excel (`.xlsx`), change regularly and may not be compatible with future versions of these programs. Text files, on the other hand, can be opened by a very wide range of currently existing programs and, more likely than not, future ones as well. Even if future researchers do not have R or a LaTeX distribution, they will still be able to open your text files and, aided by frequent comments (see below), be able to understand how you conducted your research (Bowers, 2011, 3).

Text files are also very easy to search and manipulate with a wide range of programs–such as R and RStudio–that can find and replace text characters as well as merge and separate files. Finally, text files are easy to version and changes can be tracked using programs such as Git (see Chapter 5).

2.2.3 All files should be human readable

Treat all of your research files as if someone who has not worked on the project will, in the future, try to understand them. Computer code is a way of communicating with the computer. It is 'machine readable' in that the computer is able to use it to understand what you want to do.[2] However, there is a very good chance that other people (or you six months in the future) will not understand what you were telling the computer. So, you need to make all of your files 'human readable'. To make them human readable, you should comment on your code with the goal of communicating its design and purpose (Wilson et al., 2012). With this in mind it is a good idea to *comment frequently* (Bowers, 2011, 3) and *format your code using a style guide* (Nagler, 1995). For especially important pieces of code you should use *literate programming*–where the source code and the presentation text describing its design and purpose

[1] Plain text files are usually given the file extension `.txt`. Depending on the size of your data set it may not be feasible to store it as a text file. Nonetheless, text files can still be used for analysis code and presentation files.

[2] Of course, if the computer does not understand it will usually give an error message.

appear in the same document. Doing this will make it very clear to others how you accomplished a piece of research.

Commenting

In R, everything on a line after a hash character–#–(also known as number, pound, or sharp) is ignored by R, but is readable to people who open the file. The hash character is a comment declaration character. You can use the # to place comments telling other people what you are doing. Here are some examples:

```
# A complete comment line
2 + 2 # A comment after R code

## [1] 4
```

On the first line the # (hash) is placed at the very beginning, so the entire line is treated as a comment. On the second line the # is placed after the simple equation `2 + 2`. R runs the equation and finds the answer `4`, but it ignores all of the words after the hash.

Different languages have different comment declaration characters. In LaTeX everything after the % percent sign is treated as a comment, and in Markdown/HTML comments are placed inside of `<!- ->`. The hash character is used for comment declaration in command-line shell scripts.

Nagler (1995, 491) gives some advice on when and how to use comments:

- write a comment before a block of code describing what the code does,
- comment on any line of code that is ambiguous.

In this book I follow these guidelines when displaying code. Nagler also suggests that all of your source code files should begin with a comment header. *At the least* the header should include:

- a description of what the file does,
- the date it was last updated,
- the name of the file's creator and any contributors.

You may also want to include other information in the header such as what files it depends on, what output files it produces, what version of the programming language you are using, sources that may have influenced the code, and how the code is licensed. Here is an example of a minimal file header for an R source code file that creates the third figure in an article titled 'My Article':

```
###################
# R Source code file used to create Figure 3 in My 'Article'
# Created by Christopher Gandrud
# MIT License
###################
```

Feel free to use things like the long series of hash marks above and below the header, white space, and indentations to make your comments more readable.

Style guides

In natural language writing you don't necessarily have to follow a style guide. People could probably figure out what you are trying to say, but it is a lot easier for your readers if you use consistent rules. The same is true when writing computer code. It's good to follow consistent rules for formatting your code so that it's easier for you and others to understand.

There are a number of R style guides. Most of them are similar to the Google R Style Guide.[3] Hadley Wickham also has a nicely presented R style guide.[4] You may want to use the *formatR* (Xie, 2015a) package to automatically reformat your code so that it is easier to read.

Literate programming

For particularly important pieces of research code it may be useful to not only comment on the source file, but also display code in presentation text. For example, you may want to include key parts of the code you used for your main statistical models and an explanation of this code in an appendix following your article. This is commonly referred to as literate programming (Knuth, 1992).

2.2.4 Explicitly tie your files together

If everything is just a text file, then research projects can be thought of as individual text files that have a relationship with one another. They are tied together. A data file is used as input for an analysis file. The results of an analysis are shown and discussed in a markup file that is used to create a PDF document. Researchers often do not explicitly document the relationships between files that they used in their research. For example, the results of an analysis–a table or figure–may be copied and pasted into a presentation document. It can be very difficult for future researchers to trace the table or figure back to a particular statistical model and a particular data set without

[3] See: `http://google-styleguide.googlecode.com/svn/trunk/google-r-style.html`.

[4] You can find it at `http://adv-r.had.co.nz/Style.html`.

clear documentation. Therefore, it is important to make the links between your files explicit.

Tie commands are the most dynamic way to explicitly link your files together. These commands instruct the computer program you are using to use information from another file. In Table 2.1 I have compiled a selection of key tie commands you will learn how to use in this book. We'll discuss many more, but these are some of the most important.

2.2.5 Have a plan to organize, store, and make your files available

Finally, in order for independent researchers to reproduce your work, they need to be able access the files that instruct them how to do this. Files also need to be organized so that independent researchers can figure out how they fit together. So, from the beginning of your research process you should have a plan for organizing your files and a way to make them accessible.

One rule of thumb for organizing your research in files is to limit the amount of content any one file has. Files that contain many different operations can be very difficult to navigate, even if they have detailed comments. For example, it would be very difficult to find any particular operation in a file that contained the code used to gather the data, run all of the statistical models, and create the results figures and tables. If you have a hard time finding things in a file you created, think of the difficulties independent researchers will have!

Because we have so many ways to link files together, there is really no need to lump many different operations into one file. So, we can make our files modular. One source code file should be used to complete one or just a few tasks. Breaking your operations into discrete parts will also make it easier for you and others to find errors (Nagler, 1995, 490).

Chapter 4 discusses file organization in much more detail. Chapter 5 teaches you a number of ways to make your files accessible through the cloud computing services Dropbox and GitHub.

TABLE 2.1
A Selection of Commands/Packages/Programs for Tying Together Your Research Files

Command/Package/ Program	Language	Description	Chapters Discussed
knitr	R	R package with commands for tying analysis code into presentation documents including those written in LaTeX and Markdown.	Throughout
rmarkdown	R	R package that builds on *knitr*. It allows you to use Markdown to output to HTML, PDFs compiled with LaTeX or Microsoft Word.	Throughout
`download.file`	R	Downloads a file from the internet.	6
`read.table`	R	Reads a table into R. You can use this to import a plain-text file formatted data into R.	6
`read.csv`	R	Same as `read.table` with default arguments set to import `.csv` formatted data files.	6
`source_data`	R	Reads a table stored on the internet into R. You can use it to import a plain-text formatted data file into R from secure (https) URLs.	6
`source_DropboxData`	R	Imports a plain-text data file stored in a Dropbox non-Public folder into R.	6
API-based packages	R	Various packages use APIs to gather data from the internet.	6
`merge`	R	Merges together data frames.	7
`source`	R	Runs an R source code file.	8
`source_url`	R	From the *devtools* package. Runs an R source code file from a secure (`https`) url like those used by GitHub.	8
`kable`	R	Creates tables from data frames that can be rendered using Markdown or LaTeX.	9
`toLaTeX`	R	Converts R objects to LaTeX.	2
`input`	LaTeX	Includes LaTeX files inside of other LaTeX files.	12
`include`	LaTeX	Similar to `input`, but puts page breaks on either side of the included text. Usually it is used for including chapters.	12
`includegraphics`	LaTeX	Inserts a figure into a LaTeX document.	10
`![]()`	Markdown	Inserts a figure into a Markdown document.	13
Pandoc	shell	A shell program for converting files from one markup language to another. Allows you to tie presentation documents together.	12 & 13
Make	shell	A shell program for automatically building many files at the same time.	6

3

Getting Started with R, RStudio, and knitr/rmarkdown

If you have rarely or never used R before, the first section of this chapter gives you enough information to be able to get started and understand the R code I use throughout the book. For more detailed introductions on how to use R please refer to the resources I mentioned in Chapter 1 (Section 1.6). Experienced R users might want to skip the first section. In the second section I'll give a brief overview of RStudio. I highlight the key features of the main RStudio panel (what appears when you open RStudio) and some of its key features for reproducible research. Finally, I discuss the basics of the *knitr/rmarkdown* packages, how to use them in R, and how they are integrated into RStudio.

3.1 Using R: The Basics

To get you started with reproducible research, we'll cover some very basic R syntax–the rules for talking to R. I cover key parts of the R language including:

- objects & assignment,
- component selection,
- functions and commands,
- arguments,
- the workspace and history,
- packages.

Before discussing each of these in detail, let's open R and look around.[1] When you open the R GUI program by clicking on the R icon you should get a window that looks something like Figure 3.1.[2] This window is the **R console**. Below the startup information–information about what version of R you are using, license details, and so on–you should see a > (greater-than sign). This

[1]Please see Chapter 1 for instructions on how to install R.

[2]This figure and almost all screenshots in this book were taken on a computer using the Mac OS 10.10 operating system.

prompt is where you enter R code.[3] To run R code that you have typed after the prompt, hit the `Enter` or `Return` key. Now that we have a new R session open we can get started.

FIGURE 3.1
R Startup Console

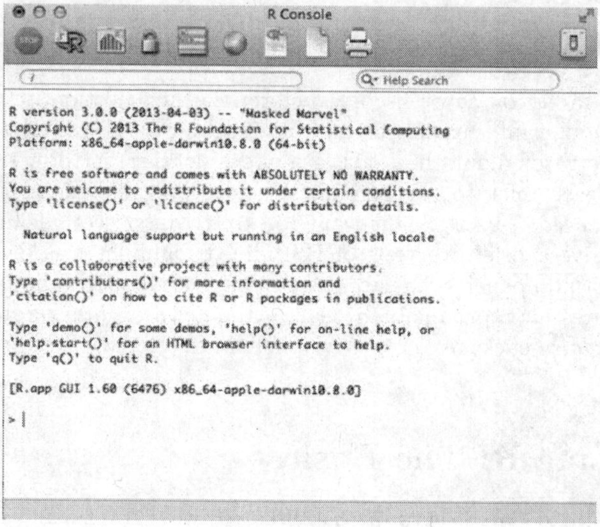

3.1.1 Objects

If you've read a description of R before, you will probably have seen it referred to as an 'object-oriented language'. What are objects? Objects are like the R language's nouns. They are things, like a vector of numbers, a data set, a word, a table of results from some analysis, and so on. Saying that R is object-oriented means that R is focused on doing actions to objects. We will talk about the actions–commands and functions–later in this section.[4] Now let's create a few objects.

---

[3] If you are using a Unix-like system such as Linux Ubuntu or Mac OS 10, you can also access R via an application called the Terminal. If you have installed R on your computer you can type `R` into the Terminal and then the `Enter` or `Return` key. This will begin a new R session. You will know you are in a new R session because the same type of startup information as in Figure 3.1 will be printed in your Terminal.

[4] Somewhat confusingly, commands and functions are themselves objects. In this chapter I treat them as distinct from other object types to avoid confusion.

Numeric & string objects

Objects can have a number of different types. Let's make two simple objects. The first is a numeric-type object. The other is a character object. We can choose almost any name we want for our objects as long as it begins with an alphabetic character and does not contain spaces.[5] Let's call our numeric object *Number*. It is a good idea to give each object a unique name to avoid conflicts and confusion. Also make sure that object names are different from the names of their components, e.g. individual variable names. This will avoid many complications like accidentally overwriting an object or confusing R about what object or component you are referring to.

To put something into the object we use the assignment operator[6] (`<-`). Let's assign the number 10 to our *Number* object.

```
Number <- 10
```

To see the contents of our object, type its name.

```
Number

## [1] 10
```

Let's briefly breakdown this output. `10` is clearly the contents of *Number*. The double hash (`##`) is included here to tell you that this is output rather than R code.[7] If you type the commands in your R console, you will not get the double hash in your output. Finally, `[1]` is the row number of the object that 10 is on. Clearly our object only has one row.

Creating an object with words and other characters–a character object–is very similar. The only difference is that you enclose the character string (letters in a word for example) inside of single or double quotation marks (`''`, or `""`).[8] To create an object called *Words* that contains the character string "Hello World":

[5] It is common for people to use either periods (`.`) or capital letters (referred to as CamelBack) to separate words in object names instead of using spaces. For example: *new.data* or *NewData* rather than *new data*. For more information on R naming conventions see Bååth (2012).

[6] The assignment operator is sometimes also referred to as the 'gets arrow'.

[7] The double hash is generated automatically by *knitr*. They make it easier to copy and paste code into R from a document created by *knitr* because R will ignore everything after a hash.

[8] Single and double quotation marks are interchangeable in R for this purpose. In this book I always use double quotes, except for *knitr* code chunk options.

```
Words <- "Hello World"
```

An object's type is important to keep in mind as it determines what we can do to it. For example, you cannot take the mean of a character object like the *Words* object:

```
mean(Words)

## Warning in mean.default(Words): argument is not numeric or
logical: returning NA

## [1] NA
```

Trying to find the mean of our *Words* object gives us a warning message and returns the value `NA`: not applicable. You can also think of `NA` as meaning "missing". To find out an object's type, use the `class` command. For example:

```
class(Words)

## [1] "character"
```

Vector & data frame objects

So far we have only looked at objects with a single number or character string.[9] Clearly we often want to use objects that have many strings and numbers. In R these are usually data frame-type objects and are roughly equivalent to the data structures you would be familiar with from using a program such as Microsoft Excel. We will be using data frames extensively throughout the book. Before looking at data frames it is useful to first look at the simpler objects that make up data frames. These are called vectors. Vectors are R's "workhorse" (Matloff, 2011). Knowing how to use vectors will be especially helpful when you cleanup raw data in Chapter 7 and make tables in Chapter 9.[10]

[9] These might be called scalar objects, though in R scalars are just vectors with a length of 1.

[10] If you want information about other types of R objects such as lists and matrices, Chapter 1 of Norman Matloff's (2011) book is a really good place to look.

Vectors

Vectors are the "fundamental data type" in R (Matloff, 2011). They are simply an ordered group of numbers, character strings, and so on.[11] It may be useful to think of basically all R objects as composed of vectors. For example, data frames are basically multiple vectors of the same length–i.e. they have the same number of rows–attached together to form columns.

Let's create a simple numeric vector containing the numbers 2.8, 2, and 14.8. To do this we will use the `c` (combine) function:

```
NumericVect <- c(2.8, 2, 14.8)

# Show NumericVect's contents
NumericVect

## [1]  2.8  2.0 14.8
```

Vectors of character strings are created in a similar way. The only major difference is that each character string is enclosed in quotation marks like this:

```
CharacterVect <- c("Albania", "Botswana", "Cambodia")

# Show CharacterVect's contents
CharacterVect

## [1] "Albania"  "Botswana" "Cambodia"
```

To give you a preview of what we are going to do when we start working with real data sets, let's combine the two vectors *NumericVect* and *CharacterVect* into a new object with the `cbind` function. This function binds the two vectors together side-by-side as columns.[12]

```
StringNumObject <- cbind(CharacterVect, NumericVect)
```

[11] In a vector, every member of the group must be of the same type. If you want an ordered group of values with different types you can use lists.

[12] If you want to combine objects as if they were rows of the same column(s), use the `rbind` function.

```
# Show StringNumObject's contents
StringNumObject

##      CharacterVect NumericVect
## [1,] "Albania"     "2.8"
## [2,] "Botswana"    "2"
## [3,] "Cambodia"    "14.8"
```

By binding these two objects together we've created a new matrix object.[13] You can see that the numbers in the *NumericVect* column are between quotation marks. Matrices, like vectors, can only have one data type.

Data frames

If we want to have an object with rows and columns and allow the columns to contain data with different types, we need to use data frames. Let's use the `data.frame` command to combine the *NumericVect* and *CharacterVect* objects.

```
StringNumObject <- data.frame(CharacterVect, NumericVect)

# Display contents of StringNumObject data frame
StringNumObject

##   CharacterVect NumericVect
## 1       Albania         2.8
## 2      Botswana         2.0
## 3      Cambodia        14.8
```

There are a few important things to notice in this output. The first is that because we used the same name for the data frame object as the previous matrix object, R deleted the matrix object and replaced it with the data frame. This is something to keep in mind when you are creating new objects. In general it is a better idea to assign elements to new objects rather than overwriting old ones. This will help avoid accidentally using an object you had not intended to. It also allows you to more easily change previously run source code.

[13] Matrices are vectors with columns as well as rows.

You can see the data frame's names attribute.[14] It is the column names. You can use the **names** command to see any data frame's names:[15]

```
names(StringNumObject)

## [1] "CharacterVect" "NumericVect"
```

You will also notice that the first column of the data set has no name and is a series of numbers. This is the row.names attribute. Data frame rows can be given any name as long as each row name is unique. We can use the **row.names** command to set the row names from a vector. For example,

```
# Reassign row.names
row.names(StringNumObject) <- c("First", "Second", "Third")

# Display new row.names
row.names(StringNumObject)

## [1] "First"  "Second" "Third"
```

You can see in this example how the **row.names** command can also be used to print the row names.[16] The row.names attribute does not behave like a regular data frame column. You cannot, for example, include it as a variable in a regression. You can use the **row.names** command to assign the row.names values to a regular column (for an example see Section 10.4.1).

You will notice in the output for *StringNumObject* that the strings in the **CharacterVect** column are no longer in quotation marks. This does not mean that they are somehow now numeric data. To prove this, try to find the mean of **CharacterVect** by running it through the **mean** command:

```
mean(StringNumObject$ChacterVect)

## Warning in mean.default(StringNumObject$ChacterVect): argument
is not numeric or logical: returning NA

## [1] NA
```

[14] Matrices can also have a names attribute.

[15] You can also use **names** to assign names for the entire data frame. For example, `names(StringNumObject) <- c("Variable1", "Variable2")`

[16] Note that this is really only useful for data frames with few rows.

3.1.2 Component selection

The last bit of code we just saw will probably be confusing. Why do we have a dollar sign ($) between the name of our data frame object name and the **CharacterVect** variable? The dollar sign is called the component selector.[17] It basically extracts a part–component–of an object. In the previous example it extracted the **CharacterVect** column from the *StringNumObject* and fed it to the `mean` command, which tried (in this case unsuccessfully) to find its mean.

We can Of course, use the component selector to create new objects with parts of other objects. Imagine that we have the *StringNumObject* and want an object with only the information in the numbers column. Let's use the following code:

```
NewNumeric <- StringNumObject$NumericVect

# Display contents of NewNumeric
NewNumeric

## [1]  2.8  2.0 14.8
```

Knowing how to use the component selector will be especially useful when we discuss making tables for presentation documents in Chapter 9.

`attach` *and* `with`

Using the component selector can create long repetitive code if you want to select many components. You have to write the object name, a dollar sign, and the component name every time you want to select a component. You can streamline your code by using commands such as `attach` and `with`.

The `attach` command attaches a database to R's search path.[18] R will then search the database for variables you specify. You don't need to use the component selector to tell R again to look in a particular data frame after you have attached it. For example, let's attach the *cars* data that comes with R. It has two variables, **speed** and **dist**.[19]

```
# Attach cars to search path
```

[17]It's also sometimes called the element name operator.

[18]You can see what is in your current search path with the `search` command. Just type `search()` into your R console.

[19]For more information on this data set, type `?cars` into your R console.

```
attach(cars)

# Display speed
head(speed)

## [1] 4 4 7 7 8 9

# Display dist
head(dist)

## [1]  2 10  4 22 16 10

# Detach cars
detach(cars)
```

We used the **head** command to see just the first few values of each variable. It is a good idea to **detach** a data frame after you are done using it, to avoid confusing R.

Similarly, you can use **with** when you run commands using a particular database (see Section 3.1.4 for more details about commands). For example, we can find the mean of *NumericVect* **with** the *StringNumObject* data frame:

```
with(StringNumObject, {
    mean(NumericVect)
    }
)

## [1] 6.533333
```

You can see that in the **with** command the data frame object goes first and then the **mean** command[20] goes second in curly brackets ({}).

For examples in this book I largely avoid using the **attach** and **with** commands. I mostly use the component selector. Though it creates longer code, I find that code written with the component selector is easier to follow. It's always clear which object we are selecting a component from. Nonetheless, **attach** and **with** are very useful for streamlining your R code.

[20]Using R terminology, the second "argument" value–the code after the comma–of the **with** command is called an "expression", because it can contain more than one R command or statement. See Section 3.1.5 for a more comprehensive discussion of R command arguments.

3.1.3 Subscripts

Another way to select parts of an object is to use subscripts. You have already seen subscripts in the output from our examples so far. They are denoted with square braces (`[]`). We can use subscripts to select not only columns from data frames but also rows and individual values. As we began to see in some of the previous output, each part of a data frame has an address captured by its row and column number. We can tell R to find a part of an object by putting the row number/name, column number/name, or both in square braces. The first part denotes the rows and separated by a comma (`,`) are the columns.

To give you an idea of how this works let's use the *cars* data set that comes with R. Use the `head` command to get a sense of what this data set looks like.

```
head(cars)

##   speed dist
## 1     4    2
## 2     4   10
## 3     7    4
## 4     7   22
## 5     8   16
## 6     9   10
```

We can see a data frame with information on various cars' speeds (**speed**) and stopping distances (**dist**). If we want to select only the third through seventh rows we can use the following subscript commands:

```
cars[3:7, ]

##   speed dist
## 3     7    4
## 4     7   22
## 5     8   16
## 6     9   10
## 7    10   18
```

The colon (`:`) creates a sequence of whole numbers from 3 to 7. To select the fourth row of the **dist** column we can type:

```
cars[4, 2]

## [1] 22
```

An equivalent way to do this is:

```
cars[4, "dist"]

## [1] 22
```

Finally, we can even include a vector of column names to select:

```
cars[4, c("speed", "dist")]

##   speed dist
## 4     7   22
```

3.1.4 Functions and commands

If objects are the nouns of the R language, functions and commands[21] are the verbs. They do things to objects. Let's use the `mean` command as an example. This command takes the mean of a numeric vector object. Remember our *NumericVect* object from before:

```
# Show contents of NumericVect
NumericVect

## [1]  2.8  2.0 14.8
```

To find the mean of this object simply type:

[21] For the purposes of this book I treat the two as the same.

```
mean(x = NumericVect)

## [1] 6.533333
```

We use the assignment operator to place a command's output into an object. For example:

```
MeanNumericVect <- mean(x = NumericVect)
```

Notice that we typed the command's name then enclosed the object name in parentheses immediately afterwards. This is the basic syntax that all commands use, i.e. `COMMAND(ARGUMENTS)`. If you don't want to explicitly include an argument *you still need to type the parentheses after the command.*

3.1.5 Arguments

Arguments modify what commands do. In our most recent example we gave the `mean` command one argument (`x = NumericVect`) telling it that we wanted to find the mean of *NumericVect*. Arguments use the `ARGUMENTLABEL = VALUE` syntax.[22] In this case `x` is the argument label.

To find all of the arguments that a command can accept, look at the **Arguments** section of the command's help file. To access the help file type: `?COMMAND`. For example,

```
?mean
```

The help file will also tell you the default values that the arguments are set to. Clearly, you do not need to explicitly set an argument if you want to use its default value.

You do have to be fairly precise with the syntax for your argument's values. Values for logical arguments must written as `TRUE` or `FALSE`.[23] Arguments that accept character strings require quotation marks.

Let's see how to use multiple arguments with the `round` command. This command rounds a vector of numbers. We can use the `digits` argument to

[22]Note: you do not have to put spaces between the argument label and the equals sign or the equals sign and the value. However, having spaces can make your code easier for other people to read.

[23]They can be abbreviated `T` and `F`.

specify how many decimal places we want the numbers rounded to. To round the object *MeanNumericVect* to one decimal place type:

```
round(x = MeanNumericVect, digits = 1)

## [1] 6.5
```

Note that arguments are separated by commas.

Some arguments do not need to be explicitly labeled. For example, we could have written:

```
# Find mean of NumericVect
mean(NumericVect)

## [1] 6.533333
```

R will do its best to figure out what you want and will only give up when it can't. This will generate an error message. However, to avoid any misunderstandings between yourself and R it can be good practice to label most of your arguments. This will also make your code easier for other people to read, i.e. it will be more reproducible.

You can stack arguments inside of other arguments. To have R find the mean of *NumericVect* and round it to one decimal place use:

```
round(mean(NumericVect), digits = 1)

## [1] 6.5
```

Stacking functions inside of each other can create code that is difficult to read. Another option that potentially makes more easily understandable code is piping using the pipe function (%>%) that you can access from the *magrittr* package (Bache and Wickham, 2014). The basic idea behind the pipe function is that the output of one function is set as the first argument of the next. For example, to find the mean of **NumericVect** and then round it to one decimal place use:

```
# Load magrittr package
library(magrittr)

# Find mean of NumericVect and round to 1 decimal place
mean(NumericVect) %>% round(digits = 1)

## [1] 6.5
```

3.1.6 The workspace & history

All of the objects you create become part of your workspace, alternatively known as the current working environment. Use the `ls` command to list all of the objects in your current workspace.[24]

```
ls()

##  [1] "CatPlot"            "CharacterVect"      "cust_coef"
##  [4] "DataDuplicates"     "DataNotDuplicates" "DataUrl"
##  [7] "Description"        "DescriptionsBound" "DescriptionsTable"
## [10] "DescriptTable"      "DispropData"        "DispropOld"
## [13] "doInstall"          "Draw1"              "Draw2"
## [16] "FCLabels"           "FertConsumpData"    "FertFactor"
## [19] "FertOutliers"       "FinalCleanedData"   "FinDataFull"
## [22] "FinRegulatorData"   "FinURL"             "GatheredFert"
## [25] "GatheredFertSub"    "GatheredInflation" "InflationData"
## [28] "InflationUrl"       "kable_ex"           "LinePlot"
## [31] "M1"                 "M2"                 "M3"
## [34] "M4"                 "M5"                 "MeanNumericVect"
## [37] "MergedData1"        "MergedData2"        "NBModel"
## [40] "NBModel2"           "NBModel2Sum"        "NBModelSum"
## [43] "NBSum2DF"           "NBSumDataFrame"     "NBTable"
## [46] "NewNumeric"         "Number"             "NumericVect"
## [49] "OldUrlAddress"      "ParentDirectory"    "SetupDirectory"
## [52] "SpreadFert"         "StringNumObject"    "temp"
## [55] "toInstall"          "UDSData"            "URL"
## [58] "UrlAddress"         "Variable"           "Words"
```

You can remove specific objects from the workspace using the `rm` command. For example, to remove the `CharacterVect` and `Words` objects type:

[24]Note: your workspace will probably include different objects than this example. These are objects created to knit the book.

```
rm(CharacterVect, Words)
```

To save the entire workspace into a binary–not plain-text–RData file use the `save.image` command. The main argument of `save.image` is the location and name of the file in which you want to save the workspace. If you don't specify the file path it will be saved into your current working directory (see Chapter 4 for information on files paths and working directories). For example, to save the current workspace in a file called *DecemberWorkspace.RData* in the current working directory type:

```
save.image(file = "DecemberWorkspace.RData")
```

Use the `load` command to load a saved workspace back into R:

```
load(file = "DecemberWorkspace.RData")
```

You should generally avoid having R automatically save your workspace when you quit and reload it when you start R again. Instead, when you return to working on a project, rerun the source code files. This avoids any complications caused when you use an object in your workspace that is left over from running an older version of the source code.[25] In general I also recommend against saving data in binary RData formatted files. Because they are not text files they are not human readable and are much less future-proof.

One of the few times when saving your workspace is very useful is when it includes an object that was computationally difficult and took a long time to create. In this case you can save only the large object with the `save` command.[26] For example, if we have a very large object called *Comp* we can save it to a file called *Comp.RData* like this:

```
save(Comp, file = "Comp.RData")
```

[25]For example, imagine you create an object, then change the source code you used to create the object. However, there is a syntax error in the new version of the source code. The old object won't be overwritten and you will be mistakenly using the old object in future commands.

[26]The `save.image` command is just a special case of `save`.

R history

When you enter a command into R it becomes part of your history. To see the most recent commands in your history use the `history` command. You can also use the up and down arrows on your keyboard when your cursor is in the R console to scroll through your history.

3.1.7 Global R options

In R you can set global options with the `options` command. This lets you set how R runs and outputs commands through an entire R session. For example, to have output rounded to one decimal place, set the `digits` argument:

```
options(digits = 1)
```

3.1.8 Installing new packages and loading functions

Commands are stored in R packages. The commands we have used so far were loaded automatically by default. One of the great things about R is the many user-created packages[27] that greatly expand the number of commands we can use. To install commands that do not come with the basic R installation you need to install the add-on packages that contain them. To do this, use the `install.packages` command. By default this command downloads and installs the packages from the Comprehensive R Archive Network (CRAN).

For the code you need to install all of the packages used in this book, see page xix. When you install a package, you will likely be given a list of mirrors from which you can download the package. Simply select the mirror closest to you.

Once you have installed a package you need to load it so that you can use its functions. Use the `library` command to load a package.[28] Use the following code to load the *ggplot2* package that we use in Chapter 10 to create figures.

---

[27]For the latest list see: `http://cran.r-project.org/web/packages/available_packages_by_name.html`.

[28]You will probably see R packages referred to as "libraries", though this is a misnomer. See this blog post by Carlisle Rainey for a discussion: `http://www.carlislerainey.com/2013/01/02/packages-v-libraries-in-r/?utm_source=rss&utm_medium=rss&utm_campaign=packages-v-libraries-in-r` (posted 2 January 2013).

```
library(ggplot2)
```

Please note that for the examples in this book I only specify what package a command is from if it is not loaded by default when you start an R session.

Finally, if you want to make sure R uses a command from a specific package you can use the double-colon operator (`::`). For example, to make sure that we use the `qplot` function from the *ggplot2* package we type:

```
ggplot2::qplot(. . .)
```

We can use the double-colon to simplify our code as we don't need to include `library(. . .)`. Using the double-colon in this way ensures that R will use the command from the particular package you want and makes it clear to a source code reader what package a command comes from. Note that it does not load all of the functions in the package, just the one you ask for.

3.2 Using RStudio

As I mentioned in Chapter 1, RStudio is an integrated development environment for R. It provides a centralized and well-organized place to do almost anything you want to do with R. As we will see later in this chapter, it is especially well integrated with literate programming tools for reproducible research. Right now let's take a quick tour of the basic RStudio window.

The default window

When you first open RStudio you should see a default window that looks like Figure 3.2. In this figure you see three window panes. The large one on the left is the *Console*. This pane functions exactly the same as the console in regular R. Other panes include the *Environment/History* panes, in the upper right-hand corner. The *Environment* pane shows you all of the objects in your workspace and some of their characteristics, like how many observations a data frame has. You can click on an object in this pane to see its contents. This is especially useful for quickly looking at a data set in much the same way that you can visually scan a Microsoft Excel spreadsheet. The *History* pane records all of the commands you have run. It also allows you to rerun code and insert it into a source code file.

In the lower right-hand corner you will see the *Files/Plots/Packages/Help/Viewer* panes. We will discuss the *Files* pane in more detail in Chapter 4. Basically, it allows you to see and organize your files. The *Plots* pane

FIGURE 3.2
RStudio Startup Panel

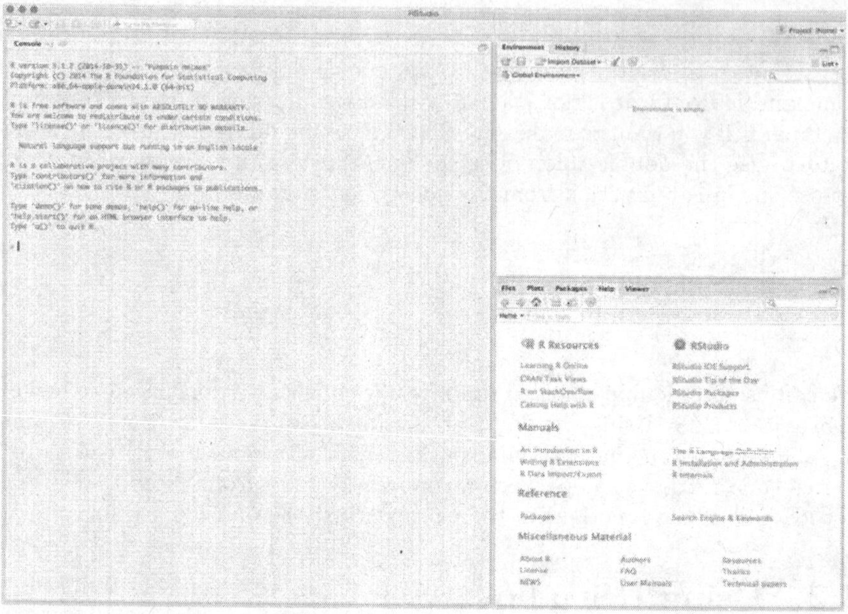

is where figures you create in R appear. This pane allows you to see all of the figures you have created in a session using the right and left arrow icons. It also lets you save the figures in a variety of formats. The *Packages* pane shows the packages you have installed, allows you to load individual packages by clicking on the dialog box next to them, access their help files (just click on the package name), update the packages, and even install new packages. The *Help* pane shows you help files. You can search for help files and search within help files using this pane. Finally, the *Viewer* pane allows you to view local web content like JavaScript graphics and Shiny web apps.

The Source *pane*

There is an important pane that does not show up when you open RStudio for the first time. This is the *Source* pane. The *Source* pane is where you create, edit, and run your source code files. It also functions as an editor for your markup files. It is the center of reproducible research in RStudio.

Let's first look at how to use the *Source* pane with regular R files. We will then cover how it works with *knitr*/*rmarkdown* in more detail in the next section.

R source code files have the file extension `.R`. When you create a new source code document, RStudio will open a new *Source* pane. Do this by going to the menu bar and clicking on `File` → `New`. In the `New` drop-down menu you have the option to create a variety of different source code documents. Select the `R Script` option. You should now see a new pane with a bar across the top that looks like the first image in Figure 3.3. To run the R code you have in your source code file simply highlight it[29] and click the `Run` icon (Run) on the top bar. This sends the code to the console where it is run. The icon to the right of `Run` simply runs the code above where you have highlighted. The `Source` icon next to this runs all of the code in the file using R's `source` command.

FIGURE 3.3
RStudio Source Code Pane Top Bars

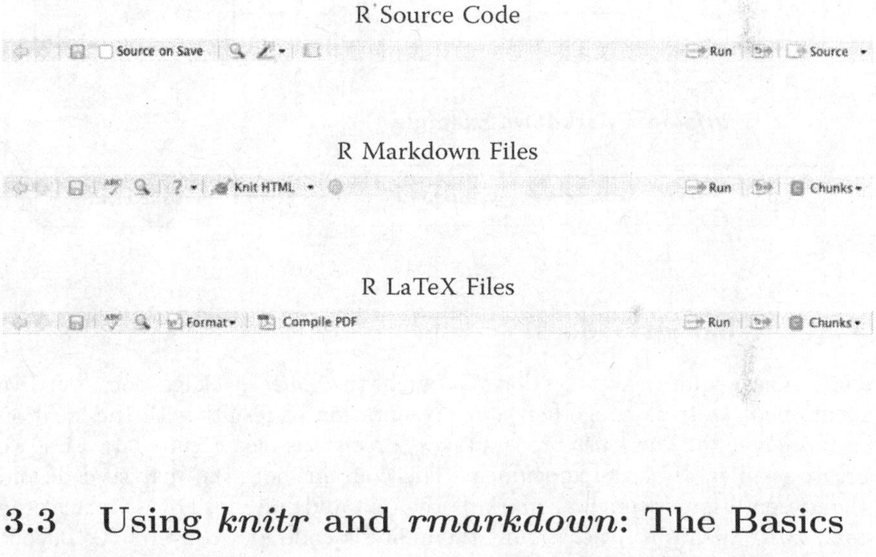

3.3 Using *knitr* and *rmarkdown*: The Basics

To get started with *knitr* and *rmarkdown* in R or RStudio we need to learn some of the basic concepts and syntax. The concepts are the same regardless of the markup language we are knitting R code with, but much of the syntax varies by markup language. *rmarkdown* relies on *knitr* and a utility called *Pandoc* to create many different types of presentation documents (HTML, PDF, or MS Word) from one document written largely using *knitr*'s R Markdown syntax.

[29] If you are only running one line of code, you don't need to highlight the code; you can simply put your cursor on that line.

FIGURE 3.4
The *knitr/rmarkdown* Process

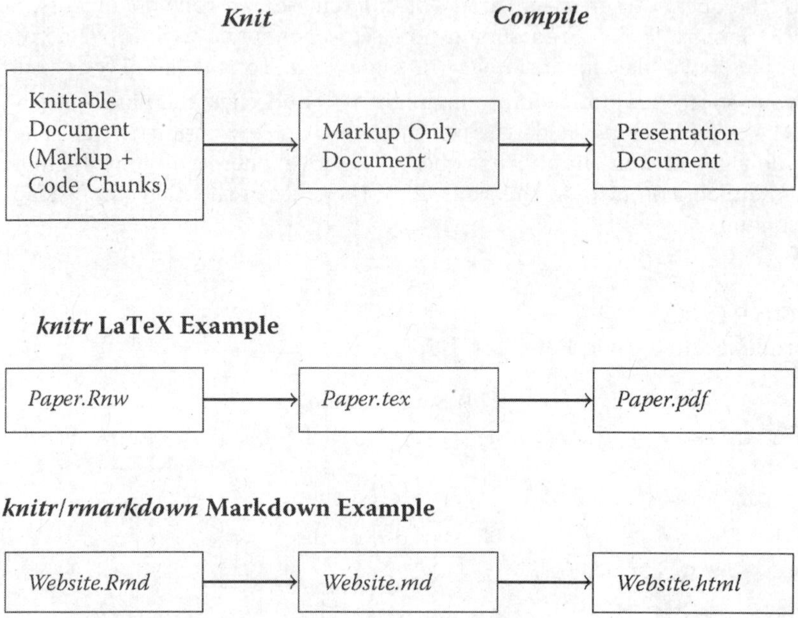

3.3.1 What *knitr* does

Let's take a quick, abstract look at what the *knitr* package does. As I've mentioned, *knitr* ties together your presentation of results with the creation of those results. The *knitr* process takes three steps (see Figure 3.4). First we create a knittable markup document. This contains both the analysis code and the presentation document's markup–the text and rules for how to format the text. *knitr* then *knits*: i.e. it runs the analysis code and converts the output into the markup language you are using according to the rules that you tell it to use. It inserts the marked-up results into a document that only contains markup for the presentation document. You *compile* this markup document as you would if you hadn't used *knitr* into your final PDF document or webpage presenting your results.

3.3.2 What *rmarkdown* does

The *rmarkdown* package implements a variation on this process that utilizes a program called Pandoc to create presentation documents in multiple formats from an a knittable document written in Markdown. The main difference between pure *knitr* markdown and *rmarkdown* documents is the inclusion of a header specifying how you want to render the document with Pandoc.[30]

The header is written in YAML.[31] The YAML header can include information such as the document's title, author, whether or not to include a table of contents, and a link to a BibTeX bibliography file. YAML is a straightforward data format that organizes information in a simple hierarchy. The header begins and ends with three dashes (`---`). Information keys–like "title" and "author"–are separated from their associated "values" by a colon (`:`). Subvalues of a hierarchy are denoted by being placed on a new line and indented.[32] Here is a basic *rmarkdown* header that indicates the document's title, author, date, and that it will be turned into a PDF document (via LaTeX).

```
---
title: "A Basic PDF Presentation Document"
author: "Christopher Gandrud"
date: "30 November 2015"
output: pdf_document:
    toc: true
---
```

The title, author, and date, will be placed at the beginning of the output document. The final line (`toc: true`) creates a table of contents near the beginning of the PDF document when we knit it. We will discuss more header options in Chapter 13.

RStudio can automatically create a basic header for the type of output document that you want when you open a new *rmarkdown* file. Simply select `File` → New File → `R Markdown...`. A window will appear that looks like Figure 3.5. Simply select the type of output document you want to create and click `Ok`.

In addition to the header, *rmarkdown* differs from *knitr* in that you can include Pandoc syntax in your R Markdown document. This can be useful for bibliographies as we will discuss in Chapter 13. Nonetheless, **remember** that apart from the header and ability to include Pandoc syntax, at the simplest level *rmarkdown* documents are *knitr* documents written in R Markdown syntax. Importantly, they have the same code chunk syntax we will see shortly.

---

[30] Note: you can also create an *rmarkdown* document without a header.

[31] YAML is a recursive acronym that means "YAML Ain't Markup Language".

[32] It doesn't matter how many spaces you use to indent, as long as all indentations have the same number of spaces.

FIGURE 3.5
The New R Markdown Options Window

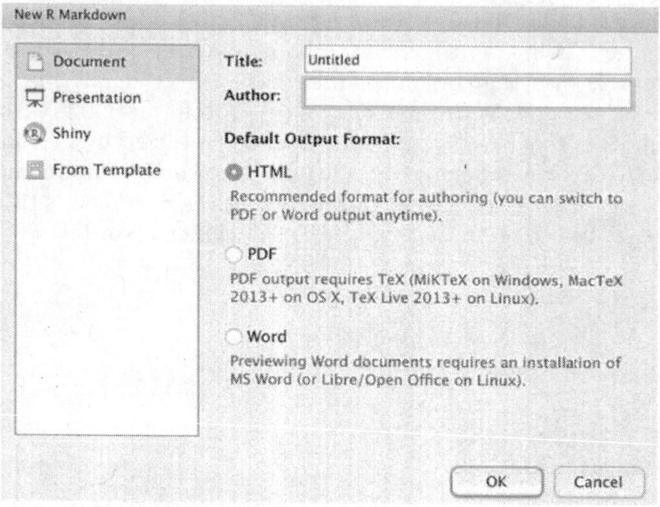

3.3.3 File extensions

When you save a knittable file, use a file extension that indicates (a) that it is knittable and (b) what markup language it is using. You can use a number of file extensions for R Markdown files including: `.Rmd` and `.Rmarkdown`.[33] LaTeX documents that include *knitr* code chunks are generally called R Sweave files and have the file extension `.Rnw`. This terminology is a little confusing. It is a holdover from *knitr*'s main literate programming predecessor *Sweave*. You can also use the less confusing file extension `.Rtex`, as regular LaTeX files have the extension `.tex`. However, the syntax for `.Rtex` files is different from that used with `.Rnw` files. We'll look at this issue in more detail below.

3.3.4 Code chunks

When you want to include R code into your markup presentation documents, place them in a code chunk. Code chunk syntax differs depending on the markup language we are using to write our documents. Let's see the syntax for R Markdown and R LaTeX files. If you are unfamiliar with basic LaTeX or Markdown syntax you might want to skim chapters 11 and 13 to familiarize yourself with it before reading this section.

[33]R Markdown files that you compile with *knitr* or *rmarkdown* have the same `.Rmd` file extension.

R Markdown

In R Markdown files we begin a code chunk by writing the head: ```{r}. A code chunk is closed–ended–simply with: ```. For example:

````
```{r}
# Example of an R Markdown code chunk
StringNumObject <- cbind(CharacterVect, NumericVect)
```
````

The R Markdown code chunk syntax is exactly the same for files you compile with *knitr* or *rmarkdown*.

R LaTeX

There are two different ways to delimit code chunks in R LaTeX documents. One way largely emulates the established *Sweave* syntax.[34] *knitr* also supports files with the .Rtex extension, though the code chunk syntax is different. I will cover both types of syntax for code chunks in LaTeX documents. Throughout the book I use the older and more established Sweave-style syntax.

Sweave-style

Traditional Sweave-style code chunks begin with the following head: «»=. The code chunk is closed with an at sign (@).

```
« »=
# Example of a Sweave-style code chunk
StringNumObject <- cbind(CharacterVect, NumericVect)
@
```

Rtex-style

Sweave-style code chunk syntax is fairly baroque compared to the Rtex-style syntax. To begin a code chunk in an Rtex file simply type double percent signs followed by begin.rcode, i.e. %% begin.rcode. To close the chunk you

[34]The syntax has its genesis in a literate programming tool called noweb (Leisch, 2002; Ramsey, 2011).

use double percent signs: `%%`. Each line in the code chunk needs to begin with a single percent sign. For example:

```
%% begin.rcode
% # Example of a Rtex-style code chunk
% StringNumObject <- cbind(CharacterVect, NumericVect)
%%
```

Code chunk labels

Each chunk has a label. When a code chunk creates a plot or the output is cached–stored for future use–*knitr* uses the chunk label for the new file's name. If you do not explicitly give the chunk a label it will be assigned one like: `unnamed-chunk-1`.

To explicitly assign chunk labels in R Markdown documents, place the label name inside of the braces after the `r`. If we wanted to use the label `ChunkLabel` we type:

````
```{r ChunkLabel}
# Example chunk label
```
````

The same general format applies to the two types of LaTeX chunks. In Sweave-style chunks we type: `«ChunkLabel»=`. In Rtex-style we use: `%% begin.rcode ChunkLabel`. Try not to use spaces or periods in your label names. Also remember that chunk labels *must* be unique.

Code chunk options

There are many times when we want to change how our code chunks are knitted and presented. Maybe we only want to show the code and not the results or perhaps we don't want to show the code at all but just a figure that it produces. Maybe we want the figure to be formatted on a page in a certain way. To make these changes and many others we can specify code chunk options.

Like chunk labels, you specify options in the chunk head. Place them after the chunk label, separated by a comma. Chunk options are written following pretty much the same rules as regular R command arguments. They have a similar `OPTION_LABEL=VALUE` structure as arguments. The option values must be written in the same way that argument values are. Character strings need to be inside of quotation marks. The logical `TRUE` and `FALSE` operators cannot be written `''true''` and `''false''`. For example, imagine we have a Markdown code chunk called `ChunkLabel`. If we want to run the *knitr* code chunk, but not show the code in the final presentation document, we can use the option `echo=FALSE`.

````
```{r ChunkLabel, echo=FALSE}
StringNumObject <- cbind(CharacterVect, NumericVect)
```
````

Note that all labels and code chunk options must be on the same line. Options are separated by commas. The syntax for *knitr* options is the same regardless of the markup language. Here is the same chunk option in Rtex-style syntax:

```
%% begin.rcode ChunkLabel, echo=FALSE
% StringNumObject <- cbind(CharacterVect, NumericVect)
%%
```

Throughout this book we will look at a number of different code chunk options. Many of the chunk options we will use in this book are listed in Table 3.1. For the full list of *knitr* options see the *knitr* chunk options page maintained by *knitr*'s creator Yihui Xie: `http://yihui.name/knitr/options`.

3.3.5 Global chunk options

So far we have only looked at how to set local options in *knitr* code chunks, i.e. options for only one specific chunk. If we want an option to apply to all of the chunks in our document we can set global chunk options. Options are 'global' in the sense that they apply to the entire document. Setting global chunk options helps us create documents that are formatted consistently without having to repetitively specify the same option every time we create a new code chunk. For example, in this book I center almost all of the figures. Instead of using the `fig.align='center'` option in each code chunk that creates a figure, I set the option globally.

To set a global option, first create a new code chunk at the beginning of your document.[35] You will probably want to set the option `include=FALSE` so

[35] In Markdown, you can put global chunk options at the very top of the document. In LaTeX they should be placed after the `\begin{document}` command (see Chapter 11 for more information on how LaTeX documents are structured).

TABLE 3.1
A Selection of *knitr* Code Chunk Options

Chunk Option Label	Type	Description
`cache`	Logical	Whether or not to save results from the code chunk in a cache database. Note: cached chunks are only run when they are changed.
`cache.vars`	Character Vector	Specify the variable names to save in the cache database.
`eval`	Logical	Whether or not to run the chunk.
`echo`	Logical	Whether or not to include the code in the presentation document.
`error`	Logical	Whether or not to include error messages.
`engine`	Character	Set the programming language for *knitr* to evaluate the code chunk with.
`fig.align`	Character	Align figures. (Note: does not work with R Markdown documents.)
`fig.path`	Character	Set the directory where figures will be saved.
`include`	Logical	When `include=FALSE` the chunk is evaluated, but the results are not included in the presentation document.
`message`	Logical	Whether or not to include R messages.
`out.height`	Numeric	Set figures' heights in the presentation document.
`out.width`	Numeric	Set figures' widths in the presentation document.
`results`	Character	How to include results in the presentation document.
`tidy`	Logical	Whether or not to have *knitr* format printed code chunks.
`warning`	Logical	Whether or not to include warnings.

These commands are discussed in more detail in Chapter 8.

that *knitr* doesn't include the code in your presentation document. Inside the code chunk use `opts_chunk$set`. You can set any chunk option as an argument to `opts_chunk$set`. The option will be applied across your document, unless you set a different local option.

Here is an example of how you can center align all of the figures in Sweave-style code chunks. Place the following code at the beginning of the document:

```
<<ChunkLabel, include=FALSE>>=
# Center align all knitr figures
opts_chunk$set(fig.align='center')
@
```

`Note`: if you want to use `opts_chunk` in a document rendered with *rmarkdown* you will need to load *knitr* in a code chunk preceding the call.

3.3.6 *knitr* package options

knitr package options affect how the package itself runs. For example, the `progress` option can be set as either `TRUE` or `FALSE`[36] depending on whether or not you want a progress bar to be displayed when you knit a code chunk. You can use `base.dir` to set the directory where you want all of your figures to be saved (see Chapter 4) or the `child.path` option to specify where child documents are located (see Chapter 12).

You set package options in a similar way as global chunk options with `opts_knit$set`. For example, include this code at the beginning of a document to turn off the progress bar when it is knitted:

```
<<ChunkLabel, include=FALSE>>=
# Turn off knitr progress bar
opts_knit$set(progress=FALSE)
@
```

3.3.7 Hooks

You can also set hooks. Hooks come in two types: chunk hooks and output hooks. Chunk hooks run a function before or after a code chunk. Output hooks

[36] It's set as `TRUE` by default.

change how the raw output is formatted. I don't cover hooks in much detail in this book. For more information on hooks, please see Yihui Xie's webpage: `http://yihui.name/knitr/hooks`.

3.3.8 *knitr*, *rmarkdown*, & RStudio

RStudio is highly integrated with *knitr*/*rmarkdown* and the markup languages that they work with. Because of this integration it is easier to create and compile *knitr*/*rmarkdown* documents in RStudio than plain R. Most of the RStudio/*knitr*/*rmarkdown* features are accessed in the *Source* pane. The *Source* pane's appearance and capabilities change depending on the type of file you have open in it. RStudio uses a file's extension and, if it is an *rmarkdown* document, its header, to determine what type of file you have open.[37] We have already seen some of the features the *Source* pane has for R source code files. Let's now look at how to use *knitr* and *rmarkdown* with R source code files as well as the markup formats we cover in this book: R Markdown and R LaTeX.

Compiling R source code Notebooks

If you want a quick well-formatted account of the code that you ran and the results that you got you can use RStudio's "Compile Notebook" capabilities. RStudio uses *rmarkdown* to create a standalone file presenting your source code and results. It will include all of the code from an R source file as well as the output. This can be useful for recording the steps you took to do an analysis. You can see an example RStudio Notebook in Figure 3.6.

If you want to create a Notebook from an open R source code file simply click the `Compile Notebook` icon ( ) in the *Source* pane's top bar.[38] Then in the window that pops up select the output type you would like (HTML, PDF or MS Word) and click the `Compile` button. For this example I selected HTML. In Figure 3.6 you can see near the top center right a small globe icon next to the word "Publish". Clicking this allows you to publish your Notebook to RPubs (`http://www.rpubs.com/`). RPubs is a site for sharing your Notebooks over the internet. You can publish not only Notebooks, but also any *knitr*/emphrmarkdown Markdown document you compile in RStudio.

R Markdown

The second image in Figure 3.3 is what the *Source* pane's top bar looks like when you have an R Markdown file open. You'll notice the familiar `Run` button for running R code. At the far right you can see a new `Chunks` drop-down menu (Chunks). In this menu you can select `Insert Chunk` to insert the basic

[37]You can manually set how you want the *Source* pane to act by selecting the file type using the drop-down menu in the lower right-hand corner of the *Source* pane.

[38]Alternatively, `File` → `Compile Notebook...`

FIGURE 3.6
RStudio Notebook Example

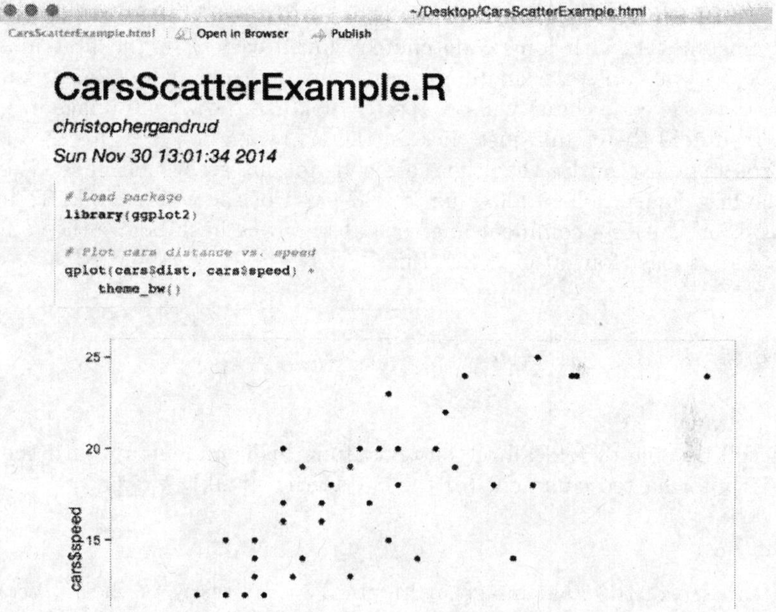

syntax required for a code chunk. There is also an option to `Run Current Chunk`–i.e. the chunk where your cursor is located–`Run Next Chunk`, and `Run All` chunks. You can navigate to a specific chunk using a drop-down menu on the bottom left-hand side of the *Source* pane (e.g. (Top Level) ÷). This can be very useful if you are working with a long document. To knit your file, click the `Knit HTML` icon on the left side of the *Source* pane's top bar. This will clearly knit it to an HTML file. If you click on the downward arrow on the right of this icon you will be given the opportunity to also knit the document to a PDF or an MS Word file using *rmarkdown*. Other useful buttons in the R Markdown *Source* pane's top bar include the `ABC` spell check icon and question mark icon, which gives you a Markdown syntax reference file in the Help pane.

Another useful RStudio *knitr*/*rmarkdown* integration feature is that RStudio can properly highlight both the markup language syntax and the R code in the *Source* pane. This makes your source code much easier to read and navigate. RStudio can also fold code chunks. This makes navigating through long documents, with long code chunks, much easier. In the first image in Figure 3.7 you can see a small downward facing arrow at line 25. If you click this arrow the code chunk will collapse to look like the second image in Figure 3.7. To unfold the chunk, just click on the arrow again.

You may also notice that there are code folding arrows on lines 27 and 34 in the first image. These allow us to fold parts of the code chunk. To enable this option, create a comment line with at least one hash before the comment text and at least four after it like this:

```
#### An RStudio Foldable Comment ####
```

You will be able to fold all of the text after this comment up until the next similarly formatted comment (or the end of the chunk).

R LaTeX

You can see in the final image in Figure 3.3 that many of the *Source* pane options for R LaTeX files are the same as R Markdown files, the key differences being that there is a `Compile PDF` icon (Compile PDF) instead of `Knit HTML`. Clicking this icon knits the file and creates a PDF file in your R LaTeX file's directory. There is also a `Format` icon instead of the question mark icon. This actually inserts LaTeX formatting commands into your document for things such as section headings and bullet lists. These commands can be very tedious to type out by hand otherwise.

Change default .Rnw knitter

By default RStudio may be set up to use *Sweave* for compiling LaTeX documents. To use *knitr* instead of *Sweave* to knit `.Rnw` files you should click on

FIGURE 3.7
Folding Code Chunks in RStudio

Not Folded

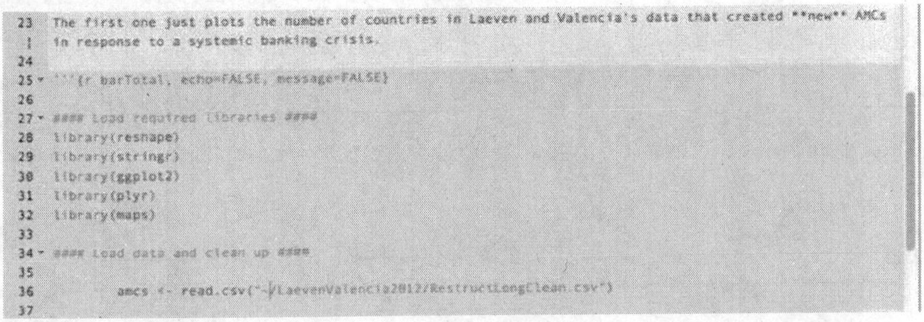

Folded

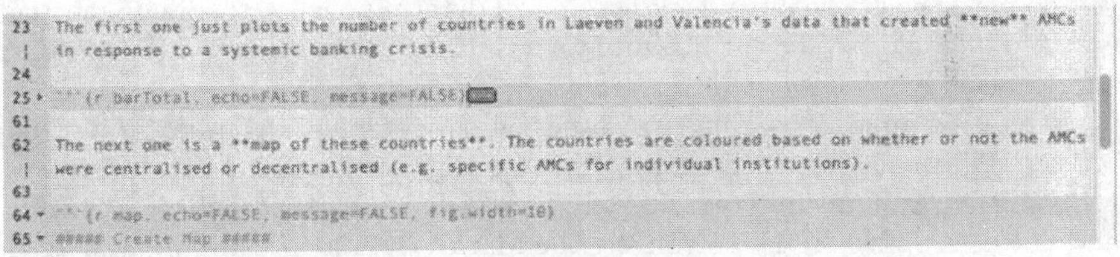

`Tools` in the RStudio menu bar then click on `Global Options...`. Once the **Options** window opens, click on the `Sweave` button. Select `knitr` from the drop-down menu for "Weave Rnw files using:". Finally, click `Apply`.[39]

In the `Sweave` options menu you can also set which LaTeX typesetting engine to use. By default it is set to the more established engine pdfLaTeX. Another option is XeLaTeX. XeLaTeX has the ability to use many more characters than pdfLaTeX as it works with UTF-8 encoded input. It can also use any font on your computer. XeLaTeX is especially useful compared to pdfLaTeX if you are using characters that are not found in standard English.

3.3.9 *knitr* & R

As *knitr* is a regular R package, you can Of course, knit documents in R (or using the console in RStudio). All of the *knitr* syntax in your markup document is the same as before, but instead of clicking a `Compile PDF` or `knit HTML` button use the `knit` function. To knit a hypothetical Markdown file *Example.Rmd* you first use the `setwd` command to set the working directory

[39]In the Mac version of RStudio, you can also access the `Options` window via `RStudio` → `Preferences` in the menu bar.

(for more details see Chapter 4) to the folder where the *Example.Rmd* file is located. In this example it is located on the desktop.[40]

```
setwd("~/Documents/")
```

Then you knit the file:

```
knit(input = "Example.Rmd", output = "Example.md")
```

You use the same steps for all other knittable document types. Note that if you do not specify the output file, *knitr* will determine what the file name and extension should be. In this example it would come up with the same name and location as we gave it.

In this example, using the `knit` function only creates a Markdown file and not an HTML file, as clicking the RStudio `knit HTML` did. Likewise, if you use `knit` on a `.Rnw` file you will only end up with a basic LaTeX `.tex` file and not a compiled PDF. To convert the Markdown file into HTML you need to further run the `.md` file through the `markdownToHTML` command from the *markdown* package, i.e.

```
mardownToHTML(file = "Example.md", output = "Example.html")
```

This is a bit tedious. Luckily, there is a command in the *knitr* package that combines `markdownToHTML` and `knit`. It is called `knit2html`. You use it like this:

```
knit2html(file = "Example.Rmd", output = "Example.html")
```

If we want to compile a `.tex` file in R we run it through the `texi2pdf` function in the *tools* package. This package will run both LaTeX and BibTeX to create a PDF with a bibliography (see Chapter 11 for more details on using BibTeX for bibliographies). Here is a `texi2pdf` example:

[40]Using the directory name `~/Documents/` is for Mac computers. Please use alternative syntax discussed in Chapter 4 on other types of systems.

```
# Load tools package
library(tools)

# Compile pdf
texi2pdf(file = "Example.tex")
```

Just like with `knit2html`, you can simplify this process by using the `knit2pdf` command to compile a PDF file from a `.Rnw` or `.Rtex` document.

3.3.10 *rmarkdown* and R

Just as *knitr* is an R package that you can run from the console, you can also run *rmarkdown* from the console. Instead of the `knit` function use `render`. Imagine that *Example.Rmd* now has an *rmarkdown* header:

```
---
title: "A Basic PDF Presentation Document"
author: "Christopher Gandrud"
date: "30 November 2015"
output:
    pdf_document:
        toc: true
    html_document:
        toc: false
---
```

This header specifies how the file can be compiled to either PDF or HTML. When compiled to PDF it will include a table of contents. When compiled to HTML it won't. Now we use `render`:

```
render("Example.Rmd")
```

This call will compile the document to a PDF in the working directory, because PDF is listed as the first output format in the header. The document will be called *Example.pdf*. Alternatively, to compile the R Markdown file to HTML use:

```
render("Example.Rmd", "html_document")
```

We could compile to both formats using:

```
render("Example.Rmd", "all")
```

or

```
render("Example.Rmd", c("pdf_document", "html_document"))
```

In all of these cases, `render` will not keep the intermediate *.md* or *.tex* document. You can have these documents saved by adding `keep_md` or `keep_tex` to the header. For example:

```
---
output:
    pdf_document:
        keep_tex: true
    html_document:
        keep_md: true
---
```

Finally, if you want to output to one format with the default rendering style, For example, the HTML document, use `html_document: default`.

Chapter summary

We've covered a lot of ground in this chapter, including R basics, how to use RStudio, and *knitr*/*rmarkdown* syntax for multiple markup languages. These tools, especially R and *knitr*/*rmarkdown*, are fundamental to the reproducible research process we will learn in this book. They enable us to create dynamic text-based files that record our research steps in detail. In the next chapter we will look at how to organize files created with these types of tools into reproducible research projects.

Appendix: knitr and Lyx

You may be more comfortable using a what-you-see-is-what-you-get (WYSIWYG) editor, similar to Microsoft Word. Lyx is a WYSIWYG LaTeX editor that can be used with *knitr*. I don't cover Lyx in detail in this book, but here is a little information to get you started.

Set Up

To set up Lyx so that it can compile `.Rnw` files, click `Document` in the menu bar then `Settings`. In the left-hand panel the second option is `Modules`. Click on `Modules` and select `Rnw (knitr)`. Click `Add` then `Ok`. Now, compile your LaTeX document in the normal Lyx way.

Code Chunks

Enter code chunks into TeX Code blocks within your Lyx documents. To create a new TeX Code block, select `Insert` from the menu bar then `TeX Code`.

4

Getting Started with File Management

Careful file management is crucial for reproducible research. Remember two of the guidelines from Chapter 2:

- Explicitly tie your files together.
- Have a plan to organize, store, and make your files available.

Apart from the times when you have an email exchange (or even meet in person) with someone interested in reproducing your research, the main information independent researchers have about the procedures is what they access in files you make available: data files, analysis files, and presentation files. If these files are well organized and the way they are tied together is clear, replication will be much easier. File management is also important for you as a researcher, because if your files are well organized you will be able to more easily make changes, benefit from work you have already done, and collaborate with others.

Using tools such as R, *knitr*/*rmarkdown*, and markup languages like LaTeX requires fairly detailed knowledge of where files are stored in your computer. Handling files to enable reproducibility may require you to use command-line tools to access and organize your files. R and Unix-like shell programs allow you to control files–creating, deleting, relocating–in powerful and really reproducible ways. By typing these commands you are documenting every step you take. This is a major advantage over graphical user interface-type systems where you organize files by clicking and dragging them with the cursor. However, text commands require you to know your files' specific addresses–their file paths.

In this chapter we discuss how a reproducible research project may be organized and cover the basics of file path naming conventions in Unix-like operating systems, such as Mac OS X and Linux, as well as Windows. We then learn how to organize them with RStudio Projects. Finally, we'll cover some basic R and Unix-like shell commands for manipulating files as well as how to navigate through files in RStudio in the *Files* pane. The skills you will learn in this chapter will be heavily used in the next chapter (Chapter 5) and throughout the book.

In this chapter we work with locally stored files, i.e. files stored on your computer. In the next chapter we will discuss various ways to store and access files remotely stored in the cloud.

4.1 File Paths & Naming Conventions

All of the operating systems covered in this book organize files in hierarchical directories, also known as file trees. To a large extent, directories can be thought of as the folders you usually see on your Windows or Mac desktop.[1] They are called hierarchical because directories are located inside of other directories, as in Figure 4.1.

4.1.1 Root directories

A root directory is the first level in a disk, such as a hard drive. It is the root out of which the file tree 'grows'. All other directories are subdirectories of the root directory.

On Windows computers you can have multiple root directories, one for each storage device or partition of a storage device. The root directory is given a drive letter assignment. If you use Windows regularly you will most likely be familiar with `C:\` used to denote the C partition of the hard drive. This is a root directory. On Unix-like systems, including Macs and Linux computers, the root directory is simply denoted by a forward slash (`/`) with nothing before it.

4.1.2 Subdirectories & parent directories

You will probably not store all of your files in the root directory. This would get very messy. Instead you will likely store your files in subdirectories of the root directory. Inside of these subdirectories may be further subdirectories and so on. Directories inside of other directories are also referred to as child directories of a parent directory.

On Windows computers separate subdirectories are indicated with a back slash (\). For example, if we have a folder called *Data* inside of a folder called *ExampleProject* which is located in the C root directory it has the address `C:\ExampleProject\Data`.[2] When you type Windows file paths into R you need to use two backslashes rather than one: e.g. `C:\\ExampleProject\\Data`. This is because the \ is an escape character in R.[3] Escape characters tell R to interpret the next character or sequence of characters differently. For example, in Section 5.1 you'll see how `\t` can be interpreted by R as a tab rather than the letter "t". Add another escape character to neutralize the escape character so that R interprets it as a backslash. In other words, use an escape character to escape the escape character. Another option for writing Windows file names in R is to use one forward slash (`/`).

On Unix-like systems, including Mac computers, directories are indicated

[1] To simplify things, I use the terms 'directory' and 'folder' interchangeably in this book.

[2] For more information on Windows file path names see this helpful website: `http://msdn.microsoft.com/en-us/library/windows/desktop/aa365247(v=vs.85).aspx`

[3] As we will see in Part IV, it is also a LaTeX and Markdown escape character.

with a forward slash (`/`). The file path of the *Data* file on a Unix-like system would be: `/ExampleProject/Data`. Remember that a forward slash with nothing before it indicates the root directory. So `/ExampleProject/Data` has a different meaning than `ExampleProject/Data`. In the former, *ExampleProject* is a subdirectory of the root. In the latter, *ExampleProject* is a subdirectory of the current working directory (see below for details about working directories). This is also true in Windows.

In this chapter I switch between the two file system naming conventions to expose you to both. For the remainder of the book I use Unix-like file paths. When you use relative paths, these will work across operating systems in R. We'll get to relative paths in a moment.

4.1.3 Working directories

When you use R, markup languages, and many of the other tools covered in this book, it is important to keep in mind what your current working directory is. The working directory is the directory where the program automatically looks for files and other directories, unless you tell it to look elsewhere. It is also where it will save files. Later in this chapter we will cover commands for finding and changing the working directory.

4.1.4 Absolute vs. relative paths

For reproducible research, collaborative research, and even if you ever change the computer you work on, it is a good idea to use relative rather than absolute file paths. Absolute file paths give the entire path of a given file or directory on a specific system. For example, `/ExampleProject/Data` is an absolute path as it specifies the path of the *Data* child directory all the way back to the root directory. However, if our current working directory is *ExampleProject* and we want to link to the *Data* child directory or a file in it, we don't need the absolute path. We could simply use `Data/`, i.e. the path relative to the working directory.

It is good practice to use relative paths when possible and organize your files such that using relative paths is easy. This makes your code less dependent on the particular file structure of a particular computer. For example, imagine you use `C:\\ExampleProject\\Data` in your source code to link to the *Data* directory. Someone–a collaborator, a researcher reproducing your work, or even you–then tries to run the code on a different computer. The code will break if they are, for instance, using a Unix-like system or have placed *ExampleProject* in a different partition of their hard drive. This can be fixed relatively straightforwardly by changing the file path in the source. However, this is tedious (often not well documented) and unnecessary if you use relative file paths.

4.1.5 Spaces in directory & file names

It is generally good practice to avoid putting spaces in your file and directory names. For example, I called the example project parent directory "ExampleProject" rather than "Example Project". Spaces in file and directory names can sometimes create problems for computer programs trying to read the file path. The program may believe that the space indicates that the path name has ended. To make multi-word names easily readable without using spaces, adopt a convention such as CamelBack. In CamelBack new words are indicated with capital letters, while all other letters are lower case. For example, "ExampleProject".

FIGURE 4.1
Example Research Project File Tree

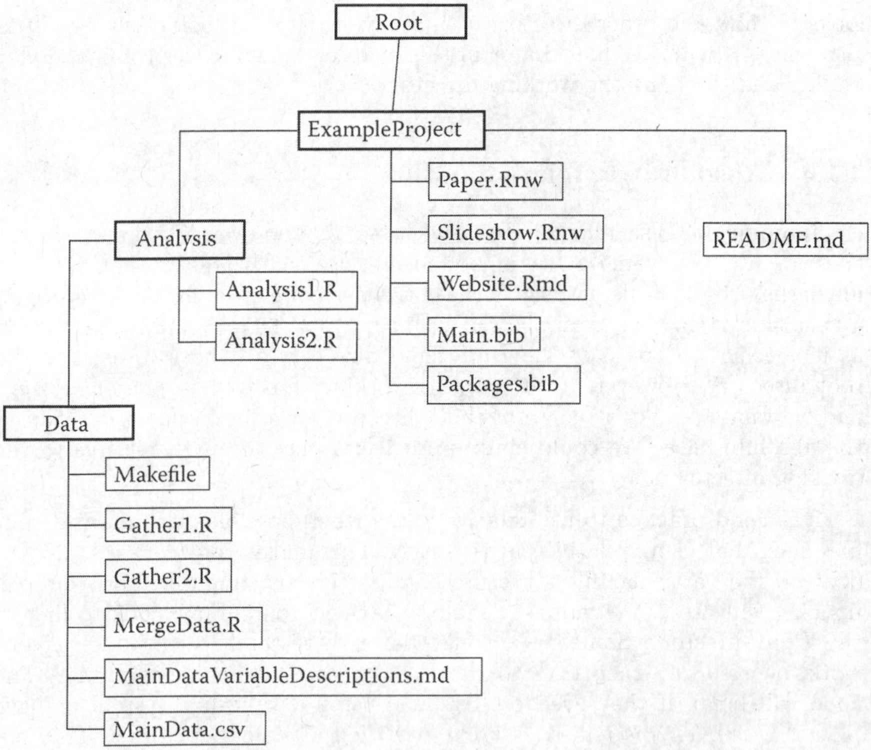

4.2 Organizing Your Research Project

Figure 4.1 gives an example of how the files in a simple reproducible research project could be organized. The project's parent directory is called *ExampleProject*. Inside this directory are the primary knittable documents (*Paper.Rnw Slideshow.Rnw*, and *Website.Rmd*). In addition there is an *Analysis* sub-directory with the R files to run the statistical analyses followed by a further *Data* child directory.

The nested file structure allows you to use relative file paths. The knittable documents can call *Analysis1.R* with the relative path *Analysis/Analysis1.R*, which in turn could call a file in the *Data/* subdirectory. If all of the directories were at the same level of the file tree then you would need to use absolute file paths.

In addition to the main files and subdirectories in *ExampleProject* you will probably notice a file called *README.md*. The *README.md* file gives an overview of all the files in the project. It should briefly describe the project including things like its title, author(s), topic, any copyright information, and so on. It should also indicate how the folders in the project are organized and give instructions for how to reproduce the project. The README file should be in the main project folder–in our example this is called *ExampleProject*–so that it is easy to find. If you are storing your project as a GitHub repository (see Chapter 5) and the file is called *README*, its contents will automatically be displayed on the repository's main page. If the *README* file is written using Markdown (e.g. *README.md*), it will also be properly formatted. Figure 5.2 shows an example of this.

FIGURE 4.2
An Example RStudio Project Menu

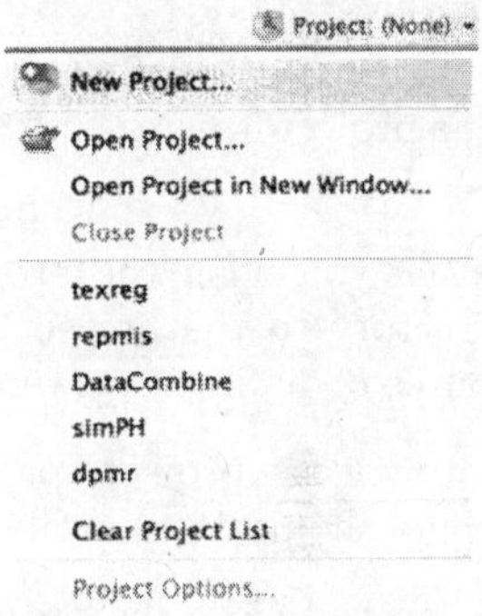

It is good practice to dynamically include the system information for the R session you used to create the project. To do this you can write your README file with R Markdown. Simply include the `sessionInfo()` command in a *knitr* code chunk in the R Markdown document. If you knit this file immediately after knitting your presentation document, it will record the information for that session.

You can also dynamically include session info in a LaTeX document. To do this, use the `toLatex` command in a code chunk. The code chunk should have the option `results='asis'`. The code is:

```
toLatex(sessionInfo())
```

4.3 Setting Directories as RStudio Projects

If you are using RStudio, you may want to organize your files as Projects. You can turn a normal directory into an RStudio Project by clicking on `File` in the RStudio menu bar and selecting `New Project...`. A new window will pop-up. Select the option `Existing Directory`. Find the directory you want to turn into an RStudio Project by clicking on the `Browse` button. Finally, select `Create Project`. You will also notice in the Create Project pop-up window that you can build new project directories and create a project from a directory already under version control (we'll do this at the end of Chapter 5). When you create a new project you will see that RStudio has put a file with the extension `.Rproj` into the directory.

Making your research project directories RStudio Projects is useful for a number of reasons:

- The project is listed in RStudio's Project menu where it can be opened easily (see Figure 4.2).
- When you open the project in RStudio it automatically sets the working directory to the project's directory and loads the workspace, history, and source code files you were last working on.
- You can set project specific options like whether PDF presentation documents should be compiled with *Sweave* or *knitr*.
- When you close the project your R workspace and history are saved in the project directory if you want.
- It helps you version control your files.
- You can build your Project–run the files in a specific way–with makefiles.
- Gives you an easy-to-use interface for managing the R packages that your project depends on.

We will look at many of these points in more detail in the next few chapters.

4.4 R File Manipulation Commands

R has a range of commands for handling and navigating through files. Including these commands in your source code files allows you to more easily replicate your actions.

getwd

To find your current working directory use the **getwd** command:

```
getwd()

## [1] "/git_repositories/Rep-Res-Book/Source/Children/Chapter4"
```

The example here shows you the current working directory that was used while knitting this chapter.

list.files

Use the **list.files** command to see all of the files and subdirectories in the current working directory. You can list the files in other directories too by adding the directory path as an argument to the command.

```
list.files()

## [1] "chapter4.Rnw" "images4"
```

You can see that the *Chapter4* folder has the file *chapter4.Rnw* (the markup file used to create this chapter) and a child directory called *images4* where I stored the original versions of the figures included in this chapter.

setwd

The **setwd** command sets the current working directory. For example, if we are on a Mac or other Unix-like computer we can set the working directory to the *GatherSource* directory in our Example Project (see Figure 4.1) like this:

```
setwd("/ExampleProject/Data/GatherSource")
```

Now R will automatically look in the *GatherSource* folder for files and will save new files into this folder, unless we explicitly tell it to do otherwise.

When working with a knittable document, setting the working directory once in a code chunk changes the working directory for all subsequent code chunks.

`root.dir`

By default the root (or working) directory for all of the code chunks in a knittable document is the directory where this document is located. You can reset the directory by feeding a new file path to the `root.dir` option. We can set this globally[4] for all of the chunks in the document by including the following code in the document's first chunk.

```
opts_knit$set(root.dir = '/ExampleProject/Analysis')
```

Here we set the */ExampleProject/Analysis* sub-directory as the root directory for all of the chunks in our presentation document.

Note: In general it is preferable to use a nested file structure, as we saw before, rather than specify `root.dir`. A nested file structure creates one less step for those trying to reproduce your work on a different computer. They do not need to change the `root.dir` file path.

`dir.create`

Sometimes you may want to create a new directory. You can use the `dir.create` command to do this.[5] For example, to create a *ExampleProject* file in the root *C* directory on a Windows computer type:

```
dir.create("C:\\ExampleProject")
```

`file.create`

Similarly, you can create a new blank file with the `file.create` command. To add a blank R source code file called *SourceCode.R* to the *ExampleProject* directory on the *C* drive use:

```
file.create("C:\\ExampleProject\\SourceCode.R")
```

[4]See the discussion of global chunk options in Chapter 3, page 53.

[5]Note: you will need the correct system permissions to be able to do this.

`cat`

If you want to create a new file and put text into it use the `cat` (concatenate and print) command. For example, to create a new file in the current working directory called *ExampleEcho.md* that includes the text "Reproducible Research with R and RStudio" type:

```
cat("Reproducible Research with R and RStudio",
    file = "ExampleCat.md")
```

In this example we created a Markdown formatted file by using the `.md` file extension. We could Of course, change the file extension to `.R` to set it as an R source code file, `.Rnw` to create a *knitr* LaTeX file, and so on.

You can use `cat` to print the contents of one or more objects to a file. **Warning:** The `cat` command will overwrite existing files with the new contents. To add the text to existing files use the `append = TRUE` argument.

```
cat("More Text", file = "ExampleCat.md",
    append = TRUE)
```

`unlink`

You can use the `unlink` command to delete files and directories.

```
unlink("C:\\ExampleProject\\SourceCode.R")
```

Warning: the `unlink` command permanently deletes files, so be very careful using this command.

`file.rename`

You can use the `file.rename` to, obviously, rename a file. It can also be used to move a file from one directory to another. For example, imagine that we want to move the *ExampleCat.md* file from the directory *ExampleProject* to one called *MarkdownFiles* that we already created.[6]

---

[6]The `file.rename` command won't create new directories. To move a file to a new directory you will need to create the directory first with `dir.create`.

```
file.rename(from = "C:\\ExampleProject\\ExampleCat.md",
            to = "C:\\MarkdownFiles\\ExampleCat.md")
```

`file.copy`

The `file.rename` fully moves a file from one directory to another. To copy the file to another directory use the `file.copy` command. It has the same syntax as `file.rename`:

```
file.copy(from = "C:\\ExampleProject\\ExampleCat.md",
          to = "C:\\MarkdownFiles\\ExampleCat.md")
```

4.5 Unix-like Shell Commands for File Management

Though this book is mostly focused on using R for reproducible research it can be useful to use a Unix-like shell program to manipulate files in large projects. Unix-like shell programs including Bash on Mac and Linux and Windows PowerShell allow you to type commands to interact with your computer's operating system.[7] We will especially return to shell commands in the next chapter when we discuss Git version control and makefiles for collecting data in Chapter 6, as well as the command-line program[8] Pandoc (Chapter 12 and 13). We don't have enough space to fully introduce shell programs or even all of the commands for manipulating files. We are just going to cover some of the basic and most useful commands for file management. For good introductions for Unix and Mac OS 10 computers see William E. Shotts Jr.'s (2012) book on the Linux command-line. For Windows users, Microsoft maintains a tutorial on Windows PowerShell at `http://technet.microsoft.com/en-us/library/hh848793`. The commands discussed in this chapter should work in both Unix-like shells and Windows PowerShell.

It's important at this point to highlight a key difference between R and Unix-like shell syntax. In shell commands you don't need to put parentheses

[7] You can access Bash via the Terminal program on Mac OS 10 and Linux computers. It is the default shell on Mac and Linux, so it loads automatically when you open the Terminal. Windows PowerShell comes installed with Windows.

[8] A command-line program is just a program you run from a shell.

around your arguments. For example, if I want to change my working directory to my Mac Desktop in a shell using the `cd` command I simply type:[9]

```
cd /Users/Me/Desktop
```

In this example `Me` is my user name.

`cd`

As we just saw, to change the working directory in the shell just use the `cd` (change directory) command. Here is an example of changing the directory in Windows PowerShell:

```
cd C:/Users/Me/Desktop
```

If you are in a child directory and want to change the working directory to the previous working directory you were in, simply type:

```
cd -
```

If, for example, our current working directory is */User/Me/Desktop* and we typed `cd` followed by a minus sign (`cd -`) then the working directory would change to */User/Me*. Note this will not work in PowerShell.

`pwd`

To find your current working directory, use the `pwd` command (present working directory). This is essentially the same as R's `getwd` command.

```
pwd

## /Users/Me/Desktop
```

[9]Many shell code examples in other sources include the shell prompt, like the `$` in Bash or `>` in PowerShell. These are like R's `>` prompt. I don't include the prompt in code examples in this book because you don't type them.

`ls`

The `ls` (list) command works very similarly to R's `list.files` command. It shows you what is in the current working directory.

```
ls

## chapter4.Rnw images4
```

As we saw earlier, R also has an `ls` command. R's `ls` command lists items in the R workspace. The shell's `ls` command lists files and directories in the working directory.

`mkdir`

Use `mkdir` to create a new directory. For example, if I wanted to create a directory in my Linux root directory called *NewDirectory* I would type:

```
mkdir /NewDirectory
```

If running this code on Mac or Linux gives you an error message like this:

```
mkdir: /NewDirectory: Permission denied
```

you simply need to use the `sudo` command to run the command with higher privileges.

```
sudo mkdir /NewDirectory
```

Running this code will prompt you to enter your administrator password.

`echo`

There are a number of ways to create new files in Unix-like shells. One of the simplest ways is with the `echo` command. This command simply prints its arguments. For example:

```
echo Reproducible Research with R and RStudio

## Reproducible Research with R and RStudio
```

If you add the greater-than symbol (`>`) after the text you want to print and then a file name, `echo` will create the file (if it doesn't already exist) in the current working directory and then print the text into the file.

```
echo Reproducible Research with R and RStudio > ExampleEcho.md
```

Using only one greater-than sign will completely erase the *ExampleEcho.md* file's contents and replace them with `Reproducible Research with R and RStudio`. To add the text at the end of an existing file, use two greater-than signs (`>>`).

```
echo More text. >> ExampleEcho.md
```

There is also a `cat` shell command. It works slightly differently than the R version of the command and I don't cover it here.

`rm`

The `rm` command is similar to R's `unlink` command. It removes (deletes) files or directories. Again, be careful when using this command, because it permanently deletes the files or directories.

```
rm ExampleEcho.md
```

As we saw in Chapter 3, R also has an `rm` command. It is different because it removes objects from your R workspace rather than files from your working directory.

`mv`

To move a file from one directory to another with the shell, use the `mv` (move) command. For example, to move the file *ExampleEcho.md* from *ExamplePro-*

jects to *MarkdownFiles* use the following code and imagine both directories are in the root directory:[10]

```
mv /ExampleProject/ExampleEcho.md /MarkdownFiles
```

Note that the *MarkdownFiles* directory must already exist, otherwise it will simply rename the file. So this command is similar to the R command `file.rename`.

`cp`

The `mv` command completely moves a file from one directory to another. To copy a version of the file to a new directory use the `cp` command. The syntax is similar to `mv`:

```
cp /ExampleProject/ExampleEcho.md /MarkdownFiles
```

`system` *(R command)*

You can run shell commands from within R using R's `system` command. For example, to run the `echo` command from within R type:

```
system("echo Text to Add > ExampleEcho.md")
```

4.6 File Navigation in RStudio

The RStudio *Files* pane allows us to navigate our file tree and do some basic file manipulations. The left panel of Figure 4.3 shows us what this pane looks like. The pane allows us to navigate to specific files and folders and delete and rename files. To select a folder as the working directory tick the dialog box next to the file then click the `More` button and select `Set As Working Directory`. Under the `More` button (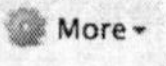

) you will also find options to `Move` and `Copy` files (see the right pane of Figure 4.3).

The *Files* pane is a GUI, so our actions in the *Files* pane are not as easily reproducible as the commands we learned earlier in this chapter.

---

[10]If they were not in the root directory we would not place a forward slash at the beginning.

FIGURE 4.3
The RStudio Files Pane

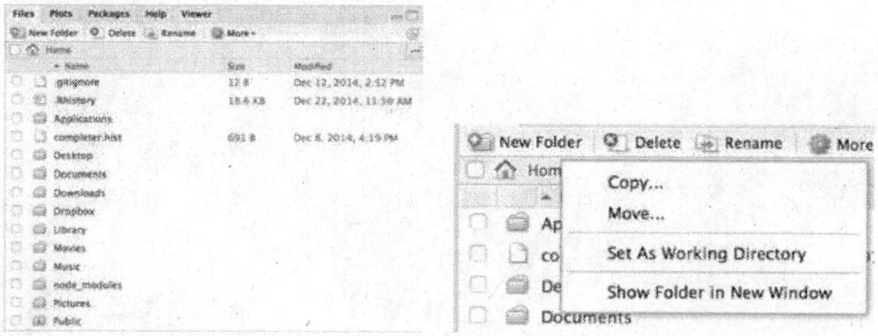

Chapter summary

In this chapter we've learned how to organize our research files to enable dynamic replication. This included not only how they can be ordered in a computer's file system, but also the file path naming conventions–the addresses–that computers use to locate files. Once we know how these addresses work we can use R and shell commands to refer to and manipulate our files. This skill is particularly useful because it allows us to place code in text-based files to manipulate our project files in highly reproducible ways. In the next few chapters we will begin to put these skills in practice when we learn how to store our files and create data files in reproducible ways.

Part II

Data Gathering and Storage

5

Storing, Collaborating, Accessing Files, and Versioning

In addition to being well organized, your research files need to be accessible for other researchers to be able to reproduce your findings. A useful way to make your files accessible is to store them on a cloud storage service[1] (see Howe, 2012). This chapter describes in detail two different cloud storage services–Dropbox and GitHub–that you can use to make your research files easily accessible to others. Not only do these services enable others to reproduce your research, they also have a number of benefits for your research workflow. Researchers often face a number of data management issues that, beyond making their research difficult to reproduce, can make doing the initial research difficult.

First, there is the problem of **storing** data so that it is protected against computer failure–virus infections, spilling coffee on your laptop, and so on. Storing data locally–on your computer–or on a flash drive is generally more prone to loss than on remote servers in the cloud.

Second, we may work on a project with different computers and mobile devices. For example, we may use a computer at work to run computationally intensive analysis, while editing our presentation document on a tablet computer while riding the train to the office. So, we need to be able to **access** our files from multiple devices in different locations. We often need a way for our **collaborators** to access and edit research files as well.

Finally, we almost never create a data set or write a paper perfectly all at once. We may make changes and then realize that we liked an earlier version, or parts of an earlier version better. This is a particularly important issue in data management where we may transform our data in unintended ways and want to go back to earlier versions. Also, when working on a collaborative project, one of the authors may accidentally delete something in a file that another author needed. To deal with these issues we need to store our data in a system that has **version control**. Version control systems keep track of changes we make to our files and allows us to access previous versions if we want to.

You can solve all of these problems in a couple of different ways using free or low cost cloud-based storage formats. In this chapter we will learn how to use Dropbox and Git/GitHub for research files:

[1] These services store your data on remote servers.

- storage,
- accessing,
- collaboration,
- version control.

5.1 Saving Data in Reproducible Formats

Before getting into the details of cloud-based data storage for all of our research files, let's consider what type of formats you should actually save your data in. A key issue for reproducibility is that others are able to not only get hold of the exact data you used in your analysis, but be able to understand and use the data now and in the future. Some file formats make this easier than others.

In general, for small to moderately-sized data sets[2] plain-text formats like comma-separated values (`.csv`) or tab-separated values[3] (`.tsv`) are good ways to store your data. These formats simply store a data set as a text file. A row in the data set is a line in the text file. Data is separated into columns with commas or tabs, respectively. These formats are not dependent on a specific program. Any program that can open text files can open them, including a wide variety of statistical programs other than R as well as spreadsheet programs like Microsoft Excel. Using text file formats helps future-proof your research. Version control systems that track changes to text–like Git–are also very effective version control systems for these types of files.

Use the `write.table` command to save data in plain-text formats from R. For example, to save a data frame called *Data* as a CSV file called *MainData.csv* in our example *DataFiles* directory (see Figure 4.1):

```
write.table(Data, "/ExampleProject/Data/DataFiles/MainData.csv",
                     sep = ",", row.names = FALSE)
```

`row.names = FALSE` prevents R from including the row names in the output

[2]I don't cover methods for storing and handling very large data sets–with high hundreds of thousands and more observations. For information on large data and R, not just storage, one place to look is this blog post from RDataMining: `http://rdatamining.wordpress.com/2012/05/06/online-resources-for-handling-big-data-and-parallel-computing-in-r/` (posted 6 May 2012). One popular service for large file storage is Amazon S3 (`http://aws.amazon.com/s3/`). I haven't used this service and can't suggest ways to integrate it with R.

[3]Sometimes this format is called tab-delimited values.

file.[4] The `sep = ","` argument specifies that we want to use commas to separate values into columns. For CSV files you can use a modified version of this command called `write.csv`. This command simply makes it so that you don't have to write `sep = ","`.[5]

If you want to save your data with values separated by tabs, rather than commas, simply set the argument `sep = "\t"` and set the file extension to `.tsv`.

R is able to save data in a wide variety of other file formats, mostly through the *foreign* package (see Chapter 6). These formats may be less future-proof than simple text-formatted data files.

One advantage of many other statistical programs' file formats is that they include not only the underlying data but also other information like variable descriptions. If you are using plain-text files to store your data you will need to include a separate file, preferably in the same directory as the data file describing the variables and their sources. In Chapter 9 (Section 9.3.6) we will look at how to automate the creation of variable description files.

5.2 Storing Your Files in the Cloud: Dropbox

In this book we'll cover two (largely) free cloud storage services that allow you to store, access, collaborate on, and version control your research files. These services are Dropbox and GitHub.[6] Though they both meet our basic storage needs, they do so in different ways and require different levels of effort to set up and maintain.

These two services are certainly not the only way to make your research files available. Research-oriented services include the SDSC Cloud,[7] the Dataverse Project,[8] figshare,[9] and RunMyCode.[10] These services include good built-in citation systems, unlike Dropbox and GitHub. They may be a very good place to store research files once the research is completed or close to completion. Some journals are beginning to require key reproducibility files be uploaded to these sites. However, these sites' ability to store, access, collaborate on, and version control files *during* the main part of the research process is mixed. Services like Dropbox and GitHub are very capable of being part of the research workflow from the beginning.

The easiest types of cloud storage for your research are services like Drop-

---

[4]Frequently the row names are just the row numbers which may have no substantive meaning.

[5]`write.csv` is a 'wrapper' for *write.table*.

[6]Dropbox provides a minimum amount of storage for free, above which they charge a fee. GitHub lets you create publicly accessible repositories–kind of like project folders–for free, but they charge for private repositories.

[7]`https://cloud.sdsc.edu/hp/index.php`

[8]`http://thedata.org/`

[9]`http://figshare.com/`

[10]`http://www.runmycode.org/`

box[11] and Google Drive.[12] These services not only store your data in the cloud, but also provide ways to share files. They even include basic version control capabilities. I'm going to focus on Dropbox because it currently offers a complete set of features that allow you to store, version, collaborate, and access your data. I will focus on how to use Dropbox on a computer. Some Dropbox functionality may be different on mobile devices.

5.2.1 Storage

When you sign up for Dropbox and install the program[13] it creates a directory on your computer's hard drive. When you place new files and folders in this directory and make changes to them, Dropbox automatically syncs the directory with a similar folder on a cloud-based server. Typically when you sign up for the service you'll receive a limited amount of storage space for free, usually a few gigabytes. This is probably enough storage space for a number of text file-based research projects.

5.2.2 Accessing data

All files stored on Dropbox have a URL address through which they can be accessed from a computer connected to the internet. Files in either the Dropbox *Public*[14] folder or in other, non-*Public* folders can be downloaded into R. Downloading files from these two different sources requires two different methods. Let's quickly look at how to download files from the Public folder. In the next chapter (see Section 6.3.2) we'll look at how to download data from non-*Public* Dropbox folders into R.

If the file is stored in the *Public* folder, right-click on the file icon in your Dropbox folder on your computer. Then click `Copy Public Link`. This copies the URL into your clipboard, from which you can paste it into your R source code (or wherever). If you are logged into the Dropbox website, right-click on files in your *Public* folder and then select `Copy public link...`.

Once you have the URL you can load the file directly into R using the `source_data` command in the *repmis* package (Gandrud, 2015) for plain-text formatted data or use the `source_url` command in the *devtools* package (Wickham and Chang, 2015a) for source code files (see Chapter 8).

Let's download data directly into R from my Dropbox Public folder. The data set's URL is: `https://dl.dropbox.com/u/12581470/code/`

[11]`http://www.dropbox.com/`

[12]`https://drive.google.com/`

[13]See `https://www.dropbox.com/downloading` for downloading and installation instructions.

[14]Note: if you created your Dropbox account after 4 October 2012 you will not automatically have a *Public* folder. To enable the folder on your account see this website: `https://www.dropbox.com/help/16/en`. You will need a Pro or Dropbox for Business account to enable a new Public folder.

`Replicability_code/Fin_Trans_Replication_Journal/Data/public.fin.msm.model.csv`.[15]

```
# Download data on Financial Regulators
# stored in a Dropbox Public folder

# Load repmis
library(repmis)

# Place the URL into the object FinURL
FinURL <- "http://bit.ly/14aS5qq"

# Download data
FinRegulatorData <- source_data(FinURL,
                                sep = ",",
                                header = TRUE)

## Downloading data from: http://bit.ly/14aS5qq
##
## SHA-1 hash of the downloaded data file is:
## 7fdcb0a9785d52e0f3d450e4bde29dbc4e2b045a

# Show variables in FinRegulatorData
names(FinRegulatorData)

## [1] "idn"         "country"    "year"         "reg_4state"
```

Let's go through this code. We already saw in our discussion of `write.table` how the `sep = ","` argument specifies that the data file's values are separated by commas. The `header = TRUE` argument tells R that the first row of the file contains the variable names. Note that from version 0.4 *repmis* automatically guesses how the columns are separated and whether or not to use the first row as the header. Because of this, we usually don't need to set the `sep` and `header` arguments explicitly. I've only done so in this example for illustration.

You're probably also wondering about the line that begins *`## SHA-1 hash of`* ... in the output. The long string of numbers and letters at the end of this line is basically a unique ID that `source_data` assigns to the file. It is called an SHA-1 hash. We'll see SHA-1 hashes more in the next section on GitHub (Section 5.3) and in Chapter 6 (Section 6.3.2). To give you a preview: it allows us to see if the file that we downloaded is the file we thought we downloaded.

To get a file's URL from your local Dropbox folder when the file is *not* in

[15] This data is from Gandrud (2013b). I've shortened the URL using Bitly (`https://bitly.com/`) so that it will fit on the page.

your *Public* folder, you also right-click on the file. Then choose `Share Dropbox Link`. This will copy the link URL into your clipboard. You can also get these URL links through the online version of your Dropbox. First, log into the Dropbox website. You can again right-click on the file name and then `Share`. This will bring up a box displaying the link for you to copy. Alternatively, when you hover your cursor over a file or folder you will see a `Share` icon (Share) appear on the far right. Clicking on this icon will also get you the link.

In either case, you cannot use the `source_data` command to download data from non-*Public* folders into R. In the next chapter we'll see how to import this type of data into R (see Section 6.3.2). To give you a preview: we'll use the `source_DropboxData` function from the *repmis* package.

5.2.3 Collaboration

Though others can easily access your data and files with Dropbox URL links, you cannot save files through the link. You must save files in the Dropbox folder on your computer or upload them through the website. If you would like collaborators to be able to modify the research files you will need to 'share' the Dropbox folder with them. You cannot fully share your *Public* folder, i.e. give others write permission, so you will need to keep the files you want collaborators to be able to modify in a *non-Public* folder. Once you create this *non-Public* folder you can share it with your collaborators by going to the Dropbox website and right-clicking on the folder's name. Then select `Invite people to collaborate...`. Enter your collaborator's email address when prompted. They will be sent an email that will allow them to accept the share request and, if they don't already have an account, sign up for Dropbox.

5.2.4 Version control

Dropbox has a simple version control system. Every time you save a document a new version is created on Dropbox. To view a previous version, navigate to the file on the Dropbox website. Then right-click on the file. In the menu that pops up select `Previous Versions`. This will take you to a webpage listing previous versions of the file, who created the version, and when it was created. A new version of a file is created every time you save a file and it is synced to the Dropbox cloud service. You can see a list of changes made to files in your Dropbox folder by going to the website and clicking on `Events`.

Note that with a free Dropbox account, previous versions of a file are only stored for **30 days**. To be able to save previous versions for more than 30 days you will need a paid account.[16]

[16] For more details see: `https://www.dropbox.com/en/help/11`.

5.3 Storing Your Files in the Cloud: GitHub

Dropbox adequately meets our four basic criteria for reproducible data storage. It is easy to set up and use. GitHub meets the criteria and more, especially when it comes to version control. It is, however, less straightforward at first. In this section we will learn enough of the basics to get you started using GitHub to store, access, collaborate on, and version control your research.

GitHub is an interface and cloud hosting service built on top of the Git version control system.[17] Git does the version control. GitHub stores the data remotely as well as providing a number of other features, some of which we look at below. GitHub was not explicitly designed to host research projects or even data. It was designed to host "socially coded" computer programs–in what Git calls "repositories"–repos for short–by making it easy for a number of collaborators to work together to build computer programs. This seems very far from reproducible research.

Remember that as reproducible researchers, we are building projects out of interconnected text files. In important ways, this is exactly the same as building a computer program. Computer programs are also basically large collections of interconnected text files. Like computer programmers, we need ways to store, version control, access, and collaborate on our text files. Because GitHub is very actively used by people with similar needs (who are also really good programmers), the interface offers many highly developed and robust features for reproducible researchers.

GitHub's extensive features and heart in the computer programming community means that it takes a longer time than Dropbox for novice users to set up and become familiar with. So we need good reasons to want to invest the time needed to learn GitHub. Here is a list of GitHub's advantages over Dropbox for reproducible research that will hopefully convince you to get started using it:[18]

Storage and access

- Dropbox simply creates folders stored in the cloud which you can share with other people. GitHub makes your projects accessible on a fully featured project website (see Figure 5.2). An example feature is that it automatically renders Markdown files called *README.md*[19] in a GitHub directory on the repository's website. This makes it easy for independent researchers to find the file and read it.

[17] I used Git version 1.7.9.6 for this book.

[18] Because many of these features apply to any service that relies on Git, much of this list of advantages also applies to alternative Git cloud storage services such as Bitbucket (`https://bitbucket.org/`).

[19] You can use a variety of other markup languages as well. See `https://GitHub.com/GitHub/markup`.

- GitHub can create and host a website for your research project that you could use to present the results, not just the replication files.

Collaboration

- Dropbox allows multiple people to share files and change them. GitHub does this and more.
- GitHub keeps meticulous records of who contributed what to a project.
- Each GitHub repository has an "Issues" area where you can note issues and discuss them with your collaborators. Basically, this is an interactive to-do list for your research project. It also stores the issues so you have a full record.
- Each repository can also host a wiki that, for example, could explain in detail how certain aspects of a research project were done.
- Anyone can suggest changes to files in a public repository. These changes can be accepted or declined by the project's authors. The changes are recorded by the Git version control system. This could be especially useful if an independent researcher notices an error.

Version control

- Dropbox's version control system only lets you see files' names, the times they were created, who created them, and revert back to specific versions. Git tracks every change you make. The GitHub website and GUI programs for Mac and Windows provide nice interfaces for examining specific changes in text files.
- Dropbox creates a new version every time you save a file. This can make it difficult to actually find the version you want as the versions quickly multiply. Git's version control system only creates a new version when you tell it to.
- All files in Dropbox are version controlled. Git allows you to ignore specific files. This is helpful if you have large binary files (i.e. not text files) that you do not want to version control because doing so will use up considerable storage space.
- Unless you have a paid account, previous file versions in Dropbox disappear after 30 days. GitHub stores previous versions indefinitely for all account types.
- Dropbox does not merge conflicting versions of a file together. This can be annoying when you are collaborating on a project and more than one author is making changes to documents at the same time. Git identifies conflicts and lets you reconcile them.

FIGURE 5.1
A Basic Git Repository with Hidden *.git* Folder Revealed

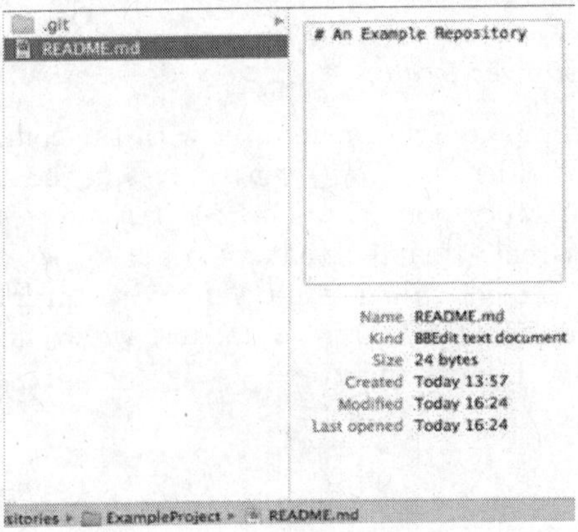

- Git is directly integrated into RStudio Projects.[20]

5.3.1 Setting up GitHub: Basic

There are at least three ways to use Git/GitHub on your computer. You can use the command-line version of Git. It's available for Mac and Linux (in the Terminal) as well as Windows through Git Bash.[21] You can also use the Graphical User Interface GitHub program. Currently, it's only available for Windows and Mac. RStudio also has GUI-style Git functionality for RStudio Projects. In this section I focus on how to use the command-line version, because it will help you understand what the GUI versions are doing and allow you to better explore more advanced Git features not covered in this book. In the next section I will mention how to use Git with RStudio Projects.

The first thing to do to set up Git and GitHub is go to the GitHub website (`https://GitHub.com/`) and sign up for an account. Second, you should go to the following website for instructions on setting up GitHub: `https://help.GitHub.com/articles/set-up-git`. The instructions on that website are very comprehensive, so I'll direct you there for the full setup information. Note that installing the GUI version of GitHub also installs Git and, on Windows, Git Bash.

---

[20]RStudio also supports the Subversion version control system, but I don't cover that here.

[21]The interface for Git Bash looks a lot like the Terminal or Windows PowerShell.

5.3.2 Version control with Git

Git is primarily a version control system, so we will start our discussion of how to use it by looking at how to version your repositories.

Setting up Git repositories locally

You can setup a Git repo on your computer with the command-line.[22] I keep my repositories in a folder called *git_repositories*,[23] though you can use Git with almost any directory you like. The *git_repositories* directory has the root folder as its parent. Imagine that we want to set up a repository in this directory for a project called *ExampleProject*. Initially it will have one README file called *README.md*. To do this, we would first type into the Terminal for Mac and Linux computers:

```
# Make new directory 'ExampleProject'
mkdir /git_repositories/ExampleProject

# Change to directory 'ExampleProject'
cd /git_repositories/ExampleProject

# Create new file README.md
echo "# An Example Repository" > README.md
```

So far we have only made the new directory and set it as our working directory (see Chapter 4). All of the examples in this section assume your current working directory is set to the repo. Then, with the `echo` shell command we created a new file named *README.md* that includes the text `# An Example Repository`. Note that the code is basically the same in Windows PowerShell or Git Bash. Also, you don't have to do these steps in the command-line. You could just create the new folders and files the same way that you normally do with your mouse in your GUI operating system.

Now that we have a directory with a file, we can tell Git that we want to treat the directory *ExampleProject* as a repository and that we want to track changes made to the file *README.md*. Use Git's `init` (initialize) command to set the directory as a repository. See Table 5.1 for the list of Git commands covered in this chapter.[24] Use Git's `add` command to add a file to the Git repository. For example,

---

[22]Much of the discussion of the command-line in this section is inspired by Nick Farina's blog post on Git (see `http://nfarina.com/post/9868516270/git-is-simpler`, posted 7 September 2012).

[23]To follow along with this code you will first need to create a folder called *git_repositories* in your root directory. Note also that throughout this section I use Unix file path conventions.

[24]For a comprehensive guide to Git commands, see `http://git-scm.com/`.

```
# Initialize the Git repository
git init

# Add README to the repository
git add README.md
```

You probably noticed that you always need to put `git` before the command. This tells the shell what program the command is from. When you initialize a folder as a Git repository, a hidden folder called *.git* is added to the directory (see Figure 5.1). This is where all of your changes are kept. If you want to add all of the files in the working directory to the Git repository type:

```
# Add all files to the repository
git add .
```

When we want Git to track changes made to files added to the repository we can use the `commit` command. In Git language we are "committing" the changes to the repository.

```
# Commit changes
git commit -a -m "First Commit, created README file"
```

Note: the files won't appear on GitHub yet. Later in the chapter we will learn how to push commits to your remote GitHub repository. The `-a` (all) option commits changes made to all of the files that have been added to the repository. You can include a message with the commit using the `-m` option like: `"First Commit, created README file"`. Messages help you remember general details about individual commits. This is helpful when you want to revert to old versions. **Remember:** Git only tracks changes when you commit them.

Finally, you can use the `status` command for details about your repository, including uncommitted changes. Generally it's a good idea to use the `-s` (short) option, so that the output is more readable.

```
# Display status
git status -s
```

TABLE 5.1
A Selection of Git Commands

Command	Description
`add`	Add a file to a Git repository.
`branch`	Create and delete branches.
`checkout`	Checkout a branch.
`clone`	Clone a repository (for example, the remote GitHub version) into the current working directory.
`commit`	Commit changes to a Git repository.
`fetch`	Download objects from the remote (or another) repository.
`.gitignore`	Not a Git command, but a file you can add to your repository to specify what files/file types Git should ignore.
`init`	Initialize a Git repository.
`log`	Show a repo's commit history.
`merge`	Merge two or more commits/branches together.
`pull`	`fetch` data from a remote repository and try to `merge` it with your commits.
`push`	Add committed changes to a remote Git repository, i.e. GitHub.
`remote add`	Add a new remote repository to an existing project.
`rm`	Remove files from Git version tracking.
`status`	Show the status of a Git repository including uncommitted changes made to files.
`tag`	Bookmark particularly significant commits.

Note: when you use these commands in the shell, you will need to precede them with `git` so the shell knows what program they are from.

FIGURE 5.2
Part of this Book's GitHub Repository Webpage

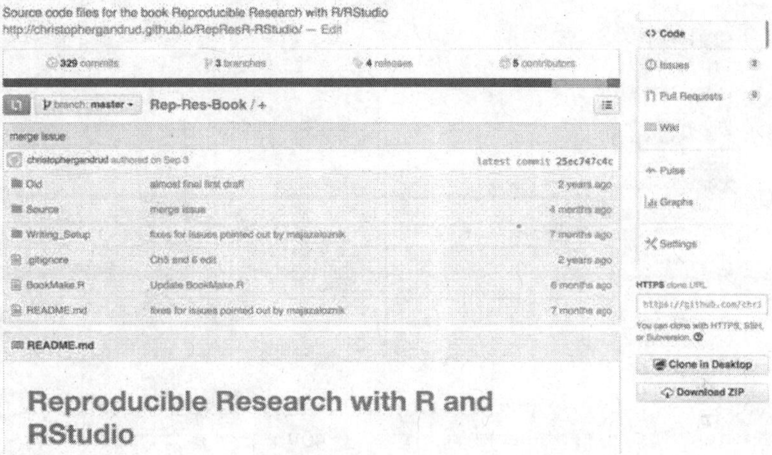

Checkout

It is useful to step back for a second and try to understand what Git is doing when you commit your changes. In the hidden *.git*, folder Git is saving all of the information in compressed form from each of your commits into a sub-folder called *objects*. Commit objects[25] are everything from a particular commit. I mean everything. If you delete all of the files in your repository (except for the *.git* folder) you can completely recover all of the files from your most recent commit with the `checkout` command:

```
# Checkout latest commit
git checkout -- .
```

Note that there is a space between the two dashed lines and the period. You can also change to any other commit or any committed version of a particular file with `checkout`. Simply replace the `--` with the commit reference. Note that the period at the end is still very important to include after the commit reference. The commit reference is easy to find and copy from a repository's GitHub webpage (see below for more information on how to create a GitHub

[25]Other Git objects include trees (sort of like directories), tags (bookmarks for important points in a repo's history), and blobs (individual files).

FIGURE 5.3
Part of this Book's GitHub Repository Commit History Page

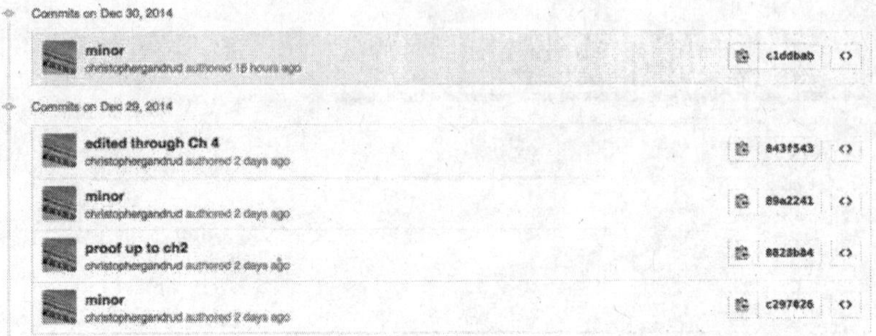

webpage).[26] For an example of a GitHub repo webpage, see Figure 5.2. Click on the link that lists the number of repo commits on the left-hand side of the repo's webpage. This will show you all of the commits. A portion of this book's commit history is shown in Figure 5.3. By clicking on the `Browse Code` icon (<>) you can see what the files at any commit looked like. Next to this button is another with a series of numbers and letters. This is the commit's SHA-1 hash.[27] For our purposes, it is the commit's reference number. Click on the `Copy SHA` button to the left of the SHA to copy it. You can then paste it as an argument to your `git checkout` command. This will revert you to that particular commit. Also include the file name if you want to revert to a particular version of a particular file.

Tags

SHA-1 hashes are a bit cumbersome to use as references. What was the hash number for that one commit? To solve this problem you can add bookmarks, known as "tags", to particularly important commits. Imagine we just committed our first full draft of a project. We want to tag it as version 0.1, i.e. "v0.1". To do this use Git's tag command:

[26] You can also search your commit history and roll back to a previous commit using only the command-line. To see the commit history use the `log` command (more details at `http://git-scm.com/book/en/Git-Basics-Viewing-the-Commit-History`). When a repo has many commits, this can be a very tedious command to use, so I highly recommend the GUI version of GitHub or the repo's GitHub website.

[27] Secure Hash Algorithm

```
# Tag most recent commit v0.1
git tag -a v0.1 -m "First draft"
```

The `-a` option adds the tag `v0.1` and `-m` lets us add a message. Now we can checkout this particular commit by using its tag, i.e.:

```
# Checkout v0.1
git checkout v0.1
```

This will create a new "branch" with a generic name *(detached from v0.1)* where you can make changes and commit them. If you plan to checkout a previous tagged version and make changes to it, it is a good idea to specifically name the branch using the `-b` argument.[28] For example, to give it the name *v0.1Branch* type:

```
# Checkout v0.1 as v0.1Brance
git checkout v0.1 -b v0.1Branch
```

What is a branch?

Branches

Sometimes you may want to work on an alternative version of your project and then merge changes made to this version back into the main one. For example, the main version could be the most stable current copy of your research, while the alternative version could be a place where you test out new ideas. Git allows you to create a new *branch* (alternative version of the repo) which can be merged back into the *master* (main) branch. To see what branch you are using type:

```
# Show git branch
git branch
```

[28] If you don't, then the new branch will have a "detached head" which will create problems using the branch in the future.

```
##   Version2
## * majorV2
##   master
```

To create a new branch use, simply enough, the `branch` command. For example, to create a new branch called *Test*:

```
# Create Test branch
git branch Test
```

You can now use `checkout` to switch to this branch.[29] Here is a shortcut for creating and checking out the branch:

```
# Create and checkout Test branch
git checkout -b Test
```

The `-b` (branch) option for `checkout` creates the new *Test* branch before switching to it.

To merge changes you commit in the *Test* branch to the *master*, `add` and `commit` your changes, `checkout` the *master* branch, then use the `merge` command.[30]

```
# Add files
git add .

# Commit changes to Test branch
git commit -a -m "Commit changes to Test"

# Checkout master branch
git checkout master

# Merge master and Test branches
git merge Test
```

[29] To delete the *Test* branch use the `-d` argument, i.e. `git branch -d Test`.

[30] Any uncommitted changes are merged with a branch when it is checked out.

Note, when you merge a branch you may encounter conflicts in the files that make it impossible to smoothly merge the files together. Git will tell you what and where these are; you then need to decide what to keep and what to delete.

Having Git ignore files

There may be files in your repository that you do not want to keep under version control. Maybe this is because they are very large files or cached files from *knitr* or other files that are byproducts of compiling an R LaTeX document (see Chapter 8). To have Git ignore particular files, simply create a file called *.gitignore*.[31] You can either put this file in the repository's parent directory to create a *.gitignore* file for the whole repository or in a subdirectory to ignore files in that subdirectory. In the *.gitignore* file, add ignore rules by simply including the names of the files that you want to have Git ignore. For example, a *.gitignore* file that is useful for ignoring files that are the byproduct of compiling an R LaTeX file would look something like this:

```
# Ignore LaTeX compile byproduct files #
########################################
*.aux
*.bbl
*.blg
cache/*
figure/*
*.log
*.pdf
*.gz
*.tex
```

The asterisk (`*`) is a "wildcard" and stands for any character. In other words, it tells Git to look for files with any name that end with a specified file extension. This is faster than writing out the full name of every file you want to ignore individually. It also makes it easy to copy the rules into new repos. You'll notice the `cache/*` and `figure/*` rules. These tell Git to ignore all of the files in the *cache* and *figure* subdirectories. These files are the product of caching code chunks and creating figures with *knitr*, respectively.

Git will not ignore files that have already been committed to a repository. To ignore these files you will first need to remove them from Git with Git's `rm` (remove) command. If you wanted to remove a file called *ExampleProject.tex* from version tracking type:

[31] Note that like *.git*, *.gitignore* files are hidden.

```
# Remove ExampleProject.tex from Git version tracking
git rm --cached ExampleProject.tex
```

Using the `-cached` argument tells Git not to track the file, but not delete it.

For more information on *.gitignore* files, see GitHub's reference page on the topic at: `https://help.GitHub.com/articles/ignoring-files`.

5.3.3 Remote storage on GitHub

So far we've been using repos stored locally. Let's now look at how to also store a repository remotely on GitHub. You can either create a new repository on GitHub and download (`clone`) it to your computer or upload (`push`) an existing repository to a new GitHub remote repo. In both cases you need to create a new repository on GitHub.

To create a new repository on GitHub go to your main GitHub account webpage and click the `New repository` button. On the next page that appears, give the repository a name, brief description, and choose whether to make it public or private. If you want to store an existing repository on GitHub give it the same name as the one that already exists on your computer. If you already have files in your local repository do not check the boxes for creating *README.md*, *LICENSE*, and *.gitignore* files. When you then click `Create Repository` you will be directed to the repository's GitHub webpage.[32]

Clone a new remote repository

If you are working with a new repository and do not have an existing version on your computer you need to "clone" the GitHub repo to your computer. The repo's GitHub page contains a button called `Clone in Desktop`. Clicking this will open GUI GitHub (if it is installed) and prompt you to specify what directory on your computer you would like to clone the repository into. You can also use the `clone` command in the shell. Imagine that the URL for a repo called *Example Project* is `https://GitHub.com/USERNAME/ExampleProject.git`. To clone it into the */git_repositories* directory type:[33]

```
# Change working directory
cd /git_repositories/
```

[32]Before the repo has any files in it, the webpage will include instructions for how to set it up on your computer.

[33]If you are on the repo's webpage the URL to copy is under `HTTPS clone URL`.

```
# Clone ExampleProject
git clone https://GitHub.com/USERNAME/ExampleProject.git
```

Push an existing repository to a new GitHub repo

If you already have a repository with files in it on your computer and you want to store them remotely in a new GitHub repo, you need to add the remote repository and `push` your files to it. Type Git's `remote add` command. For example, if your repository's GitHub URL is `https://GitHub.com/USERNAME/ExampleProject.git`, then type:

```
# Change working directory to existing local repo
cd /git_repositories/ExampleProject

# Add a remote (GitHub) repository to an existing repo
git remote add origin https://GitHub.com/USERNAME/ExampleProject.git
```

This will tell your local repository where the remote one is. Finally, push the repository to GitHub:

```
# Push local repository to GitHub for the first time
git push -u origin master
```

The `-u` (upstream tracking) option adds a tracking reference for the upstream (GitHub) repository branches.

Pushing commits to a GitHub repo

Once you have your local repository connected to GitHub you can add new commits with the `push` command. For example, if your current working directory is the Git repo you want to push and you have already added/committed the changes you want to include in the remote repo, type:

```
# Add changes to the GitHub remote master branch
git push origin master
```

The `origin` is simply the remotely stored repository on GitHub and `master` is the master branch. You can change this to another branch if you'd like. If you have not set up password caching[34] you will now be prompted to give your GitHub user name and password.

You can also push your tags to GitHub. To push all of the tags to GitHub type:

```
git push --tags
```

Now on the repo's GitHub page there will be a `Tags` section that will allow you to view and download the files in each tagged version of the repository.

5.3.4 Accessing on GitHub

Downloading into R

In general, the process of downloading data directly into R is similar to what we saw earlier for loading data from Dropbox Public folders. We can simply use the `source_data` command. First we need to find our plain-text data file's *raw* URL. To do this, go to your repository's GitHub site, navigate to the file you want to load, and click the `Raw` button on the right just above the file preview. I have data in comma-separated values format stored in a GitHub repository.[35] The URL for the raw (plain-text) version of the data is `https://raw.githubusercontent.com/christophergandrud/Disproportionality_Data/master/Disproportionality.csv`.[36]

```
# Place shortened url into URLAddress
UrlAddress <- "http://bit.ly/14aSjxB"

# Download data
DispropData <- repmis::source_data(UrlAddress)

## Downloading data from: http://bit.ly/14aSjxB
##
## SHA-1 hash of the downloaded data file is:
## 20a0b022bbcf947917878680df85f7b4dcaaf44a
```

[34]See `https://help.GitHub.com/articles/set-up-git` for more details.

[35]For full information about the disproportionality data set, please see `http://christophergandrud.github.io/Disproportionality_Data/`.

[36]It has been shortened with Bitly in the example.

```
# Show variable names
names(DispropData)

## [1] "country"               "iso2c"                 "year"
## [4] "disproportionality"
```

`source_data` downloaded the most recent version of the file from the master branch. As we saw in Section 5.2.2, running `source_data` gives us a line beginning `## SHA-1 hash of ...`. **Note:** this SHA-1 hash is different from the file's Git commit's SHA-1 hash we discussed earlier. The `source_data` SHA-1 hash is specific to the *file*, and has nothing to do with Git. We will look at this hash more in Chapter 6 (Section 6.3.2).

We can actually use `source_data` to download a particular version of a file–from a particular Git commit–directly into R. This makes reproducing a specific result much easier. To do this you just need to use a file's raw URL from a particular commit. To find a file's particular commit raw URL first click on the file on GitHub's website. Then click the `History` button (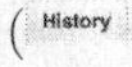

). This will take you to a page listing all of the file's versions. Click on the `Browse Code` button (

) next to the version of the file that you want to use. Click on the `Raw` button to be taken to the text-only version of the file. Finally, copy this page's URL address and use it with `source_data`.

For example, I have an old version of the disproportionality data. To download it I find this particular version of the file's URL and use it in `source_data`:

```
# Create object containing the file's URL
OldUrlAddress <- paste0("https://raw.githubusercontent.com/",
                        "christophergandrud/",
                        "Disproportionality_Data/",
                        "1a59d360b36eade3b183d6336a",
                        "2262df4f9555d1/",
                        "Disproportionality.csv")

# Download old disproportionality data
DispropOld <- repmis::source_data(OldUrlAddress)
```

In this example I did not shorten the URL, but instead used the `paste0` function to paste it together.[37] You do not have to do this. I did it here so that the URL would fit on the printed page. Notice that the URL is the same as

[37] `paste0` is the same as `paste`, but has the argument `sep = ""` so that white space is not placed between the pasted elements.

before with one exception: instead of `master` after `Disproportionality_Data` we have this strange series of number and letters: `1a59d360b36ea`.... This is the *commit's* SHA-1 hash.

As we will see in Chapter 8 (Section 8.2.3) we can use a very similar process to easily run source code files in R directly downloaded from GitHub with the `source_url` command.

Viewing files

The GitHub web user interface also allows you, your collaborators (see below) or, if the repo is public, anyone to look at text files from a web browser. Collaborators can actually also create, modify, and commit changes in the web user interface. This can be useful for making small changes, especially from a mobile device without a Git installation. Anyone with a GitHub account can suggest changes to files in a public repository on the repo's website. Simply click the `Edit` button () above the file and make edits. If the person making the edits is not a designated collaborator, their edits will be sent to the repository's owner for approval.[38] This can be a useful way for independent researchers to fix errors.

5.3.4.1 Collaboration with GitHub

Repositories can have official collaborators that can make changes to files in the repo. Public repositories can have unlimited collaborators. Anyone with a GitHub account can be a collaborator. To add a collaborator to a repository you created, click on the `Settings` button on the repository's website (see Figure 5.2). Then click the `Collaborators` button on the left-hand side of the page. You will be given a box to enter your collaborator's GitHub user name. If your collaborator doesn't have a GitHub account, they will have to create a new one. Once you add someone as a collaborator they can clone the repository onto their computer as you did earlier and push changes.

Syncing a repository

If you and your collaborators are both making changes to the files in a repo you might create conflicting changes, i.e. different changes to the same part of a file. To avoid too many conflicts, it is a good idea to sync your local repository with the remote repository **before** you push your commits to GitHub. Use the `pull command` to sync your local and remote repository. First add and commit your changes, then type:

[38] This is called a `pull` request in Git terminology. See the next section for more details.

```
# Sync repository
git pull
```

If the files you are pulling conflict with your local files you will probably want to resolve these in the individual files and commit the changes. When there are merge conflicts, Git adds both versions of a piece of text to the file. You then open the file and decide which version to keep and which one to delete. When the conflicts are resolved and changes committed, push your merged changes up to the remote repository as we did before.

5.3.5 Summing up the GitHub workflow

We've covered a lot of ground in this section. Let's sum up the basic GitHub workflow you will probably follow once your repo is set up.

1. Add any changes you've made with `git add`.
2. `commit` the changes.
3. `pull` your collaborators' changes from the GitHub repo, resolve any merge conflicts, and `commit` the changes.
4. `push` your changes to GitHub.

5.4 RStudio & GitHub

When you open a Project with a Git repository in RStudio you will see a new *Git* tab next to *Environment* and *History* (see Figure 5.6). From here you can do many of the things we covered in the previous section. Let's look at how to set up and use Git in RStudio Projects.

5.4.1 Setting up Git/GitHub with Projects

You can Git initialize new RStudio Projects, Git initialize existing projects, and create RStudio Projects from cloned repos. When you do any of these things RStudio automatically adds a *.gitignore* file telling Git to ignore *.Rproj.user*, *.Rhistory*, and *.RData* files.

Git with a new project

To create a new project with Git version control, go to `File` in the RStudio menu bar. Then click `New Project...`. In the box that appears (see Figure 5.4) select `New Directory` →`Empty Project`. Enter the Project's name

FIGURE 5.4
Creating RStudio Projects

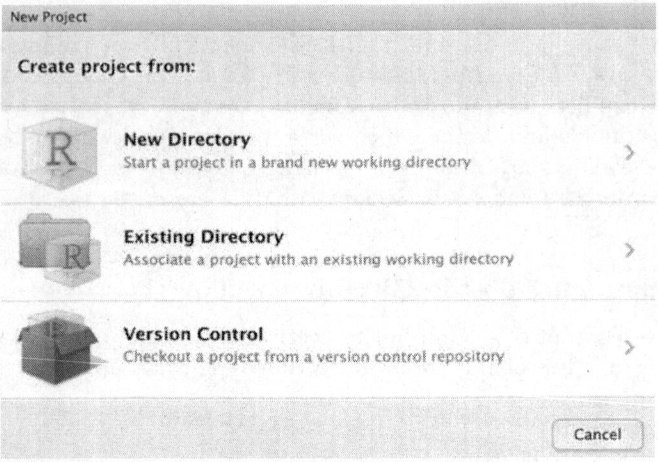

FIGURE 5.5
Creating RStudio Projects in New Directories

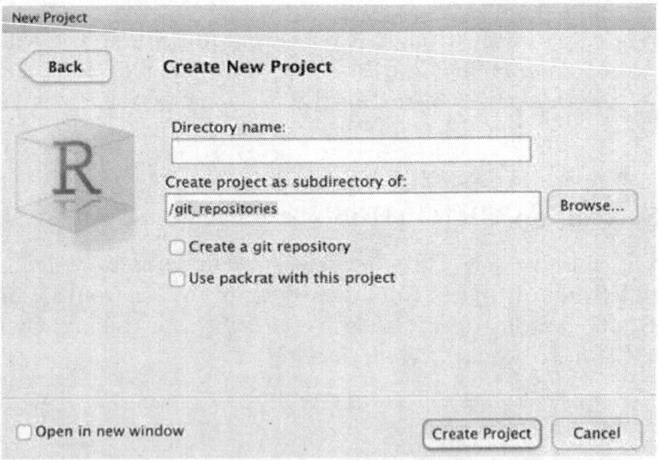

and desired directory. Make sure to check the dialog box for `Create a git repository` (see Figure 5.5).

Git initialize existing projects

If you have an existing RStudio Project and want to add Git version control to it, first go to `Tools` in the RStudio menu bar. Then select `Project Options ...`. Select the `Git/SVN` icon. Finally, select `Git` from the drop-down menu for `Version Control System:`.

Clone repository into a new project

Again go to `File` in the RStudio menu bar to create a new project from a cloned GitHub repository. Then click `New Project...`. Select the `Version Control` option and then `Git`. Finally, paste the repository's URL in the field called `Repository URL:`, enter the directory you would like to locate the cloned repo in, and click `Create Project`.

Add existing Project repository to GitHub

You can push an existing Project repository stored on your computer to a new remote repository on GitHub. To do this, first create a new repo on GitHub with the same name as your RStudio Project (see Section 5.3.3). Then copy the remote repository's URL like we saw before when we cloned a repository from GitHub (see Section 5.3.3). Open a new shell from within RStudio. To do this, click the `Shell` button in the *Git* tab's `More` drop-down menu. Now follow the same steps that we used in Section 5.3.3 to connect a locally stored repository to GitHub for the first time.

5.4.2 Using Git in RStudio Projects

The RStudio *Git* tab allows you to do many of the same things with Git that we covered in the previous section. In the top panel of Figure 5.6 you will see the *Git* tab for a new RStudio Project called *ExampleProject*. It has two files that have not been added or committed to Git. To add and commit the files to the repository, click on the dialog boxes next to the file names. In the bottom panel of Figure 5.6 you can see that I've created a new R file called *ExampleScript.R* and clicked the dialog box next to it, along with the other files. The yellow question marks in the top panel have now become green A's for "add". Clicking `Commit` opens a new window called **Review Changes** where you can commit the changes. Simply write a commit message in the box called *Commit Message* in the **Review Changes** window and click `Commit`. If you add file names to the *.gitignore* files, they will not show up in RStudio's *Git* tab.

If you are using a GitHub repo that is associated with a remote repository on GitHub, you can push and pull it with the `Pull Branches` and `Push`

FIGURE 5.6
The RStudio Git Tab

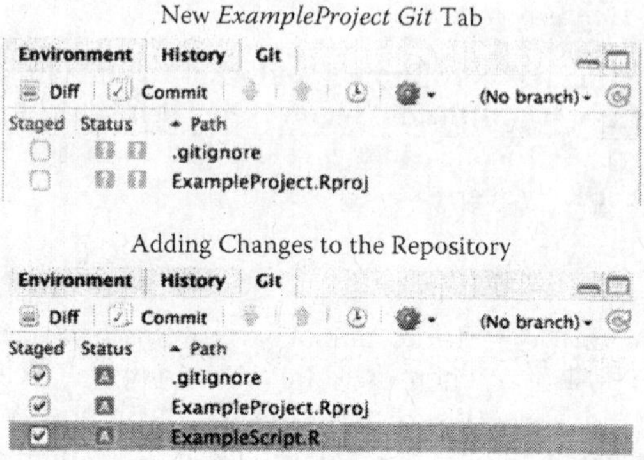

`Branch` buttons in Git menu bar (the blue and green arrows, respectively). You can use the same buttons in the **Review Changes** window. The *Git* tab also allows you to change branches, revert to previous commits, add files to `.gitignore`, and view your commit history. You can always use the `More → Shell ...` option to open a new shell with the Project set as the working directory to complete any other Git task you might want to do.

Chapter summary

In this chapter we have primarily learned how to store text-based reproducible research files in ways that allow us and others to access them easily from many locations, enable collaboration, and keep a record of previous versions. In the next chapter we will learn how to use text-based files to reproducibly gather data that we can use in our statistical analyses.

6

Gathering Data with R

How you gather your data directly impacts how reproducible your research will be. You should try your best to document every step of your data gathering process. Reproduction will be easier if your documentation–especially, variable descriptions and source code–makes it easy for you and others to understand what you have done. If all of your data gathering steps are tied together by your source code, then independent researchers (and you) can more easily regather the data. Regathering data will be easiest if running your code allows you to get all the way back to the raw data files–the rawer the better. Of course, this may not always be possible. You may need to conduct interviews or compile information from paper based archives, for example. The best you can sometimes do is describe your data gathering process in detail. Nonetheless, R's automated data gathering capabilities for internet-based information is extensive. Learning how to take full advantage of these capabilities greatly increases reproducibility and can save you considerable time and effort over the long run.

In this chapter we'll learn how to gather quantitative data in a fully reproducible way. We'll start by learning how to use data gathering makefiles to organize your whole data gathering process so that it can be completely reproduced. Then we will learn the details of how to actually load data into R from various sources, both locally on your computer and remotely via the internet. In the next chapter (Chapter 7) we'll learn the details of how to cleanup raw data so that it can be merged together into data frames that you can use for statistical analyses.

6.1 Organize Your Data Gathering: Makefiles

Before getting into the details of using R to gather data, let's start by creating a plan to organize the process. Organizing your data gathering process from the beginning of a research project improves the possibility of reproducibility and can save you significant effort over the course of the project by making it easier to add and regather data later on.

A key part of reproducible data gathering with R, like reproducible research in general, is segmenting the process into modular files that can all be run by a common "makefile". In this chapter we'll learn how to create make-like files run exclusively from R as well as GNU Make makefiles,[1] which you run from a shell.[2] Learning how to create R make-like files is fairly easy. Using GNU Make does require learning some more new syntax. However, it has one very clear advantage: it only runs a source code file that has been updated since the last time you ran the makefile. This is very useful if part of your data gathering process is very computationally and time intensive.

Segmenting your data gathering into modular files and tying them together with some sort of makefile allows you to more easily navigate research text and find errors in the source code. The makefile's output is the data set that you'll use in the statistical analyses. There are two types of source code files that the makefile runs: data gathering/cleanup files and merging files. Data cleanup files bring raw individual data sources into R and transform them so that they can be merged together with data from the other sources. Many of the R tools for data cleanup and merging will be covered in Chapter 7. In this chapter we mostly cover the ways to bring raw data into R. Merging files are executed by the makefile after it runs the data gathering/cleanup files.

It's a good idea to have the source code files use very raw data as input. Your source code should avoid directly changing these raw data files. Instead changes should be put into new objects and data files. Doing this makes it easier to reconstruct the steps you took to create your data set. Also, while cleaning and merging your data you may transform it in unintended ways, for example, accidentally deleting some observations that you wanted to keep. Having the raw data makes it easy to go back and correct your mistakes.

The files for the examples used in this section can be downloaded from GitHub at: `http://bit.ly/YnMKBG`.

6.1.1 R Make-like files

When you create make-like files in R to organize and run your data gathering you usually only need one or two commands, `setwd` and `source`. As we talked about in Chapter 4, `setwd` simply tells R where to look for and place files. `source` tells R to run code in an R source code file.[3] Let's see what an R data make file might look like for a project with a file structure similar to the example project in Figure 4.1. The file paths in this example are for Unix-like systems and the make-like file is called *Makefile.R*.

```
################
# Example R make-like file
```

[1]GNU stands for "GNU's Not Unix", indicating that it is Unix-like.

[2]To standardize things, I use the terms "R make-like file" for files created and run in R and the standard "makefile" for files run by Make.

[3]We use the `source` command more in the Chapter 8.

```
# Christopher Gandrud
# Updated 15 January 2015
################

# Set working directory
setwd("/ExampleProject/Analysis/Data/")

# Gather and cleanup raw data files.
source("Gather1.R")
source("Gather2.R")
source("Gather3.R")

# Merge cleaned data frames into data frame object CleanedData
source("MergeData.R")
```

This code first sets the working directory. Then it runs three source code files to gather data from three different sources. These files gather the data and clean it so that it can be merged together. The cleaned data frames are available in the current workspace. Next the code runs the *MergeData.R* file that merges the data frames and saves the output data frame as a CSV formatted file. The CSV file could be the main file we use for statistical analysis. *MergeData.R* also creates a Markdown file with a table describing the variables and their sources. We'll come back to how to create tables in Chapter 9.

You can run the commands in this file one by one or run the make-like file by putting it through the `source` command so that it will run it all at once.

6.1.2 GNU Make

R make-like files are a simple way to tie together a segmented data gathering process. If one or more of the source files that our example before runs is computationally intensive it is a good idea to run them only when they are updated. However, this can become tedious, especially if there are many segments. The well-established GNU Make command-line program[4] deals with this problem by comparing the output files' time stamps[5] to time stamps of the source files that created them. If a source file has a time stamp that is newer than its output, Make will run it. If the source's time stamp is older than its output, Make will skip it.

[4]GNU Make was originally developed in 1977 by Stuart Feldman as a way to compile computer programs from a series of files, its primary use to this day. For an overview see: `http://en.wikipedia.org/wiki/Make_(software)`. For installation instructions please see Section 1.5.1.

[5]A file's time stamp records the time and date when it was last changed.

In Make terminology the output files are called "targets" and the files that create them are called "prerequisites". You specify a "recipe" to create the targets from the prerequisites. The recipe is basically just the code you want to run to make the target file. The general form is:

```
TARGET ... : PREREQUISITE ...
    RECIPE
    ...
    ...
```

Note that, unlike in R, tabs are important in Make. They indicate what lines are the recipe. Make uses the recipe to ensure that targets are newer than prerequisites. If a target is newer than its prerequisite, Make does not run the prerequisite.

The basic idea of reproducible data gathering with Make is similar to what we saw before, with a few twists and some new syntax. Let's see an example that does what we did before: gather data from three sources, clean and merge the data, and save it in CSV format.

6.1.2.1 Example makefile

The first thing we need to do is create a new file called *Makefile*[6] and place it in the same directory as the data gathering files we already have. The makefile we are going to create runs prerequisite files by the alphanumeric order of their file names. So we need to ensure that the files are named in the order that we want to run them. Now let's look at the actual makefile:

```
################
# Example Makefile
# Christopher Gandrud
# Updated 1 July 2013
# Influenced by Rob Hyndman (31 October 2012)
# See: http://robjhyndman.com/researchtips/makefiles/
################

# Key variables to define
RDIR = .
MERGE_OUT = MergeData.Rout
```

[6] Alternatively you can call the file *GNUmakefile* or *makefile*.

```
# Create list of R source files
RSOURCE = $(wildcard $(RDIR)/*.R)

# Files to indicate when the RSOURCE file was run
OUT_FILES = $(RSOURCE:.R=.Rout)

# Default target
all: $(OUT_FILES)

# Run the RSOURCE files
$(RDIR)/%.Rout: $(RDIR)/%.R
    R CMD BATCH $<

# Remove Out Files
clean:
    rm -fv $(OUT_FILES)

# Remove MergeData.Rout
cleanMerge:
    rm -fv $(MERGE_OUT)
```

Ok, let's break down the code. The first part of the file defines variables that will be used later on. For example, in the first line of executable code (`RDIR = .`) we create a simple variable[7] called `RDIR` with a period (`.`) as its value. In Make and Unix-like shells, periods indicate the current directory. The next line allows us to specify a variable for the outfile created by running the *MergeData.R* file. This will be useful later when we create a target for removing this file to ensure that the *MergeData.R* file is always run.

The third executed line (`RSOURCE:= $(wildcard $(RDIR)/*.R)`) creates a variable containing a list of all of the names of files with the extension `.R`, i.e. our data gathering and merge source code files. This line has some new syntax, so let's work through it. In Make (and Unix-like shells generally) a dollar sign (`$`) followed by a variable name substitutes the value of the variable in place of the name.[8] For example, `$(RDIR)` inserts the period `.` that we defined as the value of `RDIR` previously. The parentheses are included to clearly demarcate where the variable name begins and ends.[9]

[7]Simple string variables are often referred to as "macros" in GNU Make. A common convention in Make and Unix-like shells generally is to use all caps for variable names.

[8]This is a kind of parameter expansion. For more information about parameter expansion see Frazier (2008).

[9]Braces (`{}`) are also sometimes used for this.

You may remember the asterisk (`*`) from the previous chapter. It is a "wildcard", a special character that allows you to select file names that follow a particular pattern. Using `*.R` selects any file name that ends in `.R`.

Why did we also include the actual word `wildcard`? The `wildcard` function is different from the asterisk wildcard character. The function creates a list of files that match a pattern. In this case the pattern is `$(RDIR)/*.R`. The general form for writing the `wildcard` function is: `$(wildcard PATTERN)`.

The third line (`OUT_FILES = $(RSOURCE:.R=.Rout)`) creates a variable for the `.Rout` files that Make will use to tell how recently each R file was run.[10] `$(RSOURCE:.R=.Rout)` is a variable that uses the same file name as our RSOURCE files, but with the file extension `.Rout`.

The second part of the makefile tells Make what we want to create and how to create it. In the line `all: $(OUT_FILES)` we are specifying the makefile's default target. Targets are the files that you instruct Make to make. `all:` sets the default target; it is what Make tries to create when you enter the command `make` in the shell with no arguments. We will see later how to instruct Make to compile different targets.

The next two executable lines (`$(RDIR)/%.Rout: $(RDIR)/%.R` and `R CMD BATCH $<`) run the R source code files in the directory. The first line specifies that the `.Rout` files are the targets of the `.R` files. The percent sign (`%`) is another wildcard. Unlike the asterisk, it replaces the selected file names throughout the command used to create the target.

The dollar and less-than signs (`$<`) indicate the first prerequisite for the target, i.e. the `.R` files. `R CMD BATCH` is a way to call R from a Unix-like shell, run source files, and output the results to other files.[11] The out-files it creates have the extension `.Rout`.

The next two lines specify another target: `clean`. When you type `make clean` into your shell Make will follow the recipe: `rm -fv $(OUT_FILES)`. This removes (deletes) the `.Rout` files. The `f` argument (force) ignores files that don't exist and the `v` argument (verbose) instructs Make to tell you what is happening when it runs. When you delete the `.Rout` files, Make will run all of the `.R` files the next time you call it.

The last two lines help us solve a problem created by the fact that our simple makefile doesn't push changes downstream. For example, if we make a change to *Gather2.R* and run `make`, only *Gather2.R* will be rerun. The new data frame will not be added to the final merged data set. To overcome this problem the last two lines of code create a target called `cleanMerge`, this removes only the *MergeData.Rout* file.

---

[10] The R out-file contains all of the output from the R session used while running the file. These can be a helpful place to look for errors if your makefiles give you an error like `make: *** [Gather.Rout] Error 1`.

[11] You will need to make sure that R is in your PATH. Setting this up is different on different systems. If on Mac and Linux you can load R from the Terminal by typing `R`, R is in your PATH. The usual R installation usually sets this up correctly. There are different methods for changing the file path on different versions of Windows.

Running the Makefile

To run the makefile for the first time, simply change the working directory to where the file is and type `make` into your shell. It will create the CSV final data file and four files with the extension `.Rout`, indicating when the segmented data gathering files were last run.[12]

When you run `make` in the shell for the first time you should get the output:

```
## R CMD BATCH Gather1.R
## R CMD BATCH Gather2.R
## R CMD BATCH Gather3.R
## R CMD BATCH MergeData.R
```

If you run it a second time without changing the R source files you will get the following output:

```
## make: Nothing to be done for 'all'.
```

To remove all of the `.Rout` files, set the make target to `clean`:

```
make clean
```

```
## rm -fv ./Gather1.Rout ./Gather2.Rout ./Gather3.Rout
## ./MergeData.Rout
## ./Gather1.Rout
## ./Gather2.Rout
## ./Gather3.Rout
## ./MergeData.Rout
```

If we run the following code:

[12]If you open these files you fill find the output from the R session used when their source file was last run.

FIGURE 6.1
The RStudio Build Tab

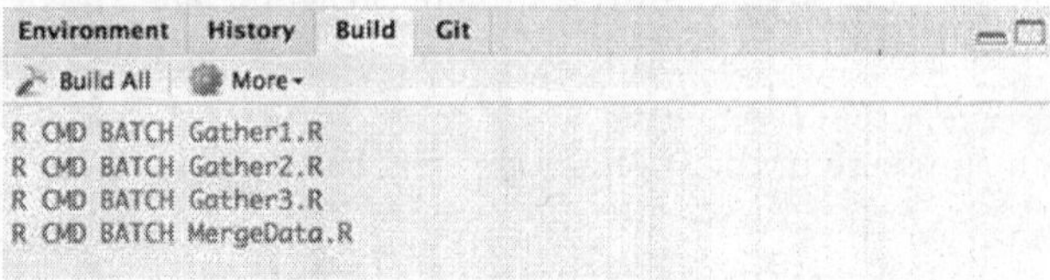


```
# Remove MergeData.Rout and make all R source files
make cleanMerge all
```

then Make will first remove the *MergeData.Rout* file (if there is one) and then run all of the R source files as need be. *MergeData.R* will always be run. This ensures that changes to the gathered data frames are updated in the final merged data set.

6.1.2.2 Makefiles and RStudio Projects

You can run makefiles from RStudio's *Build* tab. For the type of makefile we have been using, the main advantage of running it from within RStudio is that you don't have to toggle between RStudio and the shell. Everything is in one place. Imagine that the directory with our makefile is an RStudio Project. If a Project already contains a makefile, RStudio will automatically open a *Build* tab on the *Environment/History* pane, the same place where the *Git* tab appears (see Figure 6.1).[13]

The *Build* tab has buttons you can click to `Build All` (this is equivalent to `make all`), and, in the `More` drop-down menu, `Clean all` (`i.e. make clean`) and `i.e. Clean and Rebuild` (`make clean all`). As you can see in Figure 6.1, the Tab shows you the same output you get in the shell.

6.1.2.3 Other information about makefiles

Note that Make relies heavily on commands and syntax of the shell program that you are using. The above example was written and tested on a Mac. It should work on other Unix-like computers without modification.

You can use Make to build almost any project from the shell, not just

[13]If a project doesn't have a makefile you can still set up RStudio Build. Click on `Build` in the Menu bar then `Configure Build Tools . . .`. Select `Makefile` from the drop-down menu then `Ok`. You will still need to manually add a Makefile in the Project's root directory.

run R source code files. It was an integral part of early reproducible computational research (Fomel and Claerbout, 2009; Buckheit and Donoho, 1995). Rob Hyndman more recently posted a description of the makefile he uses to create a project with R and LaTeX.[14] The complete source of information on GNU Make is the official online manual. It is available at: `http://www.gnu.org/software/make/manual/`.

6.2 Importing Locally Stored Data Sets

Now that we've covered the big picture, let's learn the different tools you will need to know to gather data from different types of sources. The most straightforward place to load data from is a local file, e.g. one stored on your computer. Though storing your data locally does not really encourage reproducibility, most research projects will involve loading data this way at some point. The tools you will learn for importing locally stored data files will also be important for most of the other methods further on.

Data stored in plain-text files on your computer can be loaded into R using the `read.table` command. For example, imagine we have a CSV file called *TestData.csv* stored in the current working directory. To load the data set into R simply type:

```
TestData <- read.table("TestData.csv", sep = ",", header = TRUE)
```

See Section 5.2.2 for a discussion of the arguments in this command.

If you are using RStudio you can do the same thing with drop-down menus. To open a plain-text data file click on `Environment` → `Import Dataset...` → `From Text File...`. In the box that pops up, specify the column separator, whether or not you want the first line to be treated as variable labels, and other options. This is initially easier than using `read.table`. But it is much less reproducible.

If the data is not stored in plain-text format, but is instead saved in a format created by another statistical program such as SPSS, SAS, or Stata, we can import it using commands in the *foreign* package. For example, imagine we have a data file called *Data1.dta* stored in our working directory. This file was created by the Stata statistical program. To load the data into an R data frame object called *StataData* simply type:

---

[14] See his blog at: `http://robjhyndman.com/researchtips/makefiles/`. Posted 31 October 2012. This method largely replicates what we do in this book with *knitr*. Nonetheless, it has helpful information about Make that can be used in other tasks. It was in fact helpful for writing this section of the book.

```
# Load foreign package
library(foreign)

# Load Stata formatted data
StataData <- read.dta(file = "Data1.dta")
```

As you can see, commands in the *foreign* package have similar syntax to `read.table`. To see the full range of commands and file formats that the *foreign* package supports, use the following command:

```
library(help = "foreign")
```

If you have data stored in a spreadsheet format such as Excel's *.xlsx*, it may be best to first cleanup the data in the spreadsheet program by hand and then save the file in plain-text format. When you cleanup the data make sure that the first row has the variable names and that observations are in the following rows. Also, remove any extraneous information such as notes, colors, and so on that will not be part of the data frame.

To aid reproducibility, locally stored data should include careful documentation of where the data came from and how, if at all, it was transformed before it was loaded into R. Ideally, the documentation would be written in a text file saved in the same directory as the raw data file.

6.3 Importing Data Sets from the Internet

There are many ways to import data that is stored on the internet directly into R. We have to use different methods depending on where and how the data is stored.

6.3.1 Data from non-secure (`http`) URLs

Importing data into R that is located at a non-secure URL[15]–ones that start with `http`–is straightforward provided that:

- the data is stored in a simple format, e.g. plain-text,
- the file is not embedded in a larger HTML website.

[15]URL stands for "Uniform Resource Locator".

We already discussed the first issue in detail. You can determine if the data file is embedded in a website by opening the URL in your web browser. If you only see the raw plain-text data, you are probably good to go. To import the data, simply include the URL as the file's name in your `read.table` command.

6.3.2 Data from secure (`https`) URLs

Storing data at non-secure URLs is becoming less common. Services like Dropbox and GitHub now store their data at secure URLs.[16] You can tell if the data is stored at a secure web address if it begins with `https` rather than `http`. We have to use different commands to download data from secure URLs. Let's look at three methods for downloading data into R: `source_data`, `source_DropboxData`, and the *RCurl* package.

Loading data from secure URLs with `source_data`

As we saw in Chapter 5, we can use the `source_data` command in the *repmis* package to simplify the process of downloading data from Dropbox *Public* folders (Section 5.2.2) and GitHub (Section 5.3.4). You can use `source_data` to download data in plain-text format from almost any URL, as long as the file is not embedded in a larger HTML website.

One problem for reproducible research with sourcing data located on the internet is that data files may change without us knowing. This could change the results we get. Luckily, we can solve this problem with `source_data`. In Chapter 5 we saw that when we run the `source_data` command we not only download a data file, but also find its SHA-1 hash. The SHA-1 hash is basically a unique number for the file. If the file changes, its SHA-1 hash will change. Once we know the file's SHA-1 hash we can use `source_data`'s `sha1` argument to make sure the file that we downloaded is the same as the one we intended to download.

For example, let's find the SHA-1 hash for the disproportionality data set we downloaded in the last chapter (Section 5.3.4):[17]

```
DispropData <- repmis::source_data(UrlAddress)

## Downloading data from: http://bit.ly/14aSjxB
##
## SHA-1 hash of the downloaded data file is:
## 20a0b022bbcf947917878680df85f7b4dcaaf44a
```

[16]Dropbox used to host files in the Public folder at non-secure URLs, but switched to secure URLs.

[17]Remember we placed the file's raw GitHub URL address inside of the object *UrlAddress*.

You can see that the file's SHA-1 hash begins *20a0b022bbcf* .... Let's see what happens when we try to download an older version of the same file while placing this SHA-1 hash in `source_url`'s `sha1` argument. The URL of the alternative version of the file is in the object *OldUrlAddress*:[18]

```
DispropData <- repmis::source_data(OldUrlAddress,
       sha1 = "20a0b022bbcf947917878680df85f7b4dcaaf44a")

## Error: SHA-1 hash of downloaded file (654e38f3d56946ecdea7caab7e240642009d9e61)
##  does not match expected value (20a0b022bbcf947917878680df85f7b4dcaaf44a)
```

If we set the `sha1` argument in our replication files, others can be sure that they are using the same data files that we used to generate a particular result. It may not be practical to do this while a piece of research is under active development, as the files may be regularly updated. However, it can be very useful for source code files that underlie published results.

Loading data from Dropbox non-Public folders with `source_DropboxData`

Files stored on Dropbox non-*Public* folders are a little trickier to download. If you go to the Dropbox website and click the `Share Link` button next to a file (

) you will be given an information box. This is not the raw data file. Luckily, *repmis* includes a `source_DropboxData` command for downloading data stored in a non-Public Dropbox folder into R. It works in much the same way as `source_data`, the only difference is that instead of using the URL we need (a) the file's name and (b) its Dropbox key.

To find the file's key simply click on the `Share Link` button next to the file on the Dropbox website. Look at the URL for the webpage that appears. Here's an example: `https://dl.dropboxusercontent.com/s/exh4iobbm2p5p1v/fin_research_note.csv`

You can see that the last part of the URL (`fin_research_note.csv`) is the data file's name. The key is the string of letters and numbers just after `https://www.dropbox.com/s/`, i.e. `exh4iobbm2p5p1v`. Now that we have the file name and key we can download the data into R using `source_DropboxData`. For example:

```
# Download data from a Dropbox non-Public folder
FinDataFull <- repmis::source_DropboxData("fin_research_note.csv",
                                  "exh4iobbm2p5p1v",
                                  sep = ",", header = TRUE)
```

[18]See Section 5.3.4 for the full URL.

Loading data using RCurl

A more laborious way to download data from a secure URL that does not rely on *repmis* is to use the `getURL` command in the *RCurl* package (Temple Lang, 2015) as well as `read.table` and `textConnection`. The latter commands are in base R. The two rules about data being stored in plain text-formats and not being embedded in a larger HTML website apply to this method as well.

Let's try an example. To download the data file we used in Section 5.3.4 into R we could use this code:

```
# Put URL address into the object UrlAddress
UrlAddress <- paste0("https://raw.githubusercontent.com/",
                    "christophergandrud/Disproportionality",
                    "_Data/master/Disproportionality.csv")

# Download Electoral disproportionality data
DataUrl <- RCurl::getURL(UrlAddress)

# Convert Data into a data frame
DispropData <- read.table(textConnection(DataUrl),
                          sep = ",", header = TRUE)

# Show variables in the data
names(DispropData)

## [1] "country"              "iso2c"                "year"
## [4] "disproportionality"
```

If running `getURL(UrlAddress)` gives you an error about an SSL `certificate problem` simply add the argument `ssl.verifypeer = FALSE`. This allows you to skip certification verification and access the data.[19]

6.3.3 Compressed data stored online

Sometimes data files are large, making them difficult to store and download without compressing them. There are a number of compression methods such as Zip and Tar.[20] Zip files have the extension `.zip` and Tar files use extensions such as `.tar` and `.gz`. In most cases[21] you can download, decompress, and

[19]For more details see the *RCurl* help page at `http://www.omegahat.org/RCurl/FAQ.html`.

[20]Tar archives are sometimes referred to as 'tar balls'.

[21]Some formats that require the *foreign* package to open are more difficult. This is because functions such as `read.dta` for opening Stata `.dta` files only accept file names or URLs as arguments, not connections, which you create for unzipped files.

create data frame objects from these files directly in R. To do this you need to:[22]

- create a temporary file with `tempfile` to store the zipped file, which you will later remove with the `unlink command` at the end,
- download the file with `download.file`,
- decompress the file with one of the `connections` commands in base R,[23]
- read the file with `read.table`.

The reason that we have to go through so many extra steps is that compressed files are more than just a single file and contain a number of files as well as metadata.

Let's download a compressed file called *uds_summary.csv* from Pemstein et al. (2010). It's in a compressed file called *uds_summary.csv.gz*. At the time of writing, the file's URL address is `http://www.unified-democracy-scores.org/files/20140312/z/uds_summary.csv.gz`. Again, I shortened the URL to `http://bit.ly/1jXJgDh` because of space constraints.

```
# For simplicity, store the URL in an object called 'URL'
URL <- "http://bit.ly/1jXJgDh"

# Create a temporary file called 'temp' to put the zip file into.
temp <- tempfile()

# Download the compressed file into the temporary file.
download.file(URL, temp)

# Decompress the file and convert it into a data frame
UDSData <- read.csv(gzfile(temp, "uds_summary.csv"))

# Delete the temporary file.
unlink(temp)

# Show variables in data
names(UDSData)

## [1] "country" "year"    "cowcode" "mean"    "sd"      "median"  "pct025"
## [8] "pct975"
```

[22]The description of this process is based on a Stack Overflow comment by Dirk Eddelbuettel (see `http://stackoverflow.com/questions/3053833/using-r-to-download-zipped-data-file-extract-and-import-data?answertab=votes\#tab-top`, posted 10 June 2010.)

[23]To find a full list of commands type `?connections` into the R console.

6.3.4 Data APIs & feeds

There are a growing number of packages that can gather data directly from a variety of internet sources and import them into R. Most of these packages use the sources' web application programming interfaces (API). Web APIs allow programs to interact with a website. Needless to say, this is great for reproducible research. It not only makes the data gathering process easier as you don't have to download many Excel files and fiddle around with them before even getting the data into R, but it also makes replicating the data gathering process much more straightforward and makes it easy to update data sets when new information becomes available. Some examples of these packages include:

- The *openair* package (Carslaw and Ropkins, 2015), which beyond providing a number of tools for analyzing air quality data also has the ability to directly gather data directly from sources such as Kings College London's London Air (`http://www.londonair.org.uk/`) database.
- The *quantmod* package (Ryan, 2015) allows you to access data from Google Finance,[24] Yahoo Finance,[25] and the US Federal Reserve's FRED[26] economic database.
- The *treebase* package by Boettiger and Temple Lang (2012) allows you to access phylogenetic data from TreeBASE.[27]
- The *twitteR* package (Gentry, 2015) accesses Twitter's[28] API. This allows you to download data from Twitter including tweets and trending topics.
- The *WDI* package (Arel-Bundock, 2013) allows you to directly download data from the World Bank's Development Indicators database.[29] This database includes numerous country-level economic, health, and environment variables.
- The rOpenSci[30] group has and is developing a number of packages for accessing scientific data from web-based sources with R. They have a comprehensive set of packages for accessing biological data and academic journals. For a list of their packages see: `http://ropensci.org/packages/index.html`.
- Stack Exchange's Cross Validated website[31] also has a fairly comprehensive and regularly updated list of APIs accessible from R packages.

---

[24] `http://www.google.com/finance`
[25] `http://finance.yahoo.com/`
[26] `http://research.stlouisfed.org/fred2/`
[27] `http://treebase.org`
[28] `https://twitter.com/`
[29] `http://data.worldbank.org/data-catalog/world-development-indicators`
[30] `http://ropensci.org/`
[31] `http://stats.stackexchange.com/questions/12670/data-apis-feeds-available-as-packages-in-r`

API Package Example: World Bank Development Indicators

Each of these packages has its own syntax and it isn't possible to go over all of them here. Nonetheless, let's look at an example of accessing World Bank data with the *WDI* to give you a sense of how these packages work. Imagine that we want to gather data on fertilizer consumption. We can use *WDI*'s `WDIsearch` command to find fertilizer consumption data available at the World Bank:

```
# Load WDI package
library(WDI)

# Search World Bank for fertilizer consumption data
WDIsearch("fertilizer consumption")

##      indicator
## [1,] "AG.CON.FERT.MT"
## [2,] "AG.CON.FERT.PT.ZS"
## [3,] "AG.CON.FERT.ZS"
##      name
## [1,] "Fertilizer consumption (metric tons)"
## [2,] "Fertilizer consumption (% of fertilizer production)"
## [3,] "Fertilizer consumption (kilograms per hectare of arable land)"
```

This shows us a selection of indicator numbers and their names.[32] Let's gather data on countries' fertilizer consumption in kilograms per hectare of arable land. The indicator number for this variable is: AG.CON.FERT.ZS. We can use the command `WDI` to gather the data and put it in an object called *FertConsumpData*.

```
FertConsumpData <- WDI(indicator = "AG.CON.FERT.ZS")
```

The data we downloaded looks like this:

```
head(FertConsumpData)

##   iso2c    country AG.CON.FERT.ZS year
```

[32]You can also search the World Bank Development Indicators website. The indicator numbers are at the end of each indicator's URL.

```
## 1    1A Arab World        74.26643 2011
## 2    1A Arab World        61.26674 2010
## 3    1A Arab World        58.08116 2009
## 4    1A Arab World        64.87818 2008
## 5    1A Arab World        61.65731 2007
## 6    1A Arab World        59.43073 2006
```

You can see that `WDI` has downloaded data for four variables: **iso2c**,[33] **country**, **AG.CON.FERT.ZS** and **year**.

6.4 Advanced Automatic Data Gathering: Web Scraping

If a package does not already exist to access data from a particular website, there are other ways to automatically "scrape" data with R. This section briefly discusses some of R's web scraping tools and techniques to get you headed in the right direction to do more advanced data gathering.

The general process

Simple web scraping involves downloading a file from the internet, parsing it (i.e. reading it), and extracting the data you are interested in then putting it into a data frame object. We already saw a simple example of this when we downloaded data from the a secure HTTPS website. We downloaded a website's content from a URL address into R with the `getURL` command. We then parsed the downloaded text as a CSV formatted data file, extracted it, and put it into a new data frame object.

This was a relatively simple process, because the webpage was very simply formatted. It basically only contained the CSV formatted text. So, the process of parsing and extracting the data was very straightforward. You may not be so lucky with other data sources. Data may be stored in an HTML formatted table within a more complicated HTML marked up webpage. The *XML* package (Temple Lang, 2013) has a number of useful commands such as `readHTMLTable` for parsing and extracting this kind of data. The *XML* package also clearly has functions for handling XML formatted data.[34] In addition, the helpful *rvest* (Wickham, 2015b) package provides an easy to use set of functions with capabilities similar to and often more capable than *XML*.

[33]These are the countries' or regions' International Standards Organization's two-letter codes. For more details see: `http://www.iso.org/iso/country_codes.htm`.

[34]XML stands for "Extensible Markup Language".

If the data is stored in JSON[35] you can read it with the *rjson* (Couture-Beil, 2014) or *RJSONIO* (Temple Lang, 2014) packages.

There are more websites with APIs than R packages designed specifically to access each one. If an API is available, the *httr* package (Wickham, 2015a) may be useful. It is a wrapper for *RCurl* intended to make accessing APIs easier.

More tools to learn for web scraping

Beyond learning about the various R packages that are useful for R web scraping, an aspiring web scraper should probably invest time learning a number of other skills:

- HTML: Obviously you will encounter a lot of HTML markup when web scraping. Having a good understanding of the HTML markup language will be very helpful. W3 Schools (`http://www.w3schools.com/`) is a free resource for learning HTML as well as JSON, JavaScript, XML, and other languages you will likely come across while web scraping.

- Regular Expressions: Web scraping often involves finding character patterns. Some of this is done for you by the R packages above that parse text. There are times, however, when you are looking for particular patterns, like tag IDs, that are particular to a given website and change across the site based on a particular pattern. You can use regular expressions to deal with these situations. R has a comprehensive if bare-bones introduction to regular expressions. To access it type `?regex` into your R console.

- Looping: Web scraping often involves applying a function to multiple things, e.g. tables or HTML tags. To do this in an efficient way you will need to use loops and apply functions. Matloff (2011) provides a comprehensive overview. The *dplyr* (Wickham and Francois, 2015) for data frame manipulation is also particularly useful.

  Finally, Munzert et al. (2015) provide a comprehensive overview of web scraping and text mining with R.

Chapter summary

In this chapter we have learned how to reproducibly gather data from a number of sources. If the data we are using is available online we may be able to create really reproducible data gathering files. These files have commands that others can execute with makefiles that allow them to actually regather the exact data we used. The techniques we can use to gather online data also make it easy to update our data when new information becomes available. Of

[35] JSON means "JavaScript Object Notation"

course, it may not always be possible to have really reproducible data gathering. Nonetheless, you should always aim to make it clear to others (and yourself) how you gathered your data. In the next chapter we will learn how to clean and merge multiple data files so that they can easily be used in our statistical analyses.

7

Preparing Data for Analysis

Once we have gathered the raw data that we want to include in our statistical analyses we generally need to clean it up so that it can be merged into a single data file. In this chapter we will learn how to create the data gather and merging files we saw in the last chapter. The chapter also includes information on recoding and transforming variables. This is important for merging data and will be useful information in later chapters as well. If you are very familiar with data transformations in R you may want to skip to the next chapter.

7.1 Cleaning Data for Merging

In order to successfully merge two or more data frames we need to make sure that they are in the same format. Let's look at some of the important formatting issues and how to reformat your data frames so that they can be easily merged.

7.1.1 Get a handle on your data

Before doing anything to your data it is a good idea to take a look at it and see what needs to be done. Taking a little time to become acquainted with your data will help you avoid many error messages and much frustration.

You could type a data frame object's name into the R console. This will print the entire data frame in your console. For data frames with more than a few variables and observations this is very impractical. We have already seen a number of commands that are useful for looking at parts of your data. As we saw in Chapter 3, the `names` command shows you the variable names in a data frame object. The `head` command shows the names plus the first few observations in a data frame. The `tail` shows the last few.

Use the `dim` (dimensions) command to quickly see the number of observations and variables (the number of rows and columns) in a data frame object. For example, let's use the *FertConsumpData* object we created in Chapter 6 to test out `dim`:

```
dim(FertConsumpData)

## [1] 1736    4
```

The first number is the number of rows in the data frame (1736) and the second is the number of columns (4). You can also use the `nrow` command to find just the number of rows and `ncol` to see only the columns.

The **summary** command is especially helpful for seeing basic descriptive statistics for all of the variables in a data frame and also the variables' types. Here is an example:

```
# Summarize FertConsumpData data frame object
# This was loaded in Chapter 6
summary(FertConsumpData)

##     iso2c             country          AG.CON.FERT.ZS         year     
##  Length:1736        Length:1736        Min.   :    0.00   Min.   :2005  
##  Class :character   Class :character   1st Qu.:   19.75   1st Qu.:2006  
##  Mode  :character   Mode  :character   Median :   85.20   Median :2008  
##                                        Mean   :  240.32   Mean   :2008  
##                                        3rd Qu.:  169.78   3rd Qu.:2010  
##                                        Max.   :16532.31   Max.   :2011  
##                                        NA's   :429                     
```

We can immediately see that the variables **iso2c** and **country** are character strings. Because **summary** is able to calculate means, medians, and so on for **AG.CON.FERT.ZS** and **year**, we know they are numeric. Have a look over the summary to see if there is anything unexpected like lots of missing values (**NA's**) or unusual maximum and minimum values. You can Of course, run **summary** on a particular variable by using the component selector (**$**):

```
# Summarize fertilizer consumption variable from FertConsumpData
summary(FertConsumpData$AG.CON.FERT.ZS)

##     Min.  1st Qu.   Median     Mean  3rd Qu.     Max.     NA's 
##     0.00    19.75    85.20   240.30   169.80 16530.00      429
```

We'll come back to why knowing this type of information is important for merging and data analysis later in this chapter.

Another important command for quickly summarizing a data frame is `table`. This creates a contingency table with counts of the number of observations per combination of factor variables.

You can view a portion of a data frame object with the `View` function. This will open a new window that lets you see a selection of the data frame. If you are using RStudio, you can click on the data frame in the *Environment* tab and you will get something similar. Note that neither of these viewers are interactive in that you can't use them to manipulate the data. They are only data viewers. To be able to see similar windows that you can interactively edit, use the `fix` function in the same way that you use `View`. This can be useful for small edits, but remember that the edits are not reproducible.

7.1.2 Reshaping data

Obviously it is usually a good idea if your data sets are kept in data frame type objects. See Chapter 3 (Section 3.1.1) for how to convert objects into data frames with the `data.frame` command. Not only do data sets (generally) need to be stored in data frame objects, they also need to have the same layout before they can be merged. Most R statistical analysis tools assume that your data is in "long" format.[1] This usually means that data frame columns are variables and rows are specific observations (see Table 7.1).

TABLE 7.1
Long Formatted Data Example

Subject	Variable1
Subject1	
Subject2	
Subject3	
...	

In this chapter we will mostly use examples of time-series cross-sectional data (TSCS) that we want to have in long-format. Long formatted TSCS data is simply a data frame where rows identify observations of a particular subject at particular points in time and there are multiple observations per subject (see Table 7.2). In this chapter our TSCS data is specifically going to be countries that are observed in multiple years.

If one of our raw data sets is not in this format then we will need to reshape or, using Wickham's (2014b) terminology, "tidy" it. Some data sets are in "wide" format, where one of the columns in what would be long formatted data

[1]For an excellent discussion of ideal data formats see Wickham (2014b).

TABLE 7.2
Long Formatted Time-Series Cross-Sectional Data Example

Subject	Time	Variable1
Subject1	1	
Subject1	2	
Subject1	3	
Subject2	1	
Subject2	2	
Subject2	3	
...		

is widened to cover multiple columns. This is confusing to visualize without an example. Table 7.3 shows how Table 7.2 looks when we widen the time variable.

TABLE 7.3
Wide Formatted Data Example

Subject	Time1	Time2	Time3
Subject1			
Subject2			
...			

Tidying data is often the cause of much confusion and frustration. Though probably never easy, there are a number of useful R functions for changing data from wide format to long and vice versa. These include the matrix transpose command (`t`)[2] and the `reshape` command, both are loaded in R by default. *tidyr* (Wickham, 2014c) is a very helpful package for reshaping data. This provides more general tools for reshaping data and is worth investing some time to learn well. In this section we will look at *tidyr*'s `gather` function and

[2]See this example by Rob Kabacoff: `http://www.statmethods.net/management/reshape.html`. Note also that because the matrix transpose function is denoted with `t`, you should not give any object the name *t*.

use it to reshape a TSCS data frame from wide to long format. We will also encounter this function again in Chapter 10 when we want to transform data so that it can be graphed.

For illustration let's imagine that the fertilizer consumption data we previously downloaded from the World Bank is in wide, rather than long, format and is in a data frame object called *SpreadFert*. It looks like this:[3]

```
# Show the first 5 columns
head(SpreadFert[, 1:5])

##   iso2c        country       2005      2006      2007
## 1    AF    Afghanistan   4.240359  6.290993  3.618809
## 2    AL        Albania 111.596654 85.092466 87.167820
## 3    DZ        Algeria   7.429903 13.262651 14.961575
## 4    AS American Samoa         NA        NA        NA
## 5    AD        Andorra         NA        NA        NA
## 6    AO         Angola   2.260606  3.660000  3.305000
```

We can use the **gather** command to reshape this data from wide to long format. The term "gather" is intended to evoke an image of the many wide columns being gathered together.[4]

Let's think about how we want to tidy the data. We want to create two new columns from the many columns that are now labeled by year. Let's call the new columns **Year** and **Fert**. The **Year** column will clearly contain the year of each observation and **Fert** will contain the fertilizer consumption. **Year** will be what **gather** calls the "key" and **Fert** is the "value". In our *SpreadFert* data we don't want the **iso2c** and **country** variables to be gathered. These variables identify the data set's subjects. So we can tell **gather** that we only want columns three through nine gathered. The third column is the first one we want to gather and the ninth–the final column in the data set–is the last.

```
# Gather SpreadFert
GatheredFert <- gather(SpreadFert, Year, Fert, 3:9)

# Show GatheredFert
head(GatheredFert)
```

[3]See the chapter's Appendix (page 148) for the code I used to reshape the data from long to wide format.

[4]The opposite **spread** function is supposed to evoke an image of spreading out the data from long to wide format. See Chapter Appendix for an example using the **spread** command.

```
##   iso2c        country Year       Fert
## 1    AF    Afghanistan 2005   4.240359
## 2    AL        Albania 2005 111.596654
## 3    DZ        Algeria 2005   7.429903
## 4    AS American Samoa 2005         NA
## 5    AD        Andorra 2005         NA
## 6    AO         Angola 2005   2.260606
```

7.1.3 Renaming variables

Frequently, in the data cleaning process we want to change the names of our variables. This will make our data easier to understand and may even be necessary to properly combine data sets (see below). In the previous example, for instance, our *GatheredFert* data frame has two variables–**Year** and **Fert**. Imagine, for the sake of demonstration, that we want to rename them **year** and **FertilizerConsumption**. Renaming data frame variables is straightforward with the `rename` command in the *dplyr* package (Wickham and Francois, 2015). To rename both **variable** and **value** with the `rename` command type:

```
GatheredFert <- rename(GatheredFert,
                       year = Year,
                       FertilizerConsumption = Fert)

# Show GatheredFert
head(GatheredFert)
```

```
##   iso2c        country year FertilizerConsumption
## 1    AF    Afghanistan 2005              4.240359
## 2    AL        Albania 2005            111.596654
## 3    DZ        Algeria 2005              7.429903
## 4    AS American Samoa 2005                    NA
## 5    AD        Andorra 2005                    NA
## 6    AO         Angola 2005              2.260606
```

7.1.4 Ordering data

You may have noticed that as a result of gathering *SpreadFert* the data is now ordered by year rather than country name. Typically, TSCS data is sorted by country then year, or more generally: subject-time. Though not required for merging in R,[5] some statistical analyses assume that the data is ordered in a specific way. Well-ordered data is also easier for people to read.

We can order observations in our data set using the `order` command. For example, to order *GatheredFert* by country-year we type:

```
# Order GatheredFert by country-year
GatheredFert <- GatheredFert[order(GatheredFert$country,
                                    GatheredFert$year), ]

# Show GatheredFert
head(GatheredFert)

##        iso2c     country year FertilizerConsumption
## 1         AF Afghanistan 2005              4.240359
## 249       AF Afghanistan 2006              6.290993
## 497       AF Afghanistan 2007              3.618809
## 745       AF Afghanistan 2008              2.988068
## 993       AF Afghanistan 2009              4.521494
## 1241      AF Afghanistan 2010              4.255518
```

dplyr has a function called `arrange` that can also be useful for ordering your data. `arrange`'s syntax is much cleaner and easier to remember for data frames than the operation we did with `order`. To arrange the *GatheredFert* data as in the previous example, but with `arrange` use:

```
GatheredFert <- arrange(GatheredFert, country, year)
```

To arrange a variable in descending order, simply place it in the `desc` function from *dplyr*, e.g. `arrange(GatheredFert, country, desc(year))`.

7.1.5 Subsetting data

Sometimes you may want to use only a subset of a data frame. For example, the density plot in Figure 7.1 shows us that the *GatheredFert* data has a few very extreme values. We can use the `subset` command to examine these outliers, for example, countries that have fertilizer consumption greater-than 1000 kilograms per hectare.

[5]Unlike in other statistical programs.

FIGURE 7.1
Density Plot of Fertilizer Consumption (kilograms per hectare of arable land)

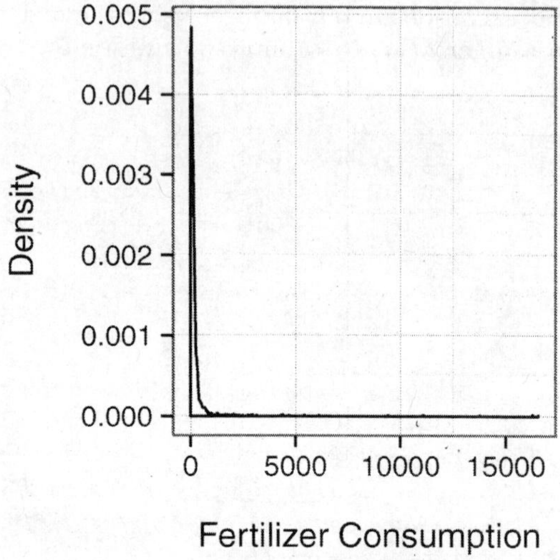

See the chapter's Appendix for the source code to create this figure.

```
# Create outlier data frame
FertOutliers <- subset(x = GatheredFert,
                       FertilizerConsumption > 1000)

# Show FertOutliers
head(FertOutliers)

##     iso2c    country year FertilizerConsumption
## 106    BH    Bahrain 2005              2906.667
## 107    BH    Bahrain 2006              9436.552
## 109    BH    Bahrain 2008              1993.333
## 111    BH    Bahrain 2010              1660.625
## 112    BH    Bahrain 2011              1178.125
## 337    CR Costa Rica 2005              1029.920
```

If we want to drop these outliers from our data set we can use `subset` again.

```
GatheredFertSub <- subset(x = GatheredFert,
                          FertilizerConsumption <= 1000)
```

In this data example, non-country units like "Arab World" are included. We might want to drop these units with the `subset` function as well. For example:

```
# Drop Arab World type from GatheredFertSub
GatheredFertSub <- subset(x = GatheredFertSub,
                          country != "Arab World")
```

We can also use `subset` to remove observations with missing values (`NA`) for **FertilizerConsumption**.

```
# Remove observations of FertilizerConsumption
# with missing values
GatheredFertSub <- subset(x = GatheredFertSub,
                          !is.na(FertilizerConsumption))

# Summarize FertilizerConsumption
summary(GatheredFertSub$FertilizerConsumption)

##    Min. 1st Qu.  Median    Mean 3rd Qu.    Max.
##    0.00   18.12   81.01  122.10  158.40  971.80
```

Let's step back one second. I've introduced a number of new logical operators and a new function in the four subsetting examples. The first example included a very simple one, the greater-than sign (`>`). The second example included the less-than or equal to operator: `<=`. The third example included the not equal operator: `!=`. In R, exclamation points (`!`) generally denote 'not'. We used this again in the final example in combination with the `is.na` command. This command indicates if an element is missing, so `!is.na` means "not missing". For a list of R's logical operators, see Table 7.4. You can use these operators and functions when subsetting data and throughout R.

7.1.6 Recoding string/numeric variables

You may want to recode your variables. In particular, when you merge data sets together you need to have **identical** identification values that R can use

TABLE 7.4
R's Logical Operators

Operator	Meaning
`<`	less-than
`>`	greater-than
`==`	equal to
`<=`	less-than or equal to
`>=`	greater-than or equal to
`!=`	not equal to
`a | b`	a or b
`a & b`	a & b
`isTRUE(a)`	determine if a is TRUE
`is.na`	missing
`!is.na`	not missing
`duplicated`	duplicated observation
`!duplicated`	not a duplicated observation

to match each observation on. If in one data set observations for the Republic of Korea are referred to as "Korea, Rep." and in another they are labeled "South Korea", R will not know to merge them. We need to recode values in the variables that we want to match our data sets on. For example, in *GatheredFertSub* the southern Korean country is labeled "Korea, Rep.". To recode it to "South Korea" we type:

```
# Recode country == "Korea, Rep."" to "South Korea"
GatheredFertSub$country[GatheredFertSub$country ==
                        "Korea, Rep."] <- "South Korea"
```

This code assigns "South Korea" to all values of the **country** variable that equal "Korea, Rep.".[6] You can use a similar technique to recode numeric variables as well. The only difference is that you omit the quotation marks. We will look at how to code factor variables later.

[6]The *countrycode* package (Arel-Bundock, 2014) is very helpful for creating standardized country identification variables.

7.1.7 Creating new variables from old

As part of your data cleanup process (or later during statistical analysis) you may want to create new variables based on existing variables. For example, we could create a new variable that is the natural logarithm of **FertilizerConsumption**. To do this we run the variable through the `log` function and assign a new variable that we'll call **logFertConsumption**.

```
GatheredFertSub$logFertConsumption <- log(
                                GatheredFertSub$FertilizerConsumption
                                )

# Summarize the log transformed variable
summary(GatheredFertSub$logFertConsumption)

##    Min. 1st Qu.  Median    Mean 3rd Qu.    Max.
##    -Inf       3       4    -Inf       5       7
```

We can use a similar procedure to create new variables from R's many other mathematical commands and arithmetic operations.[7]

Notice that when we summarize the new log transformed variable that we have a minimum (and mean) value of `-Inf`. This indicates that by logging the variable we have created observations with the value negative infinity. R calculates the natural logarithm of zero as negative infinity.[8] We probably don't want negative infinity values. There are a few ways to deal with this. We could drop all observations of **FertilizerConsumption** with the value zero before log transforming it. Another common solution is recoding zeros as some small nonnegative number like 0.001. For example:

```
# Recode zeros in Fertilizer Consumption
GatheredFertSub$FertilizerConsumption[
                          GatheredFertSub$FertilizerConsumption == 0
                          ] <- 0.001

# Natural log transform Fertilizer Consumption
GatheredFertSub$logFertConsumption <- log(
                          GatheredFertSub$FertilizerConsumption
                          )
```

[7] E.g `+`, `-`, `*`, `/`, `^` for addition, subtraction, multiplication, division, and exponentiation, respectively.

[8] R denotes positive infinity with `Inf`.

TABLE 7.5
Example Factor Levels

Number	Label	Value of **FertilizerConsumption**
1	low	< 18
2	medium low	≥ 18 & < 81
3	medium high	≥ 81 & < 158
4	high	≥ 158

```
# Summarize the log transformed variable
summary(GatheredFertSub$logFertConsumption)

##    Min. 1st Qu.  Median    Mean 3rd Qu.    Max.
##  -7.758   2.897   4.395   3.862   5.065   6.879
```

Note that this example is included to demonstrate R syntax rather than to prescribe a certain transformation of skewed data with zeros. The choice of which transformation to make should ultimately be made based on the data, model, and context. See Hyndman (2010) for more information on various alternatives including Box-Cox (Box and Cox, 1964) and inverse hyperbolic sine transformations (Burbidge and Robb, 1988).

Creating factor variables

We can create factor variables from numeric or string variables. For example, we may want to turn the continuous numeric **FertilizerConsumption** variable into an ordered categorical (i.e. factor) variable. Imagine that we want to create a factor variable called **FertConsGroup** with four levels called 'low', 'medium low', 'medium high', 'high'. To do this let's first create a new numeric variable based on the values listed in Table 7.5. Now let's use a procedure that is similar to the variable recoding we did earlier:[9]

```
#### Create numeric factor levels variable ####
# Attach GatheredFertSub data frame
attach(GatheredFertSub)
```

[9]In this code I attached the data frame *GatheredFertSub* so that it is easier to read.

```
# Created new FertConsGroup variable based on
# FertilizerConsumption
GatheredFertSub$FertConsGroup[FertilizerConsumption
                              < 18] <- 1
GatheredFertSub$FertConsGroup[FertilizerConsumption
                              >= 18 &
                              FertilizerConsumption < 81] <- 2
GatheredFertSub$FertConsGroup[FertilizerConsumption
                              >= 81 &
                              FertilizerConsumption < 158] <- 3
GatheredFertSub$FertConsGroup[FertilizerConsumption
                              >= 158] <- 4
GatheredFertSub$FertConsGroup[is.na(FertilizerConsumption)] <- NA

# Detach data frame
detach(GatheredFertSub)

# Summarize FertConsGroup
summary(GatheredFertSub$FertConsGroup)

##    Min. 1st Qu.  Median    Mean 3rd Qu.    Max.
##   1.000   2.000   3.000   2.504   4.000   4.000
```

You'll notice that we don't have a factor variable yet; our new variable is numeric. We can use the `factor` command to convert *FertConsGroup* into a factor variable with the labels we want.

```
# Create vector of factor level labels
FCLabels <- c("low", "medium low", "medium high", "high")

# Convert FertConsGroup to a factor
GatheredFertSub$FertConsGroup <- factor(GatheredFertSub$
                             FertConsGroup, labels = FCLabels)

# Summarize FertConsGroup
summary(GatheredFertSub$FertConsGroup)

##         low  medium low medium high        high
##         314         315         313         318
```

We first created a character vector with the factor-level labels and then applied using `factor`'s `labels` argument. Using `summary` with a factor variable gives us its level labels as well as the number of observations per level.

The `cut` function provides a less code-intensive way of creating factors from numeric ones and labeling factor levels. For example:

```
# Create a factor variable with the cut command
FertFactor <- cut(GatheredFertSub$FertilizerConsumption,
                  breaks = c(-0.01, 17.99, 80.99, 157.99, 999.99),
                  labels = c("low", "medium low",
                             "medium high", "high"))

# Summarize FertFactor
summary(FertFactor)

##         low  medium low medium high        high
##         314         315         313         318
```

The `labels` argument lets us specify the factor levels' names. The `breaks` argument lets us specify what values separate the factor levels. Note that we set the first break as `-0.01`, not because any country had negative fertilizer consumption, but because the intervals created by `break` exclude the left value and include the right value.[10] If we had used `0` then all of the observations where a country used effectively no fertilizer would be excluded from the "low" category.

7.1.8 Changing variable types

Sometimes a variable will have the wrong type. For example, a numeric variable may be incorrectly made a character string when a data set is imported from Excel. You can change variables' types with a number of commands. We already saw how to convert a numeric variable to a factor variable with the `factor` command. Unsurprisingly, to convert a variable to a character use `character` and `numeric` to convert it to a numeric type variable. We can place `as.` before these commands (e.g. `as.factor`) as a way of coercing a change in type.

Warning: Though these commands have straightforward names, a word of caution is necessary. Always try to understand why a variable is not of the type you would expect. Oftentimes variables have unexpected types because they are coded (or miscoded) in a way that you didn't anticipate. Changing

[10] In mathematical notation the "low" level includes all values in the interval $(-0.01, 17.99]$.

the variables' types, especially when using `as.`, can introduce new errors. Make sure that the conversion made the changes you expected.

7.2 Merging Data Sets

In the previous section we learned crucial skills for cleaning up data sets. When your data sets are (a) in the same format and (b) have variables with identically matching ID values, you can merge your data sets together. In this section we'll look at two different ways to merge data sets: binding and the `merge` command. We'll also look at ways to address a common issue when merging data: duplicated observations and columns.

7.2.1 Binding

As we saw in Chapter 3, if your data sets are in the same order–rows in all of the data sets represent the same observation of the same subject–then you can simply use the `cbind` command to bind columns from the data sets together. This situation is unusual when merging real-world data. If your data sets are not in exactly the same order you will create a data set with nonsensical rows that combine data from multiple observations. Therefore, you should avoid using `cbind` for merging most real-world data.

If you have data sets with the exact same columns and variable types and you just want to attach one under the other you can use the `rbind` command. It binds the rows in one object to the rows in another.[11] It has the same syntax as `cbind` (see page 33). Again, you should be cautious when using this command, though it is more difficult to accidentally create a nonsensical data set with `rbind`. R will give you an error if it cannot match your objects' columns.

7.2.2 The merge command

Generally, the safest and most effective way to merge two data sets together is with the `merge` command. Imagine that we want to merge our *GatheredFertSub* data frame with two other data frames we created in Chapter 6: *FinRegulatorData* and *DispropData.* The simplest way to do this is to use the merge command twice, i.e.:

```
# Merge FinRegulatorData and DispropData
MergedData1 <- merge(x = FinRegulatorData,
```

[11]Some programming languages and statistical programs refer to this type of action as "appending" one data set to another.

```
                    y = DispropData,
                    by = "iso2c",
                    all = TRUE)

# Merge combined data set with and GatheredFertSub
MergedData1 <- merge(x = MergedData1,
                    y = GatheredFertSub,
                    by = "iso2c",
                    all = TRUE)

# Show MergedData1 variables
names(MergedData1)

##  [1] "iso2c"                "idn"
##  [3] "country.x"            "year.x"
##  [5] "reg_4state"           "country.y"
##  [7] "year.y"               "disproportionality"
##  [9] "country"              "year"
## [11] "FertilizerConsumption" "logFertConsumption"
## [13] "FertConsGroup"
```

Let's go through this code. The `x` and `y` arguments simply specify which data frames we want to merge. The `by` argument specifies what variable in the two frames identify the observations so that we can match them. In this example we are merging by countries' ISO country two-letter codes.[12] We set the argument `all = TRUE` so that we keep all of the observations from both of the data frames. If the argument is set to `FALSE` only observations that are common to both data frames will be included in the merged data frame. The others will not be included.

You might have noticed that this isn't actually the merge that we want to accomplish with these data frames. Remember that observations are not simply identified in this time-series cross-section data by one country name or other country code variable. Instead they are identified by both country and year variables. To merge data frames based on the overlap of two variables (e.g. match Afghanistan-2004 in one data frame with Afghanistan-2004 in the other) we need to add the `union` command to `merge`'s `by` argument. Here is a full example:[13]

---

[12]Please see this chapter's Appendix for details on how I created an ISO country two-letter code variable in the *FinRegulatorData* data frame.

[13]You can download a modified version of this example as part of the makefile exercise from Chapter 6: `http://bit.ly/YnMKBG`.

```
# Merge FinRegulatorData and DispropData
MergedData2 <- merge(FinRegulatorData, DispropData,
                     union("iso2c", "year"),
                     all = TRUE)

# Merge combined data frame with GatheredFertSub
MergedData2 <- merge(MergedData2, GatheredFertSub,
                     union("iso2c", "year"),
                     all = TRUE)

# Show MergedData2 variable names
names(MergedData2)

##  [1] "iso2c"                  "year"
##  [3] "idn"                    "country.x"
##  [5] "reg_4state"             "country.y"
##  [7] "disproportionality"     "country"
##  [9] "FertilizerConsumption" "logFertConsumption"
## [11] "FertConsGroup"
```

After merging data frames it is always a good idea to look at the result and make sure it is what you expected. Some post-merging cleanup may be required to get the data frame ready for statistical analysis.

Big data

Before discussing post-merge cleanup it is important to highlight ways to handle large data sets. The `merge` function and many of the other data frame manipulation functions covered so far in this chapter may not perform well with very large data sets. If you are using very large data sets it might be worth investing time learning how to use either the *dplyr* or *data.table* packages (Dowle et al., 2014). They have many capabilities for working efficiently with large data sets. Another approach is to learn SQL[14] or another special purpose data handling language.[15] Once you know how these languages work, you can incorporate them into your R workflow with R packages like *dplyr*.[16]

[14] Structured Query Language

[15] w3schools has an online SQL tutorial at: `http://www.w3schools.com/sql/default.asp`.

[16] See the *dplyr* vignette on using the package with SQL databases at `http://cran.r-project.org/web/packages/dplyr/vignettes/databases.html`.

7.2.3 Duplicate values

Duplicate observations are one thing to look out for after (and before) merging. You can use the `duplicated` command to check for duplicates. Use the command in conjunction with subscripts to remove duplicate observations. For example, let's create a new object called *DataDuplicates* from the iso2c-years that are duplicated in *MergedData2*. Remember that **iso2c** and **year** are in the first and second columns of the data frame.

```
# Created a data frame of duplicated country-years
DataDuplicates <- MergedData2[duplicated(
                                MergedData2[, 1:2]), ]

# Show the number of rows in DataDuplicates
nrow(DataDuplicates)

## [1] 7
```

In this data frame there are 7 duplicated iso2c-year observations. We know this because `nrow` tells us that the data frame with the duplicated values has 7 rows, i.e. 7 observations.

To create a data set without duplicated observations (if there are duplicates) we just add an exclamation point (`!`) before `duplicated`–i.e. not duplicated–in the above code.

```
# Created a data frame of unique country-years
DataNotDuplicates <- MergedData2[!duplicated(
                                MergedData2[, 1:2]), ]
```

Note that if you do have duplicated values in your data set and you run a similar procedure on it, it will drop duplicated values that have a lower order in the data frame. To keep the lowest ordered value and drop duplicates higher in the data set, use `duplicated`'s `fromLast` argument like this: `fromLast = TRUE`.

Warning: look over your data set and the source code that created the data set to try to understand why duplicates occurred. There may be a fundamental problem in the way you are handling your data that resulted in the duplicated observations.

7.2.4 Duplicate columns

Another common post-merge cleanup issue is duplicate columns, i.e. variables. These are variables from the two data frames with the same name that were not included in `merge`'s `by` argument. For example, in our previous merged data examples there are three country name variables: **country.x**, **country.y**, and **country** to signify which data frame they are from.[17]

You should Of course, decide what to do with these variables on a case-by-case basis. But if you decide to drop one of the variables and rename the other, you can use subscripts (as we saw in Chapter 3). The *dplyr* package (Wickham and Francois, 2015) has a useful function called `select` that can also remove variables from data frames. To remove variables simply write a minus sign (`-`) and then the variable name without quotes. For example, imagine that we want to keep **country.x** and drop the other variables.[18] Let's also remove the **idn** variable:

```
# Remove country.y, country, X, and idn
FinalCleanedData <- dplyr::select(DataNotDuplicates,
                                  -country.y, -country,
                                  -idn)

# Rename country.x = country
FinalCleanedData <- dplyr::rename(FinalCleanedData,
                              country = country.x)
```

```
# Show FinalCleanedData variables
names(FinalCleanedData)

## [1] "iso2c"                "year"                 "country"
## [4] "reg_4state"           "disproportionality"   "FertilizerConsumption"
## [7] "logFertConsumption"   "FertConsGroup"
```

Alternatively, you can select specific variables to keep with the `select` function by writing the variables' names without a minus sign. **Note**: if you are merging many data sets it can sometimes be good to cleanup duplicate columns between each `merge` call.

[17]The former two were created in the first merge between *FinRegulatorData* and *DispropData*. When the second merge was completed there were no variables named **country** in the MergeData2 data frame, so **country** did not need to be renamed in the new merged data set.

[18]This version of the country variable is the most complete.

Chapter summary

This chapter has provided you with many tools for cleaning up your data to get it ready for statistical analysis. Before moving on to the next chapter to learn how to incorporate statistical analysis as part of a reproducible workflow with *knitr/rmarkdown*, it's important to reiterate that the function we've covered in this chapter should usually be embedded in the types of data creation files we saw in Chapter 6. These files can then be tied together with a makefile into a process that should be able to relatively easily take very raw data and clean it up for use in your analyses. Embedding these commands in data creation source code files, rather than just typing the commands into your R console or manually changing data in Excel, will make your research much more reproducible. It will also make it easier to backtrack and find mistakes that you may have made while transforming the data. Including new or updated data when it becomes available will also be much easier if you use a series of segmented data creation source code files that are tied together with a makefile.

Appendix

R code for turning *FertConsumData* into year-wide format:

```
# Load WDI and tidyr package
library(WDI)
library(tidyr)

# Gather fertilizer consumption data from WDI
FertConsumpData <- WDI(indicator = "AG.CON.FERT.ZS")

# Spread FertConsumpData to year wide format
SpreadFert <- spread(FertConsumpData, year, AG.CON.FERT.ZS)

# Order SpreadFert by country
SpreadFert <- arrange(SpreadFert, country)
```

R code for creating iso2c country codes with the *countrycode* package:

```
# Load countrycode package
library(countrycode)
```

```
# FinRegulatorData
FinRegulatorData$iso2c <- countrycode(FinRegulatorData$country,
                                      origin = "country.name",
                                      destination = "iso2c")
```

R code for creating Figure 7.1:

```
# Load ggplot2
library(ggplot2)

# Create density plot
ggplot(data = GatheredFert, aes(FertilizerConsumption)) +
        geom_density() +
        xlab("\n Fertilizer Consumption") + ylab("Density\n") +
        theme_bw()
```

Part III

Analysis and Results

8

Statistical Modeling and knitr

When you have your data cleaned and organized you will begin to examine it with statistical analyses. In this book we don't look at how to do statistical analysis in R (a subject that would and does take up many books). Instead we focus on how to make your analyses really reproducible. To do this you dynamically connect your data gathering and analysis source code to your presentation documents. When you dynamically connect your data gathering makefiles and analysis source code to your markup document you will be able to completely rerun your data gathering and analysis and present the results whenever you compile the presentation documents. Doing this makes it very clear how you found the results that you are advertising. It also automatically keeps the presentation of your results–including tables and figures–up-to-date with any changes you make to your data and analyses source code files.

You can dynamically tie your data gathering, statistical analyses, and presentation documents together with *knitr/rmarkdown*. In Chapter 3 you learned basic *knitr/rmarkdown* syntax. For the rest of the chapter I'll simply refer to it as "*knitr* syntax", but it applies to *rmarkdown* as well. In this chapter we will begin to learn *knitr* syntax in more detail, particularly code chunk options for including dynamic code in your presentation documents. This includes code that is run in the background, i.e. not shown in the presentation document, as well as displaying the code and output in your presentation document both as separate blocks and inline with the text. We will also learn how to dynamically include code from languages other than R. We examine how to use *knitr* with modular source code files. Finally, we will look at how to create reproducible 'random' analyses and how to work with computationally intensive code chunks.

The goal of this and the next two chapters–which cover dynamically presenting results in tables and figures–is to show you how to tie data gathering and analyses into your presentation documents so closely that every time the documents are compiled they actually reproduce your analysis and present the results. Please see the next part of this book, Part IV, for details on how to create the LaTeX and Markdown documents that can include *knitr* code chunks.

Reminder: Before discussing the details of how to incorporate your analysis into your source code, it's important to reiterate something we discussed in Chapter 2. The syntax and capabilities of R packages and R itself can change with new versions. Also, as we have seen for file path names, syntax can change depending on what operating system you are using. So it is important to have your R session info available (see Section 2.2.1 for details) to make your research more reproducible and future-proof. If someone reproducing your research has this information, they will be able to download your files and use the exact version of the software that you used. For example, CRAN maintains an archive of previous R package versions that can be downloaded.[1] Previous versions of R itself can also be downloaded through CRAN.[2]

8.1 Incorporating Analyses into the Markup

For a relatively short piece of code that you don't need to run in multiple presentation documents it may be simplest to type the code directly into chunks written in your *knitr* markup document. In this section we will learn how to set *knitr* options for handling these code chunks. For a list of many of the chunk options covered here see Table 3.1.

8.1.1 Full code chunks

By default, *knitr* code chunks are run by R, and the code and any text output (including warnings and error messages) are inserted into the text of your presentation documents in blocks. The blocks are positioned in the final presentation document text at the points where the code chunk was written in the knittable markup. Figures are inserted as well. Let's look at the main options for determining how code chunks are handled by *knitr*.

`include`

Use `include=FALSE` if you don't want to include anything in the text of your presentation document, but you still want to evaluate a code chunk. It is `TRUE` by default.

`eval`

The `eval` option determines whether or not the code in a chunk will be run. Set the `eval` option to `FALSE` if you would like to include code in the presentation document text without actually running the code. By default it is set to `TRUE`, i.e. the code is run. You can alternatively use a numerical vector with `eval`. The numbers in the vector tell *knitr* which expressions in the chunk to evaluate. For example, if you only want to evaluate the first two expressions, simply set `eval=1:2`.

[1]See: `http://cran.r-project.org/src/contrib/Archive/`.
[2]See: `http://cran.r-project.org/src/base/`.

`echo`

If you would like to hide a chunk's code from the presentation document you can set `echo=FALSE`. Note that if you also have `eval=TRUE` then the chunk will still be evaluated and the output will be included in your presentation document. Clearly, if `echo=TRUE`, then source code will be included in the presentation document. As with `eval`, you can alternatively use a numerical vector in `echo`. The numbers in the vector indicate which expressions to echo in your final document.

`results`

We will look at the `results` option in more detail in the next two chapters (see especially Section 9.1). However, let's briefly discuss the option value `hide`. Setting `results='hide'` is almost the opposite of `echo=FASLE`. Instead of showing the results of the code chunk and hiding the code, `results='hide'` shows the code, but not the results. Warnings, errors, and messages will still be printed.

`warning, message, error`

If you don't want to include the warnings, messages, and error messages that R outputs in the text of your presentation documents, just set the `warning`, `message`, and `error` options to `FALSE`. They are set to `TRUE` by default.

`cache`

If you want to run a code chunk once and the output for when you knit the document again, rather than running the code chunk every time, set the option `cache=TRUE`. When you do this the first time the document is knitted, the chunk will be run and the output stored in a subdirectory of the working directory called *cache*. When the document is subsequently knitted, the chunk will only be run if the code in the chunk changes or its options change. This is very handy if you have a code chunk that is computationally intensive to run. The `cache` option is set to `FALSE` by default. Later in this chapter (Section 8.4) we will see how to use the `cache.vars` command to cache only certain variables created by a code chunk.

`dependson`

Cached chunks are only rerun when their code changes. Sometimes one chunk will depend on the results from a prior chunk. In these cases it is good to rerun the chunk if the prior one is also rerun. The `dependson` option allows you to do this. You can specify either a vector of the labels for the chunks depended on or their numbers in order from the start of the document. For example, `dependson=c(2, 3)` specifies that if the second or third chunks are rerun, then the current chunk will also be rerun.

`cache.extra`

Sometimes to ensure reproducibility it may be useful to rerun a chunk when some other condition changes, such as when a new version of R is installed or a dependent file changes. You can feed a list of conditions to `cache.extra` to do this. For instance:

```
cache.extra=list(file.info(Data.csv)$mtime, R.version
```

Here we set two conditions under which the chunk will be rerun. The first specifies that the chunk should be rerun whenever the *Data.csv* file is modified. The `file.info` function extracts information about the file and `mtime` gives the last time that the file was modified. If this differs from when the chunk was last run, then it will be run again. This is very useful for keeping your cached chunks and the files they rely on in sync.

The second condition enabled by `R.version` reruns the chunk whenever the R version or even the operating system changes. If you only want to rerun the chunk when the version of R is different, then use `R.version.string`.

`size`

If you do want to print part or all of your code chunk into your LaTeX document, you may also want to resize the text. To do this, use the `size` option. By default it is set to `size='normalsize'`. You can use any of the LaTeX font sizes listed in Table 11.1 from Chapter 11.

8.1.2 Showing code & results inline

Sometimes you may want to have R code or output show up inline with the rest of your presentation document's text. For example, you may want to include a small chunk of stylized code in your text when you discuss how you did an analysis. Or you may want to dynamically report the mean of some variable in your text so that the text will change when you change the data. The *knitr* syntax for including inline code is different for the LaTeX and Markdown languages. We'll cover both in turn.

8.1.2.1 LaTeX

Inline static code

There are a number of ways to include a code snippet inline with your text in LaTeX. You can simply use the LaTeX command `\texttt` to have text show up in the `typewriter` font commonly used in LaTeX-produced documents to indicate that some text is code (I use typewriter font for this purpose in this book, as you have probably noticed). For example, using `\texttt{2 + 2}` will give you `2 + 2` in your text. Note that in LaTeX curly brackets (`{}`) work exactly like parentheses in R, i.e. they enclose a command's arguments.

However, the `\texttt` command isn't always ideal, because your LaTeX compiler will still try to run the code inside of the command as if it were LaTeX markup. This can be problematic if you include characters like the backslash \ or curly brackets `{}`. They have special meanings for LaTeX. The hard way to solve this problem is to use escape characters (see Chapter 4). The backslash is an escape character in LaTeX.

Probably the better option is to use the `\verb` command. It is equivalent to the `eval=FALSE` option for full *knitr* code chunks. To use the `\verb` command, pick some character you will not use in the inline code. For example, you could use the vertical bar (`|`). This will be the `\verb` delimiter. Imagine that we want to actually include '`\texttt`' in the text. We would type:

```
\verb|\texttt|
```

The LaTeX compiler will ignore almost anything from the first vertical bar up until the second bar following `\verb`. All of the text in-between the delimiter characters is put in typewriter font.[3]

Inline dynamic code

If you want to dynamically show the results of some R code in your *knitr* LaTeX-produced text you can use `\Sexpr`. This is a pseudo LaTeX command; it looks like LaTeX, but is actually *knitr*.[4] Its structure is more like a LaTeX command's structure than *knitr*'s in that you enclose your R code in curly brackets (`{}`) rather than the `<<>>= . . . @` syntax you use for block code chunks.

For example, imagine that you wanted to include the mean of a vector of river lengths–591–in the text of your document. The *rivers* numeric vector, loaded by default in R, has the lengths of 141 major rivers recorded in miles. You can simply use the `mean` command to find the mean and the `round` command to round the result to the nearest whole number:

[3]For more details see the LaTeX Wikibooks page: `http://en.wikibooks.org/wiki/LaTeX/Paragraph_Formatting#Verbatim_Text` (accessed 24 November 2012). Also, for help troubleshooting see the UK List of Frequently Asked Questions: `http://www.tex.ac.uk/cgi-bin/texfaq2html?label=verbwithin` (accessed 4 January 2012).

[4]The command directly descends from *Sweave*.

```
round(mean(rivers), digits = 0)

## [1] 591
```

To have just the output show up inline with the text of your document you would type something like:

```
The mean length of 141 major rivers in North America
is \Sexpr{round(mean(rivers), digits = 0)} miles.
```

This produces the sentence:

The mean length of 141 major rivers in North America is 591 miles.

R code included inline with `Sexpr` is evaluated using current R options. So if you want all of the output from `Sexpr` to be rounded to the same number of digits, for example, it might be a good idea to set this in a code chunk with R's `options` command. See page 44 for more details.

8.1.2.2 Markdown

Inline static code

To include static code inline in an R Markdown (and regular Markdown) document, enclose the code in single backticks (` . . . `). For example:

```
This is example R code: `MeanRiver <- mean(rivers)`.
```

produces:[5]

This is example R code: `MeanRiver <- mean(rivers)`.

Inline dynamic code

Including dynamic code in the body of your R Markdown text is similar to including static code. The only difference is that you put the letter `r` after the first single backtick. For example:

[5]The exact look of the text depends on the Cascading Style Sheets (CSS) style file you are using. The example here was created with RStudio's default style file.

```
`r mean(rivers)`
```

will include the mean value of the *rivers* vector in the text of your Markdown document.

8.1.3 Dynamically including non-R code in code chunks

You are not limited to dynamically including just R code in your presentation documents. *knitr* can run code from a variety of other languages including: Python, Ruby, Bash, Haskell, and Awk. All you have to do to dynamically include code from one of these languages is use the `engine` code chunk option to tell *knitr* which language you are using. For example, to dynamically include a simple line of Python code in an R Markdown document type:

````
```{r engine='python'}
print "Reproducible Research"
```
````

In the final HTML file you will get:[6]

```
print "Reproducible Research"
```

```
## Reproducible Research
```

Many of the programming language values `engine` can take are listed in Table 8.1. To enable more complete syntax highlighting for non-R languages you will need to download Andre Simon's *highlighter* utility. Installation instructions can be found on his website at: `http://www.andre-simon.de/zip/download.html`.

8.2 Dynamically Including Modular Analysis Files

There are a number of reasons why you might want to have your R source code located in separate files from your markup documents even if you compile them together with *knitr*.

[6] Again, this was created using RStudio's default CSS style file.

TABLE 8.1
A Selection of *knitr* `engine` Values

Value	Programming Language
`awk`	Awk
`bash`	Bash shell
`coffeescript`	CoffeeScript
`gawk`	Gawk
`haskell`	Haskell
`highlight`	Highlight
`python`	Python
`R`	R (default)
`ruby`	Ruby
`sas`	SAS
`sh`	Bourne shell

First, it can be unwieldy to edit both your markup and long R source code chunks in the same document, even with RStudio's handy *knitr* code folding and chunk management options. There are just too many things going on in one document.

Second, you may want to use the same code in multiple documents–an article and slide show presentation, for example. It is nice to not have to copy and paste the same code into multiple places. Instead, it is easier to have multiple documents link to the same source code file. When you make changes to this source code file, the changes will automatically be made across all of your presentation documents. You don't need to make the same changes multiple times.

Third, other researchers trying to replicate your work might only be interested in specific parts of your analysis. If you have the analysis broken into separate and clearly labeled modular files that are explicitly tied together in the markup file with *knitr*, it is easy for them to find the specific bits of code that they are interested in.

8.2.1 Source from a local file

Usually, in the early stages of your research, you may want to run code stored in analysis files located on your computer. Doing this is simple. The *knitr* syntax is the same as for block code chunks. The only change is that instead of writing all of your code in the chunk, you save it to its own file and use the `source` command to access it.[7] For example, in an R Markdown file we could run the R code in a file called *MainAnalysis.R* from our *ExampleProject* like this:

```
```{r, include=FALSE}
# Run main analysis
source("/ExampleProject/Analysis/MainAnalysis.R"}
```
```

Notice that we set the option `include=FALSE`. This will run the analysis and produce objects created by the analysis code that can be used by other code chunks, but the output will not show up in the presentation document's text.

Sourcing a makefile in a code chunk

In Chapter 6 we created a GNU Makefile to organize our data gathering. You can run makefiles every time you compile your presentation document. This can keep your data, analyses, figures, and tables up-to-date. One way to do this is to run the GNU makefile in an R code chunk with the `system` command (see Section 4.5). Perhaps a better way to run makefiles from *knitr* presentation documents is to include the commands in a code chunk using the Bash engine. For example, a Sweave-style code chunk for running the makefiles in our example project would look like this:

```
<<engine='bash', include=FALSE>>=
# Change working directory to /ExampleProject/Analysis/Data
cd /ExampleProject/Analysis/Data/

# Run makefile
make cleanMerge all

# Change to working directory to /ExampleProject/Analysis/
cd /ExampleProject/Analysis/
@
```

Please see page 115 for details on the `make` command arguments used here.

You can Of course, also use R's `source` command to run an R make-like data gathering file. Unlike GNU Make, this will rerun all of the data

[7]We used the `source` command in Chapter 6 in our make-like data gathering file.

gathering files, even if they have not been updated. This may become very time consuming depending on the size of your data sets and how they are manipulated.

One final note on including makefiles in your *knitr* presentation document source code: it is important to place the code chunk with the makefile before code chunks containing statistical analyses that depend on the data file it creates. Placing the makefile first will keep the others up-to-date.

8.2.2 Source from a non-secure URL (`http`)

Sourcing from your computer is fine if you are working alone and do not want others to access your code. Once you start collaborating and generally wanting people to be able to reproduce your analyses, you need to use another storage method. The simplest method is to host the replication code in your Dropbox public folder. You can find the file's public URL in the same way that you did in Chapter 5. Then use the `source` command the same way as we did before with the `read.table` command.[8]

8.2.3 Source from a secure URL (`https`)

If you are using GitHub or another service that uses secure URLs to host your analysis source code files you need to use the `source_url` command in the *devtools* package. For GitHub based source code we find the file's URL the same way we did in Chapter 5 (Section 5.3.4). Remember to use the URL for the *raw* version of the file. I have a short script hosted on GitHub for creating a scatterplot from data in R's *cars* data set. The script's shortened URL is `http://bit.ly/1D5p1w6`.[9] To run this code and create the scatterplot using `source_url` you simply type:

```
# Load devtools package
library(devtools)

# Run the source code to create the scatter plot
source_url("http://bit.ly/1D5p1w6")

## SHA-1 hash of file is ff75a88b90decfcaefc9903bbc283e1fc4cd2339
```

[8]You can also make the replication code accessible for download and either instruct others to change the working directory to the replication file or have them change the directory information as necessary. You will need to do this with GNU makefiles like those included with this book.

[9]The original URL is at `https://raw.githubusercontent.com/christophergandrud/Rep-Res-Examples/master/Graphs/SimpleScatter.R`. This is very long, so I shortened it using bitly. You may notice that the shortened URL is not secure. However, it does link to the original secure `https` URL.

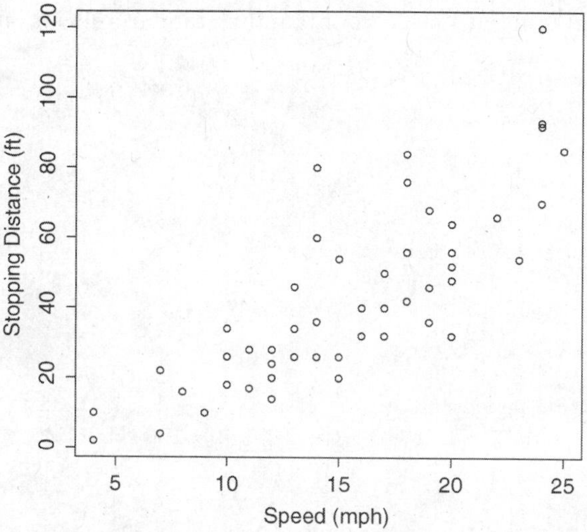

You can also use the *devtools* command `source_gist` in a similar way to source GitHub Gists. Gists are a handy way to share code over the internet. For more details see: `https://gist.GitHub.com/`.

Similar to what we saw in Chapter 5 (Section 5.3.4), if you would like to use a particular version of a file stored on GitHub, simply include that version's URL in the `source_url` call. This can be useful for replicating particular results. Linking to a particular version of a source code file will enable replication even if you later make changes to the file. To access the URL for a particular version of a file, first click on the file on GitHub's website. Then click the `History` button (
). This will take you to a page listing all of the file's versions. Click on the `Browse Code` button (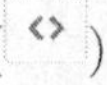
) next to the version of the file that you want to use. Finally, click on the `Raw` button to be taken to the text-only version of the file. Copy this page's URL and use it in `source_url`.

Also, just like with `source_data`, we can set the `sha1` argument to tell `source_url` to make sure that the source code file it is downloading is the one we intended. This will work regardless of whether or not the file is stored on GitHub.

8.3 Reproducibly Random: `set.seed`

If you are including simulations in your analysis it is often a good idea to specify the random number generator state you used. This will allow others to exactly replicate your 'randomly'–really pseudo-randomly–generated simulation results. Use the `set.seed` command in your source code files or code chunks to do this. For example, use the following code to set the random number generator state[10] and randomly draw 1,000 numbers from a standard normal distribution with a mean of 0 and a standard deviation of 2.

```
# Set seed as 125
set.seed(125)

# Draw 1000 numbers
Draw1 <- rnorm(1000, mean = 0, sd = 2)

# Summarize Draw1
summary(Draw1)

##     Min. 1st Qu.  Median    Mean 3rd Qu.    Max.
## -7.2110 -1.4070 -0.1040 -0.1215  1.3160  5.6770
```

The **rnorm** command draws the 1,000 simulations. The **mean** argument allows us to set the normal distribution's mean and **sd** sets its standard deviation. Just to show you that we will draw the same numbers if we use the same seed, let's run the code again:

```
# Set seed as 125
set.seed(125)

# Draw 1000 numbers
Draw2 <- rnorm(1000, mean = 0, sd = 2)

# Summarize Draw1
summary(Draw2)

##     Min. 1st Qu.  Median    Mean 3rd Qu.    Max.
## -7.2110 -1.4070 -0.1040 -0.1215  1.3160  5.6770
```

8.4 Computationally Intensive Analyses

Sometimes you may want to include computationally intensive analyses that take a long time to run as part of a *knitr* document. This can make writing

[10]See the `Random` help file for detailed information on R's random number generation capabilities by typing `?Random` into your console.

the document frustrating because it will take a long time to knit it each time you make changes. There are at least two solutions to this problem: the `cache` chunk option and makefiles. We discussed makefiles in Chapter 6, so let's look at how to work with the `cache` option.

When you set `cache=TRUE` for the code chunk that contains the analysis, the code chunk will only be run when the chunk's contents change[11] or the chunk options change. This is a very easy solution to the problem. It does have a major drawback: other chunks can't access objects created by the chunk or use commands from packages loaded in it. Solve these problems by (a) having packages loaded in a separate chunk and (b) save objects created by the cached chunk to a separate RData file that can be loaded in later chunks (see Section 3.1.6 for information on saving to RData files).[12]

Imagine that in a cached code chunk we create an object called *Sample*. Then in a later code chunk we want to use the `hist` command to create a histogram of the sample. In the cached code chunk we save *Sample* to a file called *Sample.RData*.

```
<<Sample, cache=TRUE>>=
# Create data
Sample <- rnorm(n = 1000, mean = 5, sd = 2)

# Save sample
save(Sample, file = "Sample.RData")
@
```

The latter code chunk for creating the histogram would go something like this:[13]

```
<<Histogram>>=
# Load Sample
load(file = "Sample.RData")
```

[11]Note that the chunk will not be run if only the contents of a file the chunk sources are changed. Use the `dependson` option in cases where it is important to rerun a chunk when a prior chunk changes.

[12]It's true that when `knitr` caches a code chunk it saves the chunk's objects to an `.RData` file. However, it is difficult to load this file directly because the file name changes every time the cached chunk is rerun.

[13]For reference, *Sample* was created by using the `rnorm` command to take a random sample of size 1,000 from a normal distribution with a mean of five and standard deviation of two.

```
# Create histogram
hist(Sample)
@
```

If the code chunk you want to cache creates many objects, but you only want to save a few of them, you can use *knitr*'s `cache.vars` chunk option. Simply give it a character vector of the objects' names that you want to save.

Chapter summary

In this chapter we covered in more detail key *knitr* syntax for including code chunks in our presentation documents. This and other tools we learned in this chapter are important for tying our statistical analyses directly to its advertising, i.e. our presentation documents. In the next two chapters we will learn how to take the output from our statistical analysis and, using *knitr*, present the results with dynamically created tables and figures.

9

Showing Results with Tables

Graphs and other visual methods, discussed in the next chapter, can often be more effective ways to present descriptive and inferential statistics than tables.[1] Nonetheless, tables of parameter estimates, descriptive statistics, and so on can sometimes be important tools for describing your data and presenting research findings. See Ehrenberg (1977) and Gelman (2011) for information on creating tables for effective communication.

Learning how to dynamically connect statistical results with tables in your presentation documents aids reproducibility and can ultimately save you a lot of time. Manually typing results into tables by hand is tedious, not very reproducible, and can introduce errors.[2] It's especially tedious to retype tables to reflect changes you made to your data and models. Fortunately, you don't actually need to create tables by hand. There are many ways to have R do the work for you.

The goal of this chapter is for you to learn how to dynamically create tables for your presentation documents written in LaTeX and Markdown. We will first learn the simple *knitr*/*rmarkdown* syntax we need to dynamically include tables created from R objects. Then we will learn how to actually create the tables. There are a number of ways to turn R objects into tables that can be dynamically included in LaTeX or Markdown/HTML markup. In this chapter we mostly focus on three tools for creating tables: the `kable` function from *knitr*, the *xtable* package, and the *texreg* package (Leifeld, 2015). `kable` can create tables from data frames for both LaTeX and Markdown/HTML documents. *xtable* does the same, but is much more customizable. *texreg* produces publication-quality tables from objects containing statistical model results–model objects. It allows you to combine results from multiple models into one table. Unfortunately *texreg* is less flexible with objects of classes it does not support.[3]

[1] This is especially true of the small-print, high-density coefficient estimate tables that are sometimes descriptively called 'train schedule' tables.

[2] For example, in a replication of Reinhart and Rogoff's much cited (2010) study of economic growth and public debt, Herndon et al. (2014) found a number of apparent transcription errors. Analysis results in the original spreadsheets appear to not have been entered into the paper's tables accurately.

[3] These are not the only packages available in R for creating presentation document tables from R objects. I personally really like the *stargazer* package (Hlavac, 2014). It has a similar syntax to *texreg* and is particularly good for showing results from multiple models estimated using different model types in one table.

Warning: Automating table creation removes the possibility of adding errors to the presentation of your analyses by incorrectly copying output, a big potential problem in hand-created tables. However, it is not error-free. You could easily create inaccurate tables with coding errors. So, as always, it is important to 'eyeball' the output. Does it make sense? If you select a couple values in the R output, do they match what is in the presentation document's table? If not, you need to go back to the code and see where things have gone wrong. With that caveat, let's start making tables.

9.1 Basic *knitr* Syntax for Tables

The most important `knitr`/emphrmarkdown chunk option for showing tables is `results`. The `results` option can have one of four values:

- `'hide'`,
- `'asis'`,
- `'markup'`,
- `'hold'`.

The value `hide` clearly hides the results of your code chunk from your presentation document. `hold` collects all of the output and prints it at the end of the chunk. To include tables created from R objects in your LaTeX or Markdown output you should set `results='asis'` or `results='markup'`. `asis` is the simplest option as it writes the raw markup form of the table into the presentation document, not as a highlighted code chunk, but as markup. It is then compiled as table markup with the rest of the document. `markup` uses an output hook to mark up the results in a predefined way. In this chapter we will work with examples using the `asis` option.[4]

9.2 Table Basics

Before getting into the details of how to create tables from R objects we need to first learn how generic tables are created in LaTeX and Markdown/HTML. If you are not familiar with basic LaTeX or Markdown syntax you might want to skip ahead to chapters 11 and 13, respectively, before coming back to learn about making tables in these languages.

[4] Note that the `results` option is a major difference in syntax between *knitr* and *Sweave*. In *Sweave* the equivalent option is `results=TEX`.

9.2.1 Tables in LaTeX

Tables in LaTeX are usually embedded in two environments: the `table` and `tabular` environments. What is a LaTeX environment in general?

A LaTeX environment is a part of the markup where special commands are executed. A simple environment is the `center` environment.[5] Everything typed in a center environment is, unsurprisingly, centered. Typing:

```
\begin{center}
    This is a center environment.
\end{center}
```

creates the following text in the PDF output:

This is a center environment.

LaTeX environments all follow the same general syntax:

```
\begin{ENVIRONMENT_NAME}
    . . .
    . . .
\end{ENVIRONMENT_NAME}
```

You do not have to indent the contents of an environment. Indentations neither affect how the document is compiled nor show up in the final PDF.[6] It is conventional to indent them, however, because it makes the markup easier to read.

In this chapter we will learn about two types of environments you need for tables in LaTeX. The `tabular` environment allows you to format the content of a table. The `table` environment allows you to format a table's location in the text and its caption.

The `tabular` *environment*

The `tabular` environment allows you to create tables in LaTeX. Let's work through the basic syntax for a simple table.[7]

---

[5] For a comprehensive list of LaTeX environments see: `http://latex.wikia.com/wiki/List_of_LaTeX_environments`.

[6] An aside: the `tabbing` environment is a useful way to create tabbed text in LaTeX. We don't cover this here though.

[7] For a comprehensive overview, see the LaTeX Wiki page on tables: `http://en.wikibooks.org/wiki/LaTeX/Tables`.

To begin a simple tabular environment type `\begin{tabular}{TABLE_SPEC}`. The `TABLE_SPEC` argument allows you to specify the number of columns in a table and the alignment of text in each column. For example, to create a table with three columns, the first of which is left-justified and the latter two center-justified we type:

```
\begin{tabular}{l c c}
```

The `l` argument creates a left-justified column, `c` creates a centered one. If we wanted a right-justified column we would use `r`.[8] Finally, we can add a horizontal line between columns by adding a vertical bar `|` between the column arguments.[9] For example, to place a vertical line between the first and second column in our example table we would type:

```
\begin{tabular}{l | c c}
```

Now let's enter content into our table. We saw earlier how CSV files delimit individual columns with commas. In LaTeX's `tabular` environment, columns are delimited with ampersands (`&`).[10] In CSV tables, new lines are delimited by starting a new line. In LaTeX tables you use two backslashes (`\\`).[11] Here is a simple example of the first two lines of a table:

```
\begin{tabular}{l | c c}
    Observation & Variable1 & Variable2 \\
    Subject1 & a & b \\
```

It is common to demarcate the row with a table's column names–the first

---

[8]You can also specify a column's width by using `m{WIDTH}` instead. Be sure to load the *array* package in the preamble for this to work. Using `m` will create a column of a specified width that is vertically justified in the middle. For example, `m{3cm}` would create a column with a width of 3 centimeters. Text in the column would automatically be wrapped onto multiple lines if need be. You can replace the `m` with either `p` or `b`. `p` vertically aligns the text at the top, `b` aligns it at the bottom.

[9]If you add two vertical bars (`||`) you will get two lines.

[10]If you want to include an ampersand in the text of your LaTeX document you need to escape it like this: `\&`.

[11]You can use two backslashes outside of the `tabular` environment as well to force a new line. Also, to increase the space between the line you can add a vertical width argument to the double backslashes. For example, `\\[3cm]` will give you a 3-centimeter gap between the current line and the next one.

row–with horizontal lines. A horizontal line also often visually demarcates a table's end. You can add horizontal lines in the `tabular` environment with the `\hline` command.

```
\begin{tabular}{l | c c}
    \hline
    Observation & Variable1 & Variable2 \\
    \hline \hline
    Subject1 & a & b \\
    \hline
```

Finally, we close the `tabular` environment with `\end{tabular}`. The full code (with a few extra rows added) is:

```
\begin{tabular}{l | c c}
    \hline
    Observation & Variable1 & Variable2 \\
    \hline \hline
    Subject1 & a & b \\
    Subject2 & c & d \\
    Subject3 & e & f \\
    Subject4 & g & h \\
    \hline
\end{tabular}
```

This produces the following table:

Observation	Variable1	Variable2
Subject1	a	b
Subject2	c	d
Subject3	e	f
Subject4	g	h

The `table` *float environment*

You might notice that the table we created so far lacks a title and is bunched very closely to the surrounding text. In LaTeX we can create a `table` float environment to solve this problem. Float environments allow us to separate a table from the text, specify its location, and give it a caption.[12] To begin a `table`

[12]We will see in the next chapter how to use `figure` floats as well.

TABLE 9.1
Example Simple LaTeX Table

Observation	Variable1	Variable2
Subject1	a	b
Subject2	c	d
Subject3	e	f
Subject4	g	h

float environment use `\begin{table}[POSITION_SPEC]`. The `POSITION_SPEC` argument allows us to determine the location of the table. It can be set to `h` for here, i.e. where the table is written in the text. It can also be `t` to place it on the top of a page or `b` for the bottom of the page. To set a title for the table use the `\caption` command. LaTeX automatically determines the table's number, so you only need to enter the text. You can also declare a cross-reference key for the table with the `\label` command.[13] A `table` environment is Of course, closed with `\end{table}`. Let's see a full example.

```
\begin{table}[t]
    \caption{Example Simple LaTeX Table}
    \label{ExLaTeXTable}
    \begin{center}
        \begin{tabular}{l | c c}
            \hline
            Observation & Variable1 & Variable2 \\
            \hline \hline
            Subject1 & a & b \\
            Subject2 & c & d \\
            Subject3 & e & f \\
            Subject4 & g & h \\
            \hline
        \end{tabular}
    \end{center}
\end{table}
```

Notice that the `tabular` environment is further nested in the `center` environment. This centers the table while leaving the table's title left-justified.

[13]This command works throughout LaTeX. To reference the table type in the text of your document `\ref{KEY}`, where `KEY` is what you set with the `\label` command. Use `\pageref` to reference the page number.

The final result is Table 9.1. One final tip: to have the caption placed at the bottom rather than the top of the table in the final document, simply put the `caption` command after the `tabular` environment is closed.

You can see how typing out a table in LaTeX gets very tedious very fast. For all but the simplest tables it is best to try to have R do the table-making work for you.

9.2.2 Tables in Markdown/HTML

Now we will briefly look at the syntax for creating simple Markdown and HTML tables before turning to learn how to have R create these tables for us.

Markdown tables

Markdown table syntax, as with all Markdown syntax, is generally much simpler than LaTeX's tabular syntax. The markup is much more human readable. Nonetheless, larger tables can still be tedious to create.

You do not need to declare any new environments to start creating a Markdown table. Just start typing in the content. Columns are delimited in Markdown tables with a vertical bar (`|`). Rows are started with a new line. To indicate the head of the table–usually the row(s) containing the column names–separate it from the body of the table with a row of dashes (e.g. `----`). Here is an example based on the table we created in the previous section:

```
Observation | Variable1  | Variable2
----------- | ---------- | ---------
Subject1    | a          | b
```

Note that it is not necessary to line up the vertical bars. You just need to have the same number of them on each row.

You can specify each column's text justification using colons on the dashed row. For example, this code will create the left-center-center justified formatted table we made earlier:

```
Observation | Variable1 | Variable2
:---------- | :-------: | :-------:
Subject1    | a         | b
Subject2    | c         | d
Subject3    | e         | f
Subject4    | g         | c
```

To create a left-justified column simply use a colon on only the left side of the dashes.

The ultimate look of a Markdown table is highly dependent on the CSS style file you are using (see Chapter 13 for how to change your CSS style file). The default RStudio CSS style as of late 2014 formats our table to look like this:

Observation	**Variable1**	**Variable2**
Subject1	a	b
Subject2	c	d
Subject3	e	f
Subject4	g	c

Using a different CSS style file[14] we can get something like this:

OBSERVATION	VARIABLE1	VARIABLE2
Subject1	a	b
Subject2	c	d
Subject3	e	f
Subject4	g	c

In basic Markdown you can add a caption with the heading syntax (see Section 13.1.3). In this example the three hashes (###) create the header:

```
### Example Simple Markdown Table
Observation | Variable1 | Variable2
:---------- | :-------: | :-------:
Subject1    | a         | b
```

producing something like this:

[14]The table was created using the Upstanding Citizen style from the program Marked.

Example Simple Markdown Table

OBSERVATION	VARIABLE1	VARIABLE2
Subject1	a	b
Subject2	c	d
Subject3	e	f
Subject4	g	c

HTML tables

The `texreg` function that we will learn in the next section doesn't create tables formatted with Markdown syntax. It can create tables with HTML syntax. This is useful for us because virtually any HTML markup can be incorporated into a Markdown document. In fact, Markdown table syntax is only a stepping stone for more easily producing tables with HTML syntax. So it is useful to also understand the basic syntax for HTML tables.

HTML uses element "tags" to begin and end tables. The main element we use to create tables is, well, the `tables` element. This is very similar to LaTeX's `tabular` environment. An HTML element generally begins with a start tag and ends with an end tag. Clearly this is very similar to LaTeX's `\begin{}` and `\end{}` commands. Begin tags are encapsulated in a greater-than and less-than sign and include the element tag name (`<TAG>`). End tags are similar, but include a forward slash like this `</TAG>`. The content of the element goes between the start and end tags. For example:

```
<table>
    . . .
    . . .
</table>
```

As in LaTeX you are not required to tab the content of a table element; however, it does make the markup document easier to read and, as the number of tags proliferates, easier to write.

You can specify element attributes inside of start tags.[15] For example, to add a border to the table use: <table border="1">.[16]

Table rows are put inside of tr (table rows) element tags. Individual cells are delimited with td (standard cell) tags. Here is what the first row of our example table looks like in basic HTML:

```
<table>
   <tr>
     <td>Observation</td> <td>Variable1</td> <td><Variable2/td>
   </tr>
```

We can further delimit a table's header row(s) from its body with the thead and tbody tags. Finally, before making a full table it's useful to mention that table captions can be included with caption tags. Let's put this all together:

```
<table>
    <thead>
        <tr>
            <td>Observation</td> <td>Variable1</td> <td>Variable2</td>
        </tr>
    </thead>
    <tbody>
        <tr>
            <td>Subject1</td> <td>a</td> <td>b</td>
        </tr>
        <tr>
            <td>Subject2</td> <td>c</td> <td>d</td>
        </tr>
        <tr>
            <td>Subject3</td> <td>e</td> <td>e</td>
        </tr>
        <tr>
            <td>Subject4</td> <td>f</td> <td>f</td>
        </tr>
    </tbody>
</table>
```

As with Markdown tables, the ultimate appearance of the table is highly dependent on the style files you use.

[15]These work like arguments in R in that they change how the element is evaluated.

[16]Whether or not a border appears is determined by whether or not the style sheet you are using includes borders.

9.3 Creating Tables from Supported Class R Objects

Just as the `write.csv` command turns an R data frame into a CSV formatted text file, there are a number of methods in R to take an object–e.g. a matrix, data frame–the output from a statistical analysis, and so on–and turn them into LaTeX and HTML tables. `kable`, *xtable*, and *texreg* each work most easily with specific object classes that their designers explicitly supported.

9.3.1 `kable` for Markdown and LaTeX

`kable` easily converts matrices and data frames into tables for Markdown, HTML, and LaTeX among others. Let's create a simple data frame:

```
kable_ex <- data.frame(
            Observation = c("Subject1", "Subject2",
                            "Subject3", "Subject4"),
            Variable1 = c("a", "c", "e", "g"),
            Variable2 = c("b", "d", "f", "c")
)
```

Then simply place this data frame into a `kable` call:

```
kable(kable_ex, caption = "Example kable Table")
```

This creates the following table:

Example kable Table

Observation	Variable1	Variable2
Subject1	a	b
Subject2	c	d
Subject3	e	f
Subject4	g	c

Beyond setting the tables caption with `caption`, there are a few other alterations that can be made with `kable` arguments. You can specify new column and row names by passing character vectors to `col.names` and `row.names`, respectively. These are very useful as it can be difficult, or at least irritating, for your readers to try to decode the names you give to your data frame rows and columns in R. Another useful argument is `digits`. This will round numbers in the table to a specified number of digits after the decimal place. To effectively convey your results you should *at the least* only include digits that are significant in that they meaningfully vary in the data (Ehrenberg, 1977, 281).

You can also change the markup language that the table is created in using the `format` argument. For example, to create a LaTeX formatted table use `format = 'latex'`. In general, you do not need to specify the format if you are using *knitr* or *rmarkdown* to include the table in a presentation document. This will be done automatically.

9.3.2 *xtable* for LaTeX and HTML

While `kable` allows you to quickly create simple tables, it can only do so from matrices and data frames. It also has limited customizability. The *xtable* package can create more customizable tables from a wider variety of R objects, including statistical model objects.

Different R statistical model estimation commands can produce model objects of different classes. For example, the `lm` (linear model) command creates model summaries of the `lm` class. Let's create a simple linear regression using the *swiss* data frame and `lm` command. This data frame is included with R by default. The simple linear regression model we are going to make has the *swiss* variable **Examination** as the dependent variable and **Education** as the only independent variable.[17]

```
# Fit simple linear regression model
M1 <- lm(Examination ~ Education, data = swiss)

# Show M1 class
class(M1)

## [1] "lm"
```

By using the `class` command we can see that *M1* is of the `lm` class. *M1* contains items estimated by the linear regression model[18] such as the coefficient

[17]For a description of these variables type `?swiss` into the console

[18]If you are unfamiliar with the syntax of R statistical estimation models the previous code might be confusing. In general 'response' (Y) variables are written first and are separated from the 'explanatory' (X) variables by a tilde ($\sim$). Crawley (2005, 107) notes that you can read $Y \sim X$ as 'Y is modeled as a function of X'. In later examples we will see that individual explanatory variables are generally separated by plus signs (+), indicating that

estimates and their standard errors. To get a summary of a model object's contents use the `summary` command like this:

```
# Show summary of M1 model object
summary(M1)

##
## Call:
## lm(formula = Examination ~ Education, data = swiss)
##
## Residuals:
##      Min       1Q   Median       3Q      Max
## -10.9322  -4.7633  -0.1838   3.8907  12.4983
##
## Coefficients:
##             Estimate Std. Error t value Pr(>|t|)
## (Intercept) 10.12748    1.28589   7.876 5.23e-10 ***
## Education    0.57947    0.08852   6.546 4.81e-08 ***
## ---
## Signif. codes:  0 '***' 0.001 '**' 0.01 '*' 0.05 '.' 0.1 ' ' 1
##
## Residual standard error: 5.773 on 45 degrees of freedom
## Multiple R-squared:  0.4878,Adjusted R-squared:  0.4764
## F-statistic: 42.85 on 1 and 45 DF,  p-value: 4.811e-08
```

To find a full list of object classes that *xtable* supports, type `methods(xtable)` into the R Console after you have loaded the package.

xtable *for LaTeX*

Let's look at how to create LaTeX tables with *xtable* by creating a table summarizing the estimates from the *M1* model object.

```
<<results='asis', echo=FALSE>>=
# Load xtable
library(xtable)

# Create LaTeX table from M1 and show the output markup
```

they are included in the model, not that they are added. For more information see Crawley (2005, Ch. 7).

```
xtable(M1, caption = "Linear Regression,
       Dependent Variable: Exam Score",
       label = "BasicXtableSummary",
       digits = 1)
@
```

When included in an R Sweave-style LaTeX document, this code will create a table exactly like Table 9.2.

Let's go through this code, working from the outside in. First you'll notice that we've set two *knitr* code chunk options. As we discussed earlier, `results='asis'` allows us to include the LaTeX formatted table created by *xtable*. The next option `echo=FALSE` hides the code from being shown in our final document. The *xtable* command creates the summary table of our *M1* model object. Not only does it produce both complete `tabular` and `table` environments, but also through the `caption` and `label` arguments it automatically adds in the table's title and cross-reference label, respectively. Finally, notice that I added the `digits = 1` argument. As in `kable`, this specifies that I want numbers in the table to be rounded to one decimal digit.

	Estimate	Std. Error	t value	Pr(>|t|)
(Intercept)	10.1	1.3	7.9	0.0
Education	0.6	0.1	6.5	0.0

TABLE 9.2
Linear Regression, Dependent Variable: Exam Score

xtable *for Markdown/HTML*

We can use *xtable* and the `print.xtable` command[19] to also create tables for Markdown and HTML documents. The *xtable* command produces, unsurprisingly, `xtable` class objects. We can run these through the `print` command and add arguments to customize how the table is formatted. By default, `print.xtable`'s `type` argument is set to `"latex"`. To create an HTML table that can be inserted into Markdown and HTML documents, set the `type` argument from `"latex"` to `"html"`. For example, to create an HTML version of the table summarizing *M1* and include it in an R Markdown document we type:

[19]Note: you can abbreviate `print.xtable` simply as `print`.

```
```{r, results='asis', echo=FALSE}
# Load xtable
library(xtable)

# Create an xtable object from M1
M1Table <- xtable(M1, caption = "Linear Regression, Dependent
                  Variable: Exam Score",
                  label = "BasicXtableSummary",
                  digits = 1)

# Create HTML summary table of M1Table
print.xtable(M1Table, type = "html", caption.placement = "top")
```
```

If you intend to include multiple tables in your R Markdown document you will want to set all of the tables to be printed in HTML. You can place `options("xtable.type" = "html")` in a code chunk near the beginning of your document.[20] This simply makes it so that you don't need to include `type = "html"` every time you use `print`.

Notice in the previous code example that we also added the `caption.placement = "top"` argument. This will move the caption from the bottom of the table, as it is in Table 9.2, to the top. See the *xtable* package documentation[21] for the full list of `print.xtable` options.

9.3.3 *texreg* for LaTeX and HTML

`kable` and *xtable* are limited when it comes to creating tables from statistical model objects. `kable` only works with matrices and data frames. *xtable* is easiest when working with only one model object at a time. Furthermore, by default these tools do not create output tables that present estimates from multiple statistical models in the style used by many prominent academic journals. The *texreg* package is very useful for creating these types of tables. It also supports more model object types than *xtable*.

texreg *for LaTeX*

Imagine we want to show the estimates from a number of nested regression models in LaTeX a table like Table 9.3. For example, to estimate nested regression models from the remaining variables in the *swiss* data set we would type:

[20]Of course, you will probably want to use the `include=FALSE` *knitr* option with this code chunk.

[21]`http://cran.r-project.org/web/packages/xtable/xtable.pdf`

```
# Estimated nested regression models
M2 <- lm(Examination ~ Education + Agriculture, data = swiss)

M3 <- lm(Examination ~ Education + Agriculture + Catholic,
          data = swiss)

M4 <- lm(Examination ~ Education + Agriculture + Catholic +
          Infant.Mortality, data = swiss)

M5 <- lm(Examination ~ Education + Agriculture + Catholic +
          Infant.Mortality + Fertility, data = swiss)
```

xtable *for LaTeX*

We can now include these model objects in one LaTeX table with *texreg*. Remember to include `results='asis'` in the code chunk head.

```
# Load texreg package
library(texreg)

# Create custom coefficient names
cust_coef <- c('(Intercept)', 'Education', 'Agriculture',
               'Catholic', 'Infant Mortality',
               'Fertility')

# Create nested regression model table
texreg(list(M1, M2, M3, M4, M5),
    caption = 'Nested Estimates Table with \\emph{texreg}',
    caption.above = TRUE,
    label = 'Basic_texregTable',
    custom.coef.names = cust_coef)
```

Notice that we placed the model objects in a list when we called `texreg`. `texreg` automatically created the `table` and `tabular` environments and by default centers the table.[22] We added a caption and reference label with the `caption` and `label` arguments, respectively. By default, the caption is placed

[22] Use the `center = FALSE` argument to override centering. If you would like to only create the `tabular` environment use the argument `table = FALSE`. Creating your own `table` environment can be useful in situations where you want more customizability.

TABLE 9.3
Nested Estimates Table with *texreg*

	Model 1	Model 2	Model 3	Model 4	Model 5
(Intercept)	10.13***	19.72***	18.54***	18.66**	24.57**
	(1.29)	(3.20)	(2.64)	(5.84)	(8.24)
Education	0.58***	0.36**	0.42***	0.42***	0.33*
	(0.09)	(0.10)	(0.09)	(0.09)	(0.13)
Agriculture		−0.14**	−0.07	−0.07	−0.08
		(0.04)	(0.04)	(0.04)	(0.04)
Catholic			−0.08***	−0.08***	−0.07**
			(0.02)	(0.02)	(0.02)
Infant Mortality				−0.01	0.10
				(0.23)	(0.25)
Fertility					−0.10
					(0.09)
R^2	0.49	0.59	0.73	0.73	0.73
Adj. R^2	0.48	0.57	0.71	0.70	0.70
Num. obs.	47	47	47	47	47
RMSE	5.77	5.25	4.30	4.36	4.35

$^{***}p < 0.001$, $^{**}p < 0.01$, $^{*}p < 0.05$

below the table, so we used `caption.above = TRUE` to place it on top. Finally, we created custom coefficient names with `custom.coef.names` that are a bit tidier than the variable names in our R dataset. Your readers will appreciate easily discernible coefficient names.

In the LaTeX caption you'll notice `\\emph{texreg}`. In LaTeX the `emph` command italicizes text (we'll see this again in Chapter 11). We added an additional escape character \ so that R would not try to interpret the `e` and instead feed it to LaTeX. By default, `texreg` uses `stars = c(0.001, 0.01, 0.05)` to determine at what p-values to display statistical significance stars. This is the same as the `lm` model summary default showing three sets of statistical significance stars. You can define the significance levels by assigning a different numeric vector to the `stars` argument.

There are many other changes you can make to tables created with *texreg*. You can change the column and coefficient names, determine what type of standard errors to show, and so on. For the full list of arguments, see the help file by typing `?texreg` into your R Console.

texreg *for HTML*

You can also use the *texreg* package to create tables in Markdown/HTML documents. Instead of the `texreg` function, use `htmlreg`. The syntax is largely similar, though arguments relating to LaTeX are not available, while others relating the HTML are. Here is a simple example creating Table 9.3 in an HTML document:

```
htmlreg(list(M1, M2, M3, M4, M5),
        caption = 'Nested Estimates Table in HTML Document',
        caption.above = TRUE,
        custom.coef.names = cust_coef)
```

Notice that we did not include the `label` argument as this is not available in HTML. The resulting table looks like this:

Nested Estimates Table in HTML Document

	Model 1	Model 2	Model 3	Model 4	Model 5
(Intercept)	10.13***	19.72***	18.54***	18.66**	24.57**
	(1.29)	(3.20)	(2.64)	(5.84)	(8.24)
Education	0.58***	0.36**	0.42***	0.42***	0.33*
	(0.09)	(0.10)	(0.09)	(0.09)	(0.13)
Agriculture		-0.14**	-0.07	-0.07	-0.08
		(0.04)	(0.04)	(0.04)	(0.04)
Catholic			-0.08***	-0.08***	-0.07**
			(0.02)	(0.02)	(0.02)
Infant Mortality				-0.01	0.10
				(0.23)	(0.25)
Fertility					-0.10
					(0.09)
R^2	0.49	0.59	0.73	0.73	0.73
Adj. R^2	0.48	0.57	0.71	0.70	0.70
Num. obs.	47	47	47	47	47

***p* < 0.001**, *p* < 0.01, p < 0.05

9.3.4 Fitting Large Tables in LaTeX

Sometimes you may have large tables that are difficult to fit onto a page in LaTeX. There are a number of ways to adjust tables so that they fit on the page.

LaTeX landscape tables

If your LaTeX table is very wide, e.g. because it shows results from many estimation models, you can use LaTeX's `lscape` package to create `landscape` formatting environments. Rather than orienting the text of a page so that it is in profile (a long page), a `landscape` environment turns it 90 degrees so that it has a landscape orientation (a wide page).

To use the *lscape* package, first place `\usepackage{lscape}` in your LaTeX document's preamble. Then begin a `landscape` environment with `\begin{landscape}` where you would like it located in the text. Then place the `table` environment information and *knitr* code for creating the table. Finally, close the `landscape` environment with `\end{landscape}`.

LaTeX scalebox for tables

In addition, the `scalebox` command from the *graphics* package could be useful for fitting large tables onto a PDF page. This command expands or shrinks the text in the table. `texreg` actually has a `scalebox` argument. If you use `scalebox = 0.5` it will halve the size of the table; `scalebox = 2` doubles it.

More generally, to rescale a table use:

```
\scalebox{HORIZONTAL_SCALE}[VERTICAL_SCALE]{TABLE}
```

`HORIZONTAL_SCALE` is how much to scale the table horizontally. `VERTICAL_SCALE` is how much to scale vertically and `TABLE` is the table or R code chunk to create the table.

9.3.5 *xtable* with non-supported class objects

The `kable`, *texreg*, and *xtable* packages are very convenient for model objects they know how to handle. With supported class objects the functions in these packages know where to look for the vectors containing the things–coefficient names, standard errors, and so on–that they need to create tables. With unsupported classes, however, they don't know where to look for these things. Luckily, there is a work around. You tell `xtable` where to find elements you want to include in your table. `xtable` can handle matrix and data frame class objects. The rows of these objects become table rows and the columns become the table columns. So, to create tables with non-supported class objects you need to:

1. find and extract the information from the unsupported class object that you want in the table,
2. convert this information into a matrix or data frame where the rows

and columns of the object correspond to the rows and columns of the table that you want to create,

3. use *xtable* with this object to create the table.

Imagine that you want to create a results table showing the covariate names, coefficient means, and quantiles for marginal posterior distributions estimated from a Bayesian normal linear regression using the *Zelig* package (Goodrich and Lu, 2007; Owen et al., 2013)[23] and data from the *swiss* data frame. Let's run the model:

```
# Load Zelig package
library(Zelig)

# Estimate model
NBModel <- zelig(Examination ~ Education, model = "normal.bayes",
                 data = swiss, cite = FALSE)

# Find NBModel's class
class(NBModel)

## [1] "zelig"        "normal.bayes"
```

Using the `class` command we see that the model output object in *NBModel* is of both the `zelig` and `normal.bayes` classes. These class are not supported by *xtable*. If you try to create a table summarizing the estimates in *NBTable* you will get the following error:

```
# Load xtable
library(xtable)

# Attempt to create a table with NBModel
NBTable <- xtable(NBModel)

## Error in UseMethod("xtable"): no applicable method for 'xtable'
applied to an object of class "c('zelig', 'normal.bayes')"
```

With unsupported class objects you have to create the summary yourself and extract the elements that you want from it manually. A good knowledge of vectors, matrices, and component selection is very handy for this (see Chapter 3).

[23]Remember you will need to have installed the *ZeligBayesian* package. Please see page xix for more details.

First, create a summary of your output object *NBModel*:

```
NBModelSum <- summary(NBModel)
```

This creates a new object of the class `summary.MCMCZelig`. We're still not there yet as this object contains not just the covariate names and so on but also information we don't want to include in the results table, like the estimation formula. The second step is to extract a matrix from inside *NBModelSum* called *summary* with the component selector (`$`). Remember that to find the components of an object use the `names` command.

```
names(NBModelSum)

## [1] "summary" "call"   "start"  "end"    "thin"    "nchain"
```

The *summary* matrix is where the things we want in our table are located. I find it easier to work with data frames, so let's also convert the matrix into a data frame.

```
NBSumDataFrame <- data.frame(NBModelSum$summary)
```

Here is what the model summary data frame looks like:

```
# Show NBSumDataFrame
NBSumDataFrame

##                 Mean         SD       X2.5.       X50.      X97.5.
##(Intercept) 10.13971 1.31673464 7.5578575 10.1565881 12.7058298
## Education   0.57863 0.09117789  0.3963458  0.5781419  0.7609409
## sigma2     34.97026 7.81259626 22.9566816 33.8781995 53.2172104
```

Now we have a data frame object *xtable* can handle. After a little cleaning up (see the chapter's Appendix for more details) you can use *NBSumdata frame* with *xtable* as before to create Table 9.4.

It may take some hunting to find what you want, but a similar process can be used to create tables from objects of virtually any class.[24] Hunting for

[24]This process can also be useful for creating graphics as we will see in Chapter 10.

	Mean	2.5%	50%	97.5%
(Intercept)	10.14	7.56	10.16	12.71
Education	0.58	0.40	0.58	0.76
sigma2	34.97	22.96	33.88	53.22

TABLE 9.4
Coefficient Estimates Predicting Examination Scores in Swiss Cantons (1888) Found Using Bayesian Normal Linear Regression

what you want can be easier if you look inside of objects by clicking on them in RStudio's tab.

9.3.6 Creating variable description documents with *xtable*

You can use *xtable* to create a table describing variables in your data set and insert these into Markdown documents created with the concatenate and print (`cat`) command (see Section 4.4). This is useful because our data so far has been stored in plain-text files. Unlike binary Stata or SAS data files, plain-text data files do not include variable descriptions.

Imagine that we want to create a Markdown file with a table describing the variables from the *swiss* data frame. First we will create two vectors: one for the variable names and the other for the variable descriptions.

```
# Create variable vector from column names
Variable <- names(swiss)

# Create variable description vector
Description <- c("common standardized fertility measures",
                 "% of males involved in agriculture as occupation",
                 "% draftees receiving highest mark on army examination",
                 "% education beyond primary school for draftees",
                 "% 'catholic' (as opposed to 'protestant')",
                 "% live births who live less-than 1 year"
                 )
```

In the first line we use the **names** command to create a vector of the *swiss* data frame's column names. Then we simply create a vector of descriptions with the combine command (`c`). Now we can combine these vectors into a matrix and use it to create an HTML table.

```
# Combine Variable and Description variables into a matrix
DescriptionsBound <- cbind(Variable, Description)

# Create an xtable object from DescriptionsBound
DescriptionsTable <- xtable(DescriptionsBound)

# Format table in HTML
DescriptTable <- print.xtable(DescriptionsTable, type = "html")
```

Finally, we can use `cat` to create our Markdown variable description file.

```
# Create variable description file
cat("# Swiss Data Variable Descriptions \n",
    "### Source: Mosteller and Tukey, (1977) \n",
    DescriptTable,
    file = "SwissVariableDescriptions.md"
    )
```

The first part of the `cat` command here is the title of the document. As we will see in Chapter 13, hashes (`#`) create headers. The `\n` creates a new line in the Markdown document. The next line is information on the *swiss* data frame's source. We then include the HTML table in the *DescriptTable* object and save it to a file called *SwissVariableDescriptions.md*.

It is convenient to simply include the creation of this table in your data gathering makefiles and have it saved into the same directory as your data. This way it will be easy to update as you update your data and easy to find. If you are storing your data on GitHub it will automatically render the variable description Markdown file and make it easy for others to read. See this book's makefile example for more information: `http://bit.ly/1AaOuDx`.[25]

Chapter summary

In this chapter we have learned how to take the results from our statistical analyses and other information from our data and dynamically present it in LaTeX and Markdown documents with *knitr*/*rmarkdown*. In the next chapter we will do the same thing with figures.

[25]The long URL is: `https://GitHub.com/christophergandrud/Rep-Res-Examples/tree/master/DataGather_Merge`.

Appendix

Source code for cleaning *NBSumDataFrame* and using it to create a LaTeX table:

```
# Load packages
library(dplyr)
library(xtable)

# Change quantile variable names
NBSumDataFrame <- rename(NBSumDataFrame, "2.5%" = X2.5.)
NBSumDataFrame <- rename(NBSumDataFrame, "50%" = X50.)
NBSumDataFrame <- rename(NBSumDataFrame, "97.5%" = X97.5.)


# Reorder variables and remove the standard deviation variable
NBTable <- NBSumDataFrame[, c("Mean", "2.5%", "50%", "97.5%")]

# Create table
xtable(NBTable, caption = "Coefficient Estimates Predicting
                           Examination Scores in Swiss Cantons
                           (1888) Found Using Bayesian Normal
                           Linear Regression")
```

Note that the new variable names are in quotation marks, in contrast to the example from Chapter 7. The quotation marks allow us to specify a name that begins with a number and has special characters like %.

10

Showing Results with Figures

One of the main reasons that many people use R is to take advantage of its comprehensive and powerful set of data visualization tools. Visually displaying information with graphics is often a much more effective way of presenting both descriptive statistics and analysis results than the tables we covered in the last chapter.[1]

Nonetheless, dynamically incorporating figures with *knitr*/*rmarkdown* has many of the same benefits as dynamically including tables, especially the ability to have data set or analysis changes automatically cascade into your presentation documents. The basic process for including figures in knitted presentation documents is also very similar to including tables, though there are some important extra considerations we need to make to properly size the figures and be able to include interactive visualizations in our presentation documents.

In this chapter we will first briefly learn how to include non-knitted graphics in LaTeX and Markdown documents before turning to look at how to dynamically knit R graphics into presentation documents. In the remainder of the chapter we will look at how to actually create graphics with R including some of the fundamentals of R's default graphics package, as well as the *ggplot2* (Wickham and Chang, 2015b) and *googleVis* (Gesmann and de Castillo, 2015) packages. In each case we will focus on how to include the figures created by these packages in knitted presentation documents.

10.1 Including Non-knitted Graphics

Understanding how *knitr*/*rmarkdown* dynamically include figures is easier if you understand how figures are normally included in LaTeX and Markdown. Unlike a word processing program like Microsoft Word, in LaTeX, Markdown, HTML, and other markup languages you don't copy and paste figures into your document. Instead you link to an image file outside of your markup

[1]There are, of course, a number of exceptions to this rule of thumb. van Belle (2008, Ch. 9) argues that a few numbers should be listed in a sentence, many numbers shown in tables, and relationships between numbers are best shown with graphs. Similarly, Tufte (2001) argues that tables tend to outperform graphics for displaying 20 or fewer numbers. Graphics often outperform tables for showing larger data sets and relationships within the data.

document. Typically these image files are in formats such as *PDF*, *PNG*, and *JPEG*.[2]

There are three advantages to this method of including graphics over cut and paste. The first is that whenever the image files are changed, the changes are updated in the final presentation document when it is compiled, no re-copying and pasting. The second advantage is that the images are sized and placed with the markup code rather than pointing and clicking. This is tedious at first, but saves considerable time and frustration when a document becomes larger. It also makes it easy to consistently format multiple images in a document. Finally, because the image is not actually loaded in the markup file, you won't notice any sluggishness while editing the markup document that you get in a traditional word processor if there are many images.

If the image files are in the same directory as the markup document, we don't need to specify the image's file path, only its name. If they are in another directory, we need to include additional file path information. Remember to use relative paths when possible. In this section we will learn how to include graphics files in documents created with LaTeX and Markdown.

10.1.1 Including graphics in LaTeX

The main way to include graphics (graphs, photos, and so on) in LaTeX documents is to use the `includegraphics` command to link to image files. To have the full range of features for `includegraphics`, make sure to load the *graphicx* package in your document's preamble. Imagine that we wanted to include an image of butterflies stored in a file called *HeliconiusMimicry.png* in a LaTeX-produced document.[3] We type:

```
\includegraphics[scale=0.8]{HeliconiusMimicry.png}
```

In the square brackets you'll notice `scale=0.8`. This formats the image to be included at 80 percent of its actual size. You can use other options such as `height` to specify the height, `width` to specify the width, and `angle` to specify

[2]PDF: Portable Document Format, PNG: Portable Network Graphic, JPEG: Joint Photographic Experts Group.
A quick note about file formats: By default *knitr* creates PDF formatted figure files when knitting R LaTeX documents. These figures, generally built with vector graphics, allow you to zoom in on them by any amount without them becoming pixelated. This means that your images will be crisp in PDF presentation documents. For Markdown documents, *knitr* creates PNG images. PNG images are usually relatively high quality and can be rendered directly on websites, unlike PDFs. JPEG formatted files usually take up less disk space than PDF and PNG files. However, their quality is also worse and can often look very pixelated. For more information, Wikipedia has a comprehensive comparison of graphics file formats at: `http://en.wikipedia.org/wiki/Comparison_of_graphics_file_formats`.

[3]The image used here is from Meyer (2006).

the angle at which to rotate the image. You can add more than one option if they are separated by commas. Rather than hard coding the width in exact centimeters, you can determine its width as a proportion of the text width using `\textwidth`.[4] For example, to set our image at 80 percent of the text width we can type:

```
\includegraphics[width=0.8\textwidth]{HeliconiusMimicry.png}
```

`figure` *float environment*

Most often you will want to include LaTeX figures in a `figure` float environment. The *figure* environment works almost exactly the same way as the `table` environment we saw in the last chapter. It allows you to separate the figure from the text, add a caption, and label the figure. We begin the environment with `\begin{figure}[POSITION_SPEC]`. `POSITION_SPEC` can have the same values as we saw earlier with tables (page 172). We can then include a `caption` and `label` command. The environment is closed with `\end{figure}`. For example, to create Figure 10.1, I used the following code:[5]

```
\begin{figure}[ht]
    \caption{An Example Figure in LaTeX}
    \label{ExampleLaTeXFigure}
        \begin{center}
            \includegraphics[scale=0.8]{HeliconiusMimicry.png}
        \end{center}
    {\scriptsize{Source: \cite{Meyer2006}}}
\end{figure}
```

Notice that after the call to end the `center` environment we include `{\scriptsize{Source: \cite{Meyer2006}}}`. This simply includes a note in the figure environment giving the image's source. The note moves with the figure and is separate from the text. The `scriptsize` command transforms the text to smaller than normal size font. See Chapter 11 (Section 11.1.7) for more details on LaTeX font sizes. The command `\cite{Meyer2006}` inserts a citation from the bibliography for Meyer (2006). We will discuss bibliographies in more detail in the next chapter (Section 11.2).

[4]Note there are a number of other ways to set the size of a figure relative to a page element. See: LaTeX Wiki Book for more details: `http://en.wikibooks.org/wiki/LaTeX/Page_Layout`.

[5]For simplicity, this code does not include the full image's actual file path.

FIGURE 10.1
An Example Figure in LaTeX

Source: Meyer (2006)

10.1.2 Including graphics in Markdown/HTML

Markdown has a similar command as LaTeX's `includegraphics`. It goes like this: `![ALT_TEXT](FILE_PATH)`. This syntax may seem strange now, but it will hopefully make more sense when we cover Markdown hyperlinks in Chapter 13 (Section 13.1.7) as this is what it is intended to imitate. `ALT_TEXT` refers to HTML's `alt` (alternative text) attribute. This should be a very short description of the image that will appear if it fails to load in a web browser. `FILE_PATH` specifies the image's file path.[6] Here is an example using the image we worked with before.

```
![ButterflyImage](HeliconiusMimicry.png)
```

Note that the file path can be a URL. You may, for example, store an image in the Dropbox Public folder or on GitHub and use its URL to link to it in the Markdown document.[7]

Markdown does not include ways to resize or re-position an image, so that the syntax would stay simple. If you want to resize or position your image you will have to use HTML markup. Probably the simplest way to include images with HTML is by using the `img` (image) element tag. To create the equivalent of what we just did in Markdown with HTML we type:

[6]You can also include a title in quotation marks after the file path. This specifies the HTML `title` attribute. However, this attribute does not create a title for the image in the way that `caption` does for LaTeX float figures. Instead it creates a tooltip, a small box that appears when you place your cursor over the image. Specifying descriptive alt text is very useful for screen readers that help visually impaired people access web content.

[7]For images stored on GitHub use the URL for the raw version of the file.

```
<img src="HeliconiusMimicry.png" alt="ButterflyImage"></img>
```

The `src` (script) attribute specifies the file path. To change the width and height of the image we can use the `width` and `height` attributes. For example:

```
<img src="HeliconiusMimicry.png" alt="ButterflyImage"
     width="100px" height="100px"></img>
```

creates an image that is 100 pixels (`px`) wide by 100 pixels high.[8] It is also possible to specify the alignment of figures in Markdown with a custom CSS style file. I don't cover how to do that here.

10.2 Basic *knitr*/*rmarkdown* Figure Options

So far we have looked at how to include images that have already been created into our LaTeX and Markdown documents. *knitr*, and by extension *rmarkdown*, allow us to combine a figure's creation by R with its inclusion in a presentation document. They are tied together and update together. We use *knitr* chunk options to specify how the figure will look in the presentation document and where it will be saved. Let's learn some of the more important chunk options for figures.

10.2.1 Chunk options

`fig.path`

When you use *knitr* to create and include figures in your presentation documents it (1) runs the code you give it to create the figure, (2) automatically saves it into a particular directory,[9] and (3) includes the necessary LaTeX or Markdown code to include the figure in the final presentation document. By default *knitr* saves images into a folder (it creates) called *figure* located in the working directory.[10] You can tell *knitr* where to save the images with the `fig.path` option. Simply use the file path naming conventions suitable for your system and include the new path in quotation marks.

[8] A pixel is the smallest discrete part of images displayed on a screen. See the "pixel" Wikipedia page for more details: `http://en.wikipedia.org/wiki/Pixel`.

[9] If a code chunk creates more than one figure, *knitr* automatically saves each into its own file in the same directory.

[10] File names are based on the code chunk label where they were created.

`out.height`

To set the height that a figure will be in the final presentation document use the `out.height` option. In R LaTeX documents you can set the width using centimeters, inches, or as a proportion of a page element. In R Markdown documents you use pixels to set the height. For example, to set a figure's height in an R Markdown document to 200 pixels use `out.height='200px'`.

`out.width`

Similarly, we can set the width of a *knitr* created figure using the `out.width` option. The same rules apply as with `out.width`. For example, to have a figure shown up at 80 percent of the text width in an R LaTeX document use: `out.width='0.8\\textwidth'`. Notice that that there are two backslashes before `textwidth`. As we saw earlier, the LaTeX command only has one. However, all *knitr* code chunk options must be written as they would be in R. We need to escape the backslash with the backslash escape character, i.e. use two backslashes.

`fig.align`

You can set a knitted figure's alignment using `fig.align`. The option can be set to `left`, `center`, or `right`. To center a figure, add `fig.align='center'`.

Other figure chunk options

The previous options are probably the most commonly used ways of adjusting figures with *knitr*. However, *knitr* has many other chunk options to help you adjust your figures so that they are incorporated into your presentation documents the way that you want. The option `fig.cap` allows you to set a figure's LaTeX caption and `fig.lb` allows you to set the label.[11] As we will see below (page 198), you can use the `dev` option to choose the figure's output file format, e.g. PDF, PNG, JPEG. Please see the official *knitr* code chunk options webpage for more information on figure chunk options: `http://yihui.name/knitr/options#chunk_options`.

10.2.2 Global options

If you want all of your figures to share the same options–e.g. same height and alignment–you can set global figure options at the beginning of your document with `opts_chunk$set`. Imagine that we are making an R LaTeX Sweave-style document and want all of our figures to be center aligned and 80 percent of the text width. We type:

[11] In this chapter we will set these options in the markup rather than the code chunk. I prefer doing this because *knitr* options need to be on the same line and so can sometimes result in very long lists of options that are difficult to read.

```
<<include=FALSE>>=
opts_chunk$set.(fig.align = "center",
                out.width = "0.8\\textwidth")
@
```

You can also set some global figure options, such as `fig_height` and `fig_width` in your *rmarkdown* YAML header.

10.3 Knitting R's Default Graphics

R's *graphics* package–loaded by default–includes commands to create numerous plot types. These include `hist` for histograms, `pairs` for scatterplot matrices, `boxplot` for creating boxplots, and the versatile `plot` for creating x-y plots–including scatterplots and bar charts depending on the data's type.

There are many useful resources for learning how to fully utilize R's default graphics capabilities. These include Paul Murrell's (2011) very comprehensive *R Graphics* book. The Cookbook for R[12] and Quick-R[13] websites are also very helpful. Winston Chang, the maintainer of the Cookbook for R, also has a full book devoted to creating R graphics (2012).

In this section we are going to see how to include R's default graphics in our LaTeX and Markdown presentation documents. We will also see an example of how to source the creation of a graph from a segmented analysis file. Most of R's default graphics capabilities create static graphics. They are not animations or interactive. The discussion in this section is exclusively about using static graphics with *knitr/rmarkdown*. Later in the chapter we will discuss how to knit interactive graphics.

Let's look at an example we first saw at the end of Chapter 8 (Section 8.2.3). Remember that we accessed an R source code file stored on GitHub to create a simple scatterplot of cars' speed and stopping distances using R's *cars* data set, which is loaded by default. We haven't yet seen the code in the R source file that created the plot. The variable **speed** contains the stopping speed and **dist** contains the stopping distances. Here is the code to create the plot:

```
# Create simple scatterplot of cars' speed and stopping distance
plot(x = cars$speed, y = cars$dist,
```

[12] `http://www.cookbook-r.com/Graphs/`
[13] `http://www.statmethods.net/advgraphs/`

```
     xlab = "Speed (mph)",
     ylab = "Stopping Distance (ft)",
     cex.lab = 1.5)
```

We select the variables from *cars* to plot on the x and y axes of our graph with the component selector (`$`). Then we use the `xlab` and `ylab` arguments to specify the x and y axis labels. We could have added a title for the plot using the `main` argument. We didn't do this because we will give the plot a title in the LaTeX `figure` environment. The `cex.lab` argument increased the labels' font size. The argument specifically determines how to scale the labels relative to the default size. 1.5 means 50 percent larger than the default.

Now let's see how to create this plot with *knitr* and include it in a LaTeX `figure` environment.

```
\begin{figure}[ht]
    \caption{Example Simple Scatter Plot Using \texttt{plot}}
    \label{BasicFigureExample}
<<echo=FALSE, fig.align='center', out.width='8cm', out.height='8cm'>>=
plot(x = cars$speed, y = cars$dist,
     xlab = "Speed (mph)",
     ylab = "Stopping Distance (ft)",
     cex.lab = 1.5)
@
\end{figure}
```

This code produces Figure 10.2.[14] If you are familiar with R graphics you will notice that we did not need to tell *knitr* to save the file in a particular format. Instead, behind the scenes it automatically saves the plot as a PDF file in a folder called *figure* that is a child of the current working directory. You can choose the figure file's format with the `dev` (graphical device) chunk option. For example, to save the figure in a PNG formatted file simply add the chunk option `dev='PNG'`. You can choose any graphical device format supported by R. For a full list of R's graphical devices type `?Devices` into your console. One reason you might want to change the format is to reduce your presentation document's file size. Using a bitmap format like PNG will create smaller files than PDFs, though lower-quality images.

We could Of course, simply link to the original R source code file stored on GitHub with the `source_url` command. Let's look at an example of this

[14]Note that I did not specify the center environment. This is because it is specified in a *knitr* global chunk option.

FIGURE 10.2
Example Simple Scatter Plot Using `plot`

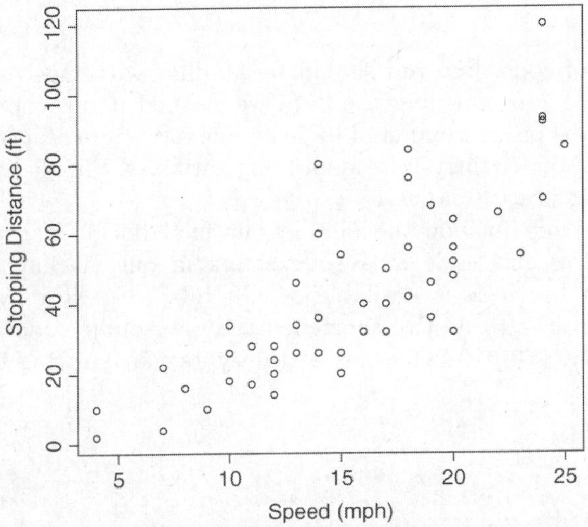

with a different source code file. Remember in Chapter 6 we used a makefile to gather data from three different sources on the internet. The CSV is called *MainData.csv* and is stored on GitHub at: `http://bit.ly/V0ldsf`.[15] We can download this data into R and make a scatterplot matrix with this code:

```
# Download data
MainData <- repmis::source_data("http://bit.ly/V0ldsf")

# Subset MainData so that it only includes the year 2003
SubData <- subset(MainData, year == 2003)

# Remove iso2c, country, year variables
# Keep reg_4state, disproportionality, FertilizerConsumption
SubData <- SubData[, c("reg_4state",
                       "disproportionality",
                       "FertilizerConsumption")]
```

[15]The full version of the URL is: `https://raw.githubusercontent.com/christophergandrud/Rep-Res-Examples/master/DataGather_Merge/MainData.csv`

```
# Create a scatterplot matrix
pairs(x = SubData)
```

This is a lot of code, but you should be familiar with most of it. You will notice that after downloading the data we cleaned it up in preparation for plotting with the `pairs` command by removing data from all years other than 2003 and all of the country-year identifying variables. Finally, we created the scatterplot matrix with `pairs`.

To dynamically include the plot in our final document, we don't need to include all of this code in a code chunk in our markup document. A file containing the code is available on GitHub.[16] So we only need to use `source_url` to link to it. I've shortened the raw source code file's URL to: `http://bit.ly/TEOgTc`. Let's look at the syntax for knitting this into an R Markdown file:

```
### Scatterplot Matrix Created from MainData.csv
```{r, echo=FALSE, warning=FALSE, message=FALSE, out.width='500px', out.height='500px'}
# Create scatterplot matrix from MainData.csv
devtools::source_url("http://bit.ly/TEOgTc")
```
```

This code creates the plot that we see in Figure 10.3. Because we have linked all the way back to the original data set *MainData.csv*, any time it is updated by the makefile, the update will automatically cascade all the way through to our final presentation document the next time we knit it.

10.4 Including *ggplot2* Graphics

The *ggplot2* package[17] (Wickham and Chang, 2015b) is probably one of the most popular recent developments in R graphics. It greatly expands the aesthetic and substantive tools R has for displaying quantitative information. Figures created with *ggplot2* are (generally) static,[18] so they are included in knitted documents the same way as most of R's default graphics.

There are a number of very good resources for learning how to use *ggplot2*. These include Hadley Wickham's *ggplot2* book (2009) and article (2010). The

[16] See: `https://raw.githubusercontent.com/christophergandrud/Rep-Res-Examples/master/Graphs/ScatterPlotMatrix.R`.

[17] "GG" stands for grammar of graphics and "2" indicates that it is the second major version of the package.

[18] It is possible to combine a series of figures created with *ggplot2* into an animation. For a nice example of an animation using *ggplot2* see Jerzy Wieczorek's animation of 2012 US presidential campaigning: `http://bit.ly/UUVKka`.

FIGURE 10.3
Example of a Scatterplot Matrix in a Markdown Document

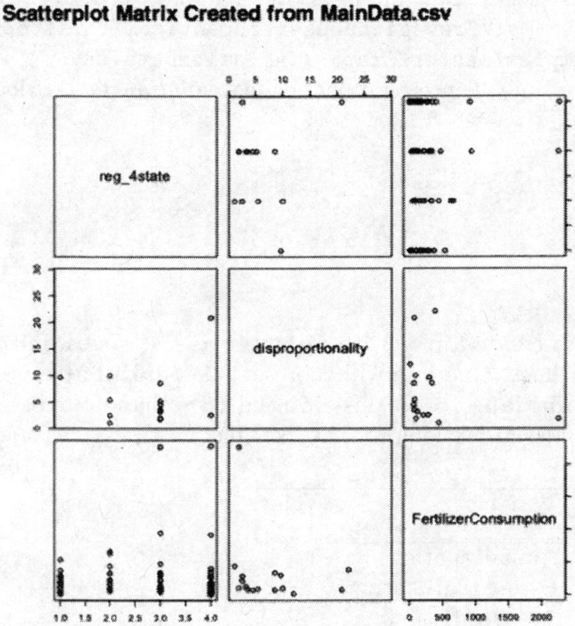

official *ggplot2* website[19] has up-to-date information. I've also found the Cookbook for R website helpful.[20]

Given that there is already extensive good documentation on *ggplot2* we are not going to learn the full details of how to use the package here. Instead, let's look at some examples of how to manipulate a data frame and a regression results object so that they can be graphed with *ggplot2*. First we will create a multi-line time series plot. Then we will create a caterpillar plot of regression results. Along with giving you a general sense of how *ggplot2* works, the examples illuminate how *ggplot2* can be made part of a fully reproducible research workflow.[21]

Sometimes we may want to show how multiple variables change together overtime. For example, imagine we have data on inflation in the United States along with inflation forecasts made by the US Federal Reserve two quarters beforehand. The data is stored on GitHub at: `https://raw.githubusercontent.com/christophergandrud/Rep-Res-Examples/master/Graphs/InflationData.csv`.[22] I've loaded the data into R and put it into an object called *InflationData*. It looks like this:

```
names(InflationData)

## [1] "Quarter"              "ActualInflation"    "EstimatedInflation"
```

We want to create a plot with **Quarter** as the x axis, inflation as the y axis, and two lines. One line will represent **ActualInflation** and the other **EstimatedInflation**. To do this we need to reshape our data so that the inflation variables are in long format like this:

Quarter	Variable	Value
1969.1	ActualInflation	
1969.1	EstimatedInflation	
1969.2	ActualInflation	
1969.2	EstimatedInflation	
...		

We can use the `gather` command from *tidyr* that we first saw in Chapter 7 (Section 7.1.2) to reshape the data. The variable identifying the observations

[19]`http://docs.ggplot2.org/current/`

[20]`http://wiki.stdout.org/rcookbook/Graphs/`

[21]Note that everything we do here with *ggplot2* can also be done with R's default graphics, though the appearance will be different.

[22]This data is from Gandrud and Grafström (2015). The example here partially recreates Figure 1 from that paper.

in this case is `Quarter`. The **ActualInflation** and **EstimatedInflation** variables (in columns two and three) are the variables that we want to gather. So let's gather the data:

```
# Load tidyr
library(tidyr)

# Gather InflationData
GatheredInflation <- gather(InflationData, variable,
                            value, 2:3)

# Show GatheredInflation variables
head(GatheredInflation)

##   Quarter        variable value
## 1  1969.1 ActualInflation    NA
## 2  1969.2 ActualInflation   3.5
## 3  1969.3 ActualInflation   3.5
## 4  1969.4 ActualInflation   3.3
## 5  1970.1 ActualInflation   3.7
## 6  1970.2 ActualInflation   3.7
```

Now we have a data set we can use to create our line graph with *ggplot2*.

Let's cover a few basic *ggplot2* ideas that will help us understand the following code better. First, plots are composed of layers including the coordinate system, points, labels, and so on. Each layer has aesthetics, including the variables plotted on the x and y axes, label sizes, colors, and shapes. Aesthetic elements are defined by the `aes` argument. Finally, the main layer types are called geometrics, including lines, points, bars, and text. Commands that set geometrics usually begin with `geom`. For example, the geometric to create lines is `geom_line`.

```
# Load ggplot2
library(ggplot2)

# Create plot
LinePlot <- ggplot(data = GatheredInflation, aes(x = Quarter,
                                                 y = value,
                                                 color = variable,
                                                 linetype = variable)) +
                  geom_line() +
                  scale_color_discrete(name = "", labels = c("Actual",
                                                            "Estimated")) +
```

```
                scale_linetype(name = "", labels = c("Actual",
                                                     "Estimated")) +
                xlab("\n Quarter") + ylab("Inflation\n") +
                theme_bw(base_size = 15)

# Print plot
print(LinePlot)
```

You can see we set the x and y axes using the **Quarter** and **value** variables. We told *ggplot* that elements in the geometric layer should have lines with different colors and line types (dashed, dotted, and so on) based on the value of **variable** that they represent. `geom_line` specifies that we want to add a line geometric layer.[23] `scale_color_discrete` and `scale_linetype` are used here to hide the plot's legend title with `name = ""` and customize the legend's labels with `labels = . . .`. You can also use them to determine the specific colors and line types you would like to use. `xlab` and `ylab` set the axes' labels. You can add a title with `ggtitle`. Finally, I added `theme_bw` so that the plot would use a simple black-and-white theme. We added the argument `base_size = 15` to increase the plot's font size.

All of the code required to create this graph is on GitHub at: `http://bit.ly/VEvGJG`.[24] So to knit the graph like Figure 10.4 into an R Sweave-style LaTeX document we type:

```
\begin{figure}[ht]
    \caption{Example Multi-line Time Series Plot Created with \emph{ggplot2}}
    \label{ggplot2Line}
        \begin{center}
<<echo=FALSE, message=FALSE, warning=FALSE, out.width='10cm', out.height='8cm'>>=
# Create plot
devtools::source_url("http://bit.ly/VEvGJG")
@
        \end{center}
\end{figure}
```

The syntax for including this and other *ggplot2* figures in an R Markdown document is the same as we saw for default R graphics.

10.4.1 Showing regression results with caterpillar plots

Many packages that estimate statistical models from data in R have built-in plotting capabilities. For example, the *survival* package (Therneau, 2015) has

[23]Remember from Chapter 3 that commands must be followed by parentheses. These layers are commands so they need to be followed by parentheses.

[24]The full URL is: `https://raw.githubusercontent.com/christophergandrud/Rep-Res-Examples/master/Graphs/InflationLineGraph.R`.

FIGURE 10.4
Example Multi-line Time Series Plot Created with *ggplot2*

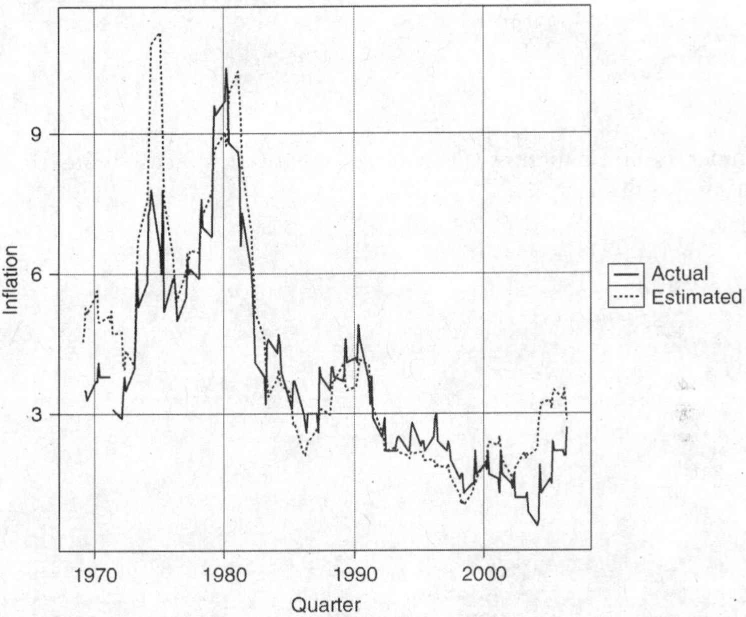

a `plot.survfit` command for plotting survival curves created using event history analysis. These plots can Of course, be knitted into presentation documents like the plots we have seen already.

However, sometimes either a package doesn't have built-in commands for plotting model results the way you want to and/or you want to use *ggplot2* to improve the aesthetic quality of the plots they do create by default. In either case you can almost always create the plot that you want by first breaking into the model results object, extracting what you want, then plotting it with *ggplot2*. The process is very similar to what we did in Chapter 9 to create custom tables (see Section 9.3.5).

To illustrate how this can work, let's create a caterpillar plot, like Figure 10.5, showing the mean coefficient estimates and the uncertainty surrounding them from a Bayesian normal linear regression model using the *swiss* data frame. Here is our model:

```
# Load Zelig package
library(Zelig)

# Estimate model
```

```
NBModel2 <- zelig(Examination ~ Education + Agriculture +
                  Catholic + Infant.Mortality,
                  model = "normal.bayes",
                  data = swiss, cite = FALSE)
```

Remember from Chapter 9 that we can create an object summarizing our estimation results like this:

```
# Create summary object
NBModel2Sum <- summary(NBModel2)

# Create summary data frame
NBSum2DF <- data.frame(NBModel2Sum$summary)

# Show data frame
NBSum2DF

##                          Mean         SD      X2.5.          X50.
## (Intercept)       18.646073922 5.92866455  7.0304647 18.650330129
## Education          0.424875818 0.09096933  0.2425198  0.425472599
## Agriculture       -0.067268833 0.04251411 -0.1514878 -0.067515362
## Catholic          -0.079682496 0.01807005 -0.1152748 -0.079836855
## Infant.Mortality -0.007320696 0.23553784 -0.4687978 -0.009074999
## sigma2            19.895381339 4.56803021 12.8441084 19.254808241
##                        X97.5.
## (Intercept)       30.42487387
## Education          0.60039594
## Agriculture        0.01549064
## Catholic          -0.04403703
## Infant.Mortality  0.45926573
## sigma2            30.69690658
```

We want to use *ggplot2* to create credibility intervals for each variable with **X2.5.** as the minimum value and **X97.5.** as the maximum value. These are the lower and upper bounds of the middle 95 percent of the estimates' marginal posterior distributions, i.e. the 95 percent credibility intervals.[25] We will also create a point at the **mean** of each estimate. To do this we will use *ggplot2*'s `geom_pointrange` command.

[25]The procedures used here are also generally applicable for graphing frequentist confidence intervals once you have calculated the confidence intervals. One useful command for doing this is `confint`.

First we need to do a little tidying up.

```
# Convert row.names to normal variable
NBSum2DF$Variable <- row.names(NBSum2DF)

# Keep only coefficient estimates
## This allows for a more interpretable scale
NBSum2DF <- subset(NBSum2DF, Variable != "(Intercept)")
NBSum2DF <- subset(NBSum2DF, Variable != "sigma2")
```

The first line of executable code creates a proper variable out of the data frame's row.names attribute. In this case row.names contains the names of the variables included in the regression. The second and third executable lines remove the estimates *(Intercept)* and *sigma2*. This allows the variable's coefficient estimates to be plotted on a scale that enables easier interpretation.

Now we can create our caterpillar plot.

```
# Load ggplot2
library(ggplot2)

# Make caterpillar plot
ggplot(data = NBSum2DF, aes(x = reorder(Variable, X2.5.),
                            y = Mean,
                            ymin = X2.5., ymax = X97.5.)) +
       geom_pointrange(size = 1.4) +
       geom_hline(aes(intercept= 0), linetype = "dotted") +
       xlab("Variable\n") + ylab("\n Coefficient Estimate") +
       coord_flip() +
       theme_bw(base_size = 20)
```

There are some new pieces of code in here, so let's take a look. First, the data frame is reordered from the highest to lowest value of **X2.5.** using the `reorder` command. This makes the plot easier to read. The middle point of the point range is set with `y` and the lower and upper bounds with `ymin` and `ymax`. The `geom_hline` command used here creates a dotted horizontal line at 0, i.e. no effect. `coord_flip` flips the plot's coordinates so that the variable names are on the y axis. We can include this plot in a knitted document the same way as before.

FIGURE 10.5
An Example Caterpillar Plot Created with *ggplot2*

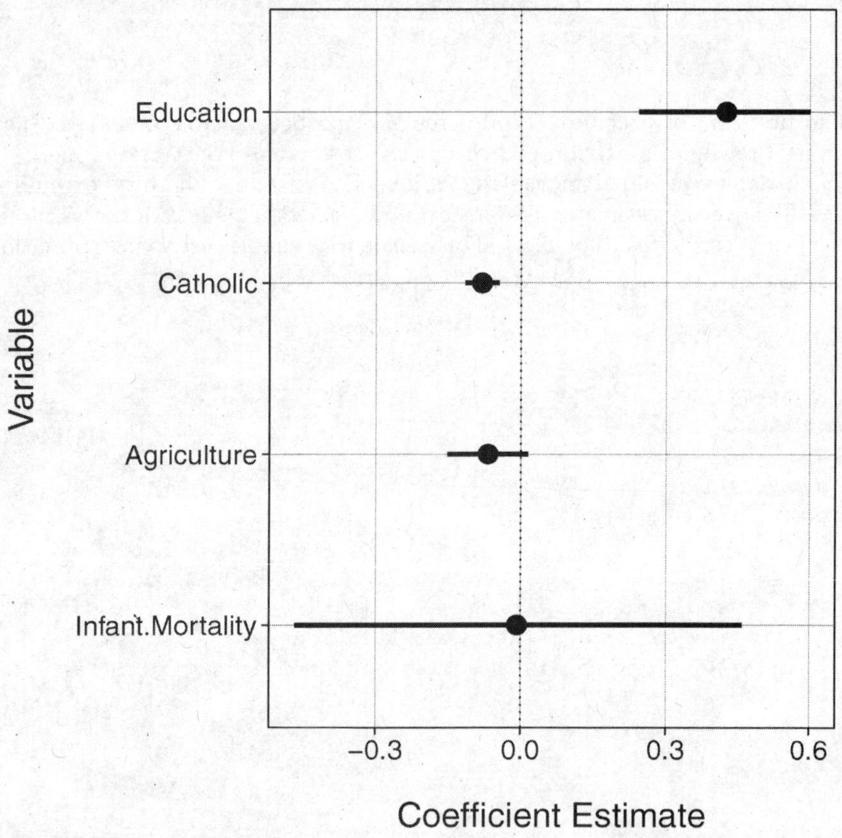

10.5 JavaScript Graphs with *googleVis*

Markus Gesmann and Diego de Castillo's *googleVis* package (2015) allows us to use Google's Visualization API from within R to create interactive tables, plots, and maps with Google Chart Tools. Because the visualizations are written in JavaScript they can be included in HTML presentation documents created by R Markdown. Unfortunately, they cannot be directly[26] included in LaTeX-produced PDFs. The *animation* package (Xie, 2014) does have some limited features for including interactive visualizations in PDFs (as well as HTML documents) and is worth investigating if you want to do this.

Basic googleVis figures

Let's briefly look at how to make one type of figure with *googleVis*: a choropleth map. This is created with the `gvisGeoChart` function. We will use this example to illustrate how to incorporate *googleVis* figures into R Markdown.[27]

Imagine that we want to map global fertilizer consumption in 2003 using the World Bank data we gathered in Chapter 6. Remember that the data was highly right skewed, so we will actually map the natural logarithm of the **FertilizerConsumption** variable.[28] Assuming that we have already loaded the *MainData.csv* data set, here is the code:

```
# Load googleVis
library(googleVis)

# Subset MainData so that it only includes 2003
SubData <- subset(MainData, year == 2003)

# Keep values of FertilizerConsumption greater-than 0.1
SubData <- subset(SubData, FertilizerConsumption > 0.1)

# Find the natural logarithm of FertilizerConsumption.
## Round the results to one decimal digit.
SubData$LogConsumption <- round(log(SubData$FertilizerConsumption),
                                digits = 1)

# Make a map of Fertilizer Consumption
```

[26]The example in this chapter is a from a screenshot.

[27]For demonstrations of the full range of plotting functions available, visit the *googleVis* website: `http://code.google.com/p/google-motion-charts-with-r/wiki/GadgetExamples#googleVis_Examples`.

[28]You'll notice in the code below that we remove all values of **FertilizerConsumption** less-than 0.1. This is so that we can calculate integer values with the natural logarithm. See Section 7.1.7 for more details.

```
FCMap <- gvisGeoChart(data = SubData,
                locationvar = "iso2c",
                colorvar = "LogConsumption",
                options = list(
                    colors = "['#ECE7F2', '#A6BDDB', '#2B8CBE']",
                    width = "780px",
                    height = "500px"))
```

The `locationvar` argument specifies the variable with information on each observation's location. Google Chart Tools can use ISO two-letter country codes to determine each country's location. `colorvar` specifies the variable with the values to map for each country. We can determine other options by creating a list-type object with arguments specifying characteristics such as the map's width, height, and colors. The colors here are written using hexadecimal values. This is a commonly used format for specifying colors on websites.[29]

To view the figure on your computer simply use *googleVis*'s `plot` command. For example, to view our map we type:

```
plot(FCMap)
```

Note that you need to be connected to the internet to view figures created by *googleVis*, otherwise your image will not be able to access the required JavaScript files from the Google Visualization API.

Including googleVis *in knitted documents*

Typing `print(FCMap, tag = "chart")` in a knittable document would print the entire JavaScript code needed to create the map. Much like we saw with tables produced with *xtable* and *texreg* in Chapter 9, we need to change the code chunk `results` option to include the map as a map rather than as JavaScript markup. To have the visualization show up in your HTML output, rather than the code block, simply set the code chunk option to `results='asis'`.[30] For example, the full code needed to create and print *FCMap* is available at:

[29] You can also use hexadecimal values in *ggplot2*. The Color Brewer 2 website (`http://colorbrewer2.org/`) is very helpful for picking hexadecimal color palettes, among others.

[30] You can use `results='asis'` to include almost any type of JavaScript graphics. For an example using the D3 JavaScript library and *knitr* see this page by Yihui Xie: `http://yihui.name/knitr/demo/javascript/`.

FIGURE 10.6
Screenshot of a *googleVis* Geo Chart

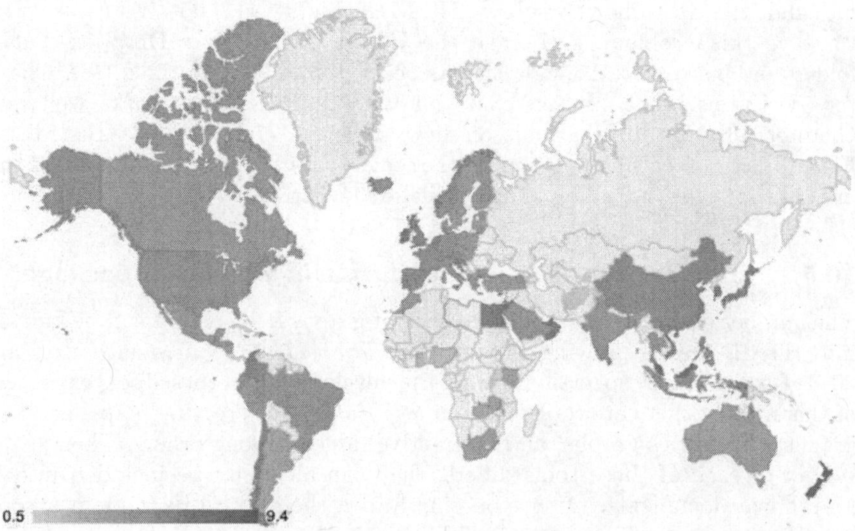

http://bit.ly/VNnZxS.[31] To knit the map into an R Markdown document we type:

```
```{r, echo=FALSE, message=FALSE, results='asis'}
# Create and print geo map
devtools::source_url("http://bit.ly/VNnZxS")
```
```

Note for Motion Charts

You may notice that Google motion charts[32] do not show up in the RStudio **Preview HTML** window or even in your web browser when you open the knitted HTML version of the file. You just see a big blank space where you had hoped the chart would be. It will show up, however, if you use the `plot` command on a `gvis` motion chart object in the console. Motion charts can only

[31]The full URL is: `https://raw.githubusercontent.com/christophergandrud/Rep-Res-Examples/master/Graphs/GoogleVisMap.R`.

[32]You can use the `gvisMotionChart` command to make these.

be displayed when they are hosted on a web server or located in a directory 'trusted' by Flash Player.[33]

The `plot` command opens a local server, but simply opening the HTML file and the RStudio **Preview HTML** window do not. An easy way to solve this problem is to save the HTML file in your Dropbox *Public* folder and access it through the associated public URL link (see Chapter 5). Publishing a motion chart on GitHub Pages also works well (see Chapter 13). For information on how to set a directory as 'trusted' by Flash Player see: `http://www.macromedia.com/support/documentation/en/flashplayer/help/settings_manager04.html`.

10.5.1 JavaScript Graphs with *htmlwidgets*-based packages

The number of tools for creating JavaScript graphs from R that can be knitted into HTML files is growing rapidly. The *htmlwidgets* (Vaidyanathan et al., 2014) framework is especially making the development of these tools easier. As of this writing there are tools built on *htmlwidgets* for creating maps, network graphs, time series graphs, and interactive tables, among others. Though the syntax of each of these tools differs, they can all easily be included into R Markdown documents. Often you simply run their core functions in a code chunk, without needing to use an additional call to `print` or `plot`.

Chapter summary

In this chapter we have learned how to take results from our statistical analyses and other information from our data and dynamically present them in figures. In the next three chapters we will learn the details of how to create the LaTeX and Markdown presentation documents we use to present the tables we created in Chapter 9 and the figures we created in this chapter.

[33]This is because motion charts and annotated time line charts rely on Flash, unlike the other Google visualizations. For more information see Markus Gesmann's blog post at: `http://www.magesblog.com/2012/05/interactive-reports-in-r-with-knitr-and.html`.

Part IV

Presentation Documents

11

Presenting with knitr/*LaTeX*

We have already begun to see how LaTeX works for presenting research results. This chapter gives you a more detailed and comprehensive introduction to basic LaTeX document structures and commands. It is not a complete introduction to all that LaTeX is capable of, but we will cover enough that you will be able to create an entire well-formatted article and slideshow with LaTeX that you can use to dynamically present your results. In the next chapter (Chapter 12) we will build on these skills by learning how to use *knitr* to create more complex LaTeX documents.

For basic LaTeX documents, such as short articles or simple presentations, it may often be quicker and simpler to write the markup using an R Markdown document and compile it to PDF with the *rmarkdown* package. As we will see in Chapter 13, Markdown syntax is much simpler than normal LaTeX. However, there are at least two reasons why it is useful to become familiar with LaTeX syntax. First, understanding LaTeX syntax will help you debug issues you might encounter when using *rmarkdown* with LaTeX that would otherwise be mysterious if you were only familiar with Markdown. Second, R Markdown has limited capabilities for creating more complex documents such as books and documents with highly customizable formatting needs. Using *kntr* and LaTeX can be useful in these situations.

In this chapter we will learn about basic LaTeX document structures and syntax as well as how to dynamically create LaTeX bibliographies with BibTeX, R, and *knitr*. Finally, we will look at how to create PDF beamer slideshows with LaTeX and *knitr*.

Note: Chapter 11 and the following chapter are unusual for this book in that they do not refer to both *knitr* and *rmarkdown*. Instead they focus on capabilities largely exclusive to *knitr*.

11.1 The Basics

In this section we will look at how to create a LaTeX article including what editor programs to use, the basic structure of a LaTeX document, including preamble and body, LaTeX syntax for creating headings, paragraphs, lines, text formatting, math, lists, footnotes, and cross-references. I will assume that you already have a fully functioning TeX distribution installed on your computer. See Section 1.5.1 for information on how to install TeX.

11.1.1 Getting started with LaTeX editors

As I mentioned earlier, RStudio is a fully functional LaTeX editor in addition to being an integrated development environment for R. If you want to create a new LaTeX document you can click `File` in the menu bar then `New` → `R Sweave`.

Remember from Chapter 3 that R Sweave files are basically LaTeX files that can include *knitr* code chunks. You can use RStudio to knit and compile a document with the click of one button: **Compile PDF** (Compile PDF). You can use this button to compile R Sweave files like regular LaTeX files in RStudio even if they do not have code chunks. If you use another program to compile them you might need to change the file extension from `.Rnw` to `.tex`. You can also insert many of the items we will cover in this section into your documents with RStudio's LaTeX `TeX Format` button. See Figure 11.1.

FIGURE 11.1
RStudio TeX Format Options

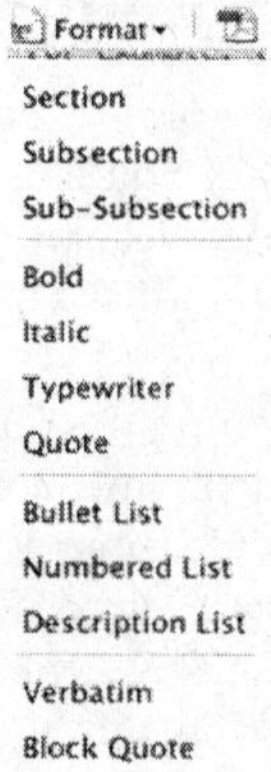

There are many other LaTeX editors[1] and many text editors that can be modified to compile LaTeX documents. For example, alongside writing this book in RStudio, I typed much of the LaTeX markup in the Sublime Text[2] text editor. None of these options have RStudio's high-level integration with *knitr*, however.[3]

If you are new to LaTeX you may be more comfortably using Lyx. Lyx has a Microsoft Word-type interface, but creates actual LaTeX documents. It also has *knitr* integration. See Chapter 3's Appendix for how to set up and use *knitr* and Lyx.

11.1.2 Basic LaTeX command syntax

As you probably noticed in Part III's examples, LaTeX commands start with a backslash (\). For example, to create a section heading you use the `\section` command. The arguments for LaTeX commands are written inside of curly braces (`{}`) like this:

[1] Wikipedia has collated a table that comprehensively compares many of these editors: `http://en.wikipedia.org/wiki/List_of_text_editors`.

[2] http://www.sublimetext.com/

[3] Andrew Wheiss has created a Sublime Text plugin called *KnitrSublime*. It enables some R LaTeX integration. For more details see: `https://GitHub.com/andrewheiss/KnitrSublime`.

```
\section{My Section Name}
```

Probably one of the biggest sources of errors that occur when compiling a LaTeX document to PDF are caused by curly brackets that aren't closed, i.e. an open bracket ({) is not matched with a subsequent closed bracket (}). Watch out for this and use an editor (like RStudio) that highlights brackets' matching pairs. As we will see, unlike in R with parentheses, if your LaTeX command does not have an argument you do not need to include the curly brackets at all.

There are a number of places to find comprehensive lists of LaTeX commands. The Netherlands TeX users group has compiled one: `http://www.ntg.nl/doc/biemesderfer/ltxcrib.pdf`.

11.1.3 The LaTeX preamble & body

All LaTeX documents require a preamble. The preamble goes at the very beginning of the document. The preamble usually starts with the `documentclass` command. This specifies what type of presentation document you are creating–e.g. an article, a book, a slideshow,[4] and so on. LaTeX refers to these as classes. Classes specify a document's formatting. You can add options to `documentclass` to change the format of the entire document. For example, if we wanted to create an article class document with two columns we would type:

```
\documentclass[twocolumn]{article}
```

In the preamble you can also specify other style options and load any extra packages you may want to use.[5]

The preamble is often followed by the body of your document. It is specified with the `body` environment. See Chapter 9 (Section 9.2.1) for more details about LaTeX environments. You tell LaTeX where the body of your document starts by typing `\begin{document}`. The very last line of your document is usually `\end{document}`, indicating that your document has ended. When you open a new R Sweave file in RStudio it creates an article class document with a very simple preamble and body like this:

[4] "Slideshow" is not a valid class. One slideshow class that we discuss later is called "beamer".

[5] The command to load a package in LaTeX is `\usepackage`. For example, if you include `\usepackage{url}` in the preamble of your document you will be able to specify URL links in the body with the command `\url{SOMEURL}`.

```
\documentclass{article}

\begin{document}



\end{document}
```

This is all you need to get a very basic article class document working. If you want the document to be of another class, simply change `article` to something else, a `book` for example.

Let's begin to modify the markup. First we will include in the preamble the (`hyperref`) for clickable hyperlinks and `natbib` for bibliography formatting. We will discuss `natbib` in more detail below. Note that in general, and unlike in R, almost all of the LaTeX packages you will use are installed on your computer when you installed the TeX distribution.

Next, it's often a good idea to include *knitr* code chunks that specify features of the document as a whole. These can include global chunk options as well as loading data and packages used throughout the document.

Then it's a good idea to specify title information just after the `document` environment begins. Use the `title` command to add a title, the `author` command to add author information, and `date` to specify the date.[6] Then include the `maketitle` command. This will place your title and author information in the body of the document. If you are writing an article you may also want to follow `maketitle` with an abstract. Unsurprisingly, you can use the `abstract` environment to include this.

Here is a full LaTeX article class document with all of these changes added:

```
%%%%%%%%%%%%%  Article Preamble %%%%%%%%%%%%%
\documentclass{article}

%%%% Load LaTeX packages
\usepackage{hyperref}
\usepackage[authoryear]{natbib}

%%%% Set knitr global options and gather data
<<Global, include=FALSE>>=
#### Set chunk options ####
opts_chunk$set(fig.align='center')

#### Load and cite R packages ####
```

[6]In some document classes the current data will automatically be included if you don't specify the date.

```
# Create list of packages
PackagesUsed <- c("knitr", "ggplot2", "repmis")

# Load PackagesUsed and create .bib BibTeX file
# Note must have repmis package installed.
repmis::LoadandCite(PackagesUsed, file = "Packages.bib", install = FALSE)

#### Gather Democracy data from Pemstein et al. (2010) ####
# For simplicity, store the URL in an object called 'url'.
url <- "http://bit.ly/1jXJgDh"

# Create a temporary file called 'temp' to put the zip file into.
temp <- tempfile()

# Download the compressed file into the temporary file.
download.file(url, temp)

# Decompress the file and convert it into a data frame
# class object called 'data'.
UDSData <- read.csv(gzfile(temp, "uds_summary.csv"))

# Delete the temporary file.
unlink(temp)

@

%%%% Start document body
\begin{document}

%%%%%%%%%%%% Create title %%%%%%%%%%%%%%%
\title{An Example knitr LaTeX Article}
\author{Christopher Gandrud \\
Hertie School of Governance\thanks{Email: \href{mailto:gandrud@hertie-school.org}
{gandrud@hertie-school.org}}}
\date{January 2015}
\maketitle

%%%%%%%%%%%% Abstract %%%%%%%%%%%%%%%%%%
\begin{abstract}
  Here is an example of a knittable article class LaTeX document.
\end{abstract}

%%%%%%%%%%% Article Main Text %%%%%%%%%%%%
\section{The Graph}

I gathered data from \cite{Pemstein2010} on countries' democracy level. They call their
democracy measure the Unified Democracy Score (UDS). Figure \ref{DemPlot} shows the mean
UDS scores over time for all of the countries in their sample.

\begin{figure}
    \caption{Mean UDS Scores}
    \label{DemPlot}
<<echo=FALSE, message=FALSE, warning=FALSE, out.width='7cm', out.height='7cm'>>=
# Graph UDS scores
ggplot(UDSData, aes(x = year, y = mean)) +
    geom_point(alpha = I(0.1)) +
    stat_smooth(size = 2) +
    ylab("Democracy Score") + xlab("") +
    theme_bw()
@
\end{figure}

%%%%%%%%%%% Reproducing the Document %%%%%
```

```
\section{Appendix: Reproducing the Document}

This document was created using R version
\Sexpr{paste0(version$major, ".", version$minor)}
and the R package \emph{knitr}
\citep{R-knitr}. It also relied on the R packages
\emph{ggplot2} \citep{R-ggplot2} and \emph{repmis} \citep{R-repmis}.
The document can be completely reproduced from
source files available on GitHub at:
\url{https://GitHub.com/christophergandrud/Rep-Res-Examples}.

%%%%%%%% Bibliography %%%%%%%%%%%%%%%%%%
\bibliographystyle{apa}
\bibliography{Main.bib,Packages.bib}

\end{document}
```

The *knitr* code chunk syntax should be familiar to you from previous chapters, so let's unpack the LaTeX syntax from just after the first code chunk, including the "Create Title" and "Abstract" parts. New syntax shown in later parts of this example is discussed in the remainder of this section and the next section on bibliographies.

First, remember that the percent sign (%) is LaTeX's comment character. Using it to comment your markup can make it easier to read. Second, as we saw in Chapter 9 (Section 9.2.1), double backslashes (\\), like those after the author's name, force a new line in LaTeX. We will discuss the `emph` command in a moment. Third, using the `thanks` command allows us to create a footnote for author contact information[7] that is not numbered like the other footnotes (see below). Finally, you'll notice `\href{mailto: . . . . .org}}`. This creates an email address in the final document that will open the reader's default email program when clicked.

Finally, you may have noticed the following line:

```
\Sexpr{paste0(version$major, ".", version$minor)}
```

This code finds the current version of R being used and prints the version number into the presentation document.

11.1.4 Headings

Earlier in the chapter we briefly saw how to create section-level headings with `section`. There are a number of other sub-section-level headings including `subsection`, `subsubsection`, `paragraph`, and `subparagraph`. Headers are

[7]Frequently it also includes thank-yous to people who have helped the research.

numbered automatically by LaTeX.[8] To have an unnumbered section, place an asterisk in it like this: `\section*{Unnumbered Section}`. In book class documents you can also use `chapter` to create new chapters and `part` for collections of chapters.

11.1.5 Paragraphs & spacing

In LaTeX, paragraphs are simply created by adding a blank line between lines. It will format all of the tabs for the beginning of paragraphs based on the document's class rules. As we discussed before, writing tabs in the markup version of your document does nothing in the compiled document. They are generally used just to make the markup easier for people to read.

Note that adding more blank lines between paragraphs will not add extra space between the paragraphs in the final document. To specify the space following paragraphs (or almost any line) use the `vspace` (vertical space) command. For example, to add three centimeters of vertical space on a page type: `\vspace{3cm}`. This gives us the following space:

Similarly, adding extra spaces between words in your LaTeX markup won't create extra spaces between words in the compiled document. To add horizontal space use the `hspace` command in the same way as `vspace`.

11.1.6 Horizontal lines

Use the `hrulefill` command to create horizontal lines in the text of your document. For example, `\hrulefill` creates:

Inside of a `tabular` environment, use the `hline` command rather than `hrulefill`.

11.1.7 Text formatting

Let's briefly look at how to do some of the more common types of text formatting in LaTeX and how to create some commonly used diacritics and special characters.

[8] The `paragraph` level does not have numbers.

TABLE 11.1
LaTeX Font Size Commands

Huge
huge
LARGE
Large
large
normalsize
small
footnotesize
scriptsize
tiny

Italics & Bold

To italicize a word in LaTeX use the `emph` (emphasis) command. For bold use `textbf`. You can nest commands inside of one another to combine their effect. For example, to ***italicize and bold*** a word use: `\emph{textbf{italicize and bold}}`.

Font size

You can specify the base font size of an entire document with a `documentclass` option. For example, to create an article with 12-point font use: `\documentclass[12pt]{article}`.

There are a number of commands to set the size of specific pieces of text relative to the base size. See Table 11.1 for the full list. Usually a slightly different syntax is used for these commands that goes like this: `{\SIZE_COMMAND . . . }`. For example, to use the tiny size in your text use: `{\tiny{tiny size}}`.

You can change the size of code chunks that *knitr* places in presentation documents using these commands. Just place the code chunk inside of `{\SIZE_COMMAND . . . }`. This is similar to using the `size` code chunk option.

Diacritics

You cannot directly enter letters with diacritics–e.g. accent mark–into LaTeX. For example, to create a letter c with a cedilla (ç) you need to type `\c{c}`. To create an ‘a’ with an acute accent (á) type: `\'{a}`. There are obviously many types of diacritics and commands to include them within

LaTeX-produced documents. For a comprehensive discussion of the issue and a list of commands see the LaTeX Wikibook page on the topic: `http://en.wikibooks.org/wiki/LaTeX/Special_Characters`. If you regularly use non-English alphabets you might also be interested in reading the LaTeX Wikibook page on on internationalization: `http://en.wikibooks.org/wiki/LaTeX/Internationalization`.

Quotation marks

To specify double left quotation marks (“) use two back ticks (``` `` ```). For double right quotes (”) use two apostrophes (`''`). Single quotes follow the same format (`` `' ``).

11.1.8 Math

LaTeX is particularly popular among quantitative researchers and mathematicians because it is very good at rendering mathematics. A complete listing of every math command would take up quite a bit of space.[9] I am briefly going to discuss how to include math in a LaTeX document. This discussion includes a few math syntax examples.

To include math inline with your text, place the math syntax in between backslashes and parentheses, i.e. `\( . . . \)`. For example, `\( s^{2} = \frac{\sum(x - \bar{x})^2}{n - 1} \)` produces $s^2 = \frac{\sum(x-\bar{x})^2}{n-1}$ in our final document.[10] We can display math separately from the text by placing the math commands inside of backslashes and square brackets: `\[ . . . \]`.[11] For example,

```
\[
s^{2} = \frac{\sum(x - \bar{x})^2}{n - 1}
\]
```

gives us:

$$s^2 = \frac{\sum(x - \bar{x})^2}{n - 1}$$

[9]See the Netherlands TeX user group list mentioned earlier for an extensive compilation of math commands.

[10]Instead of backslashes and parentheses you can also use a pair of dollar signs (`$...$`).

[11]Equivalently, use two pairs of dollar signs (`$$...$$`) or the `display` environment. Though it will still work in most cases, the double dollar sign math syntax may cause errors. You can also number display equations using the `equation` environment.

11.1.9 Lists

To create bullet lists in LaTeX use the `itemize` environment. Each list item is delimited with the `item` command. For example:

```
\begin{itemize}
    \item The first item.
    \item The second item.
    \item The third item.
\end{itemize}
```

gives us:

- The first item.
- The second item.
- The third item.

To create a numbered list use the `enumerate` environment instead of `itemize`. You can create sublists simply by nesting lists inside of lists like this:

```
\begin{itemize}
    \item The first item.
    \item The second item.
    \begin{itemize}
        \item A sublist item
    \end{itemize}
    \item The third item.
\end{itemize}
```

which gives us:

- The first item.
- The second item.
    - A sublist item
- The third item.

11.1.10 Footnotes

Plain, non-bibliographic footnotes are easy to create in LaTeX. Simply place `\footnote{` where you would like the footnote number to appear in the text. Then type the footnote's text. Of course, remember to close the footnote with a `}`. LaTeX does the rest, including formatting and numbering.

11.1.11 Cross-references

LaTeX will also automatically format cross-references. We were already partially introduced to cross-references in chapters 9 and 10. At the place where you would like to reference, add a `label` such as `\label{ACrossRefLabel}`. It doesn't really matter what label you choose, though make sure they are not duplicated in the document. Also, it can be a good idea to use the same conventions that we learned for labeling R objects (see Section 3.1.1). Then place a `ref` command (e.g. `\ref{ACrossRefLabel}`) at the place in the text where you want the cross-reference to be.

If you place the `label` on the same line as a heading command, `ref` will place the heading number. If `label` is in a `table` or `figure` environment you will get the table or figure number. You can also use `pageref` instead of `ref` to include the page number. Finally, loading the *hyperref* package makes cross-references (or footnote) clickable. Clicking on them will take you to the items they refer to.

11.2 Bibliographies with BibTeX

LaTeX can take advantage of very comprehensive bibliography-making capabilities. All major TeX distributions come with BibTeX. BibTeX is basically a tool for creating databases of citation information. In this section, we are going to see how to incorporate a BibTeX bibliography into your LaTeX documents. Then we will learn how use R to automatically generate a bibliography of packages used to create a knitted document. For more information on BibTeX syntax see the LaTeX Wikibook page on Bibliography management: `http://en.wikibooks.org/wiki/LaTeX/Bibliography_Management`.

11.2.1 The *.bib* file

BibTeX bibliographies are stored in plain-text files with the extension `.bib`. These files are databases of citations.[12] The syntax for each citation goes like this:

[12] The order of the citations does not matter.

```
@DOCUMENT_TYPE{CITE_KEY,
    title = {TITLE},
    author = {AUTHOR},
    . . . = {. . .}
}
```

DOCUMENT_TYPE specifies what type of document–article, book, webpage, and so on–the citation is for. This determines what items the citation can and needs to include. Then we have the CITE_KEY. This is the reference's label that you will use to include the citation in your presentation documents. We'll look more at this later in the section. Each citation must have a unique CITE_KEY. A common way to write these keys is to use the author's surname and the publication year, e.g. Donoho2009. The cite key is followed by the other citation attributes such as **author**, **title**, and **year**. These attributes all follow the same syntax: ATTRIBUTE = {. . .}.

It's worth taking a moment to discuss the syntax for the BibTeX author attribute. First, multiple author names are separated by **and**. Second, BibTeX assumes that the last word for each author is their surname. If you would like multiple words to be taken as the "surname" then enclose these words in curly brackets. If we wanted to cite the World Bank as an author we write {World Bank}; otherwise it will be formatted "Bank, World" in the presentation document.

Here is a complete BibTeX entry for Donoho et al. (2009):

```
@article{Donoho2009,
  author = {David L Donoho and Arian Maleki and Morteza
  Shahram and Inam Ur Rahman and Victoria Stodden},
  title = {Reproducible research in computational harmonic
    analysis},
  journal = {Computing in Science & Engineering},
  year = {2009},
  volume = {11},
  number = {1},
  pages = {8--18}
}
```

Each item of the entry must end in a comma, except the last one.[13]

11.2.2 Including citations in LaTeX documents

When you want to include citations from a BibTeX file in your LaTeX document you first use the `bibliography` command. For example, if the BibTeX file is called *Main.bib* and it is in the same directory as your markup document, then type: `\bibliography{Main.bib}`. You can use a bibliography stored in another directory; just include the appropriate file path information. Usually `bibliography` is placed right before `\end{document}` so that it appears at the end of the compiled presentation document.

You can also specify how you would like the references to be formatted using the `bibliographystyle` command. For example, this book uses the American Psychological Association (APA) style for references. To set this I included `\bibliographystyle{apa}` directly before `bibliography`. The default style[14] is to number citations (e.g. [1]) rather than include author-year information[15] used by the APA. You will need to include the LaTeX package *natbib* in your preamble to be able to use author-year citation styles. This book includes `\usepackage[authoryear]{natbib}` in its preamble.

Place the `cite` command in your document's text where you want to place a reference. You include the `CITE_KEY` for the reference in this command, e.g. `\cite{Donoho2009}`. You can include multiple citations in `cite`, just separate the `CITE_KEY`s with commas. You can add options such as the page numbers or other text to a citation using square brackets ([]). For example, if we wanted to cite the tenth page of Donoho et al. (2009) we type: `\cite[10]{Donoho2009}`. The author-year style in-text citation that this produces looks like this: (Donoho et al., 2009, 10). You can add text at the beginning of a citation with another set of square brackets. Typing `\cite[see][10]{Donoho2009}` gives us: (see Donoho et al., 2009, 10).

If you are using an author-year style you can use a variety of *natbib* commands to change what information is included in the parentheses. For a selection of these commands and examples, see Table 11.2.

11.2.3 Generating a BibTeX file of R package citations

Researchers are pretty good about citing others' articles and data. However, citations of R packages used in analyses is very inconsistent. This is unfortunate not only because correct attribution is not being given to those who worked to create the packages, but also because it makes reproducibility harder. Not citing packages obscures important steps that were taken in the research process, primarily which package versions were used. Fortunately, there are R

[13]This is very similar to how we create vectors in R, though in BibTeX you can actually have a comma after the last attribute.

[14]It is referred to in LaTeX as the plain style.

[15]This is sometimes referred to as the "Harvard" style.

TABLE 11.2
A Selection of *natbib* In-text Citation Style Commands

Command Example	Output
`\cite{Donoho2009}`	Donoho et al. (2009)
`\citep{Donoho2009}`	(Donoho et al., 2009)
`\citeauthor{Donoho2009}`	Donoho et al.
`\citeyear{Donoho2009}`	2009
`\citeyearpar{Donoho2009}`	(2009)

tools for quickly and dynamically generating package BibTeX files, including the versions of the packages you are using. They will automatically update the citations each time you compile your document to reflect any changes made to the packages.

You can automatically create citations for R packages using the `citation` command inside of a code chunk. For example, if you want the citation information for the `xtable` package you simply type:

```
citation("xtable")

##
## To cite package 'xtable' in publications use:
##
##   David B. Dahl (2014). xtable: Export tables to LaTeX or HTML. R
##   package version 1.7-4. http://CRAN.R-project.org/package=xtable
##
## A BibTeX entry for LaTeX users is
##
##   @Manual{,
##     title = {xtable: Export tables to LaTeX or HTML},
##     author = {David B. Dahl},
##     year = {2014},
##     note = {R package version 1.7-4},
##     url = {http://CRAN.R-project.org/package=xtable},
##   }
##
## ATTENTION: This citation information has been auto-generated from
## the package DESCRIPTION file and may need manual editing, see
## 'help("citation")'.
```

This gives you both the plain citation as well as the BibTeX version. If you only want the BibTeX version of the citation you can use the `toBibtex` command.

```
toBibtex(citation("xtable"))

## @Manual{,
##   title = {xtable: Export tables to LaTeX or HTML},
##   author = {David B. Dahl},
##   year = {2014},
##   note = {R package version 1.7-4},
##   url = {http://CRAN.R-project.org/package=xtable},
## }
```

The *knitr* package creates BibTeX bibliographies for R packages with the `write_bib` command. Let's make a BibTeX file called *Packages.bib* containing citation information for the *xtable* package.

```
# Create package BibTeX file
knitr::write_bib("xtable",
                 file = "Packages.bib")
```

`write_bib` automatically assigns each entry a cite key using the format `R-PACKAGE_NAME`, e.g. `R-xtable`.

Warning: *knitr*'s `write_bib` command currently does not have the ability to append package citations to an existing file, but instead writes them to a new file. If there is already a file with the same name, it will overwrite the file. So, be very careful using this command to avoid accidental deletions. It is a good idea to have `write_bib` always write to a file specifically for automatically generated package citations. You can include more than one bibliography in LaTeX's `bibliography` command. All you need to do is separate them with a comma.

```
\bibliography{Main.bib,Packages.bib}
```

We can use these techniques to automatically create a BibTeX file with citation information for all of the packages used in a research project. Simply make a character vector of the names of packages that you would like to include in your bibliography. Then run this through `write_bib`.

You can make sure you are citing all of the key packages used in a knitted document by (a) creating a vector of all of the packages and then (b) using this in the following code to both load the packages and write the bibliography:

```
# Package list
PackagesUsed <- c("ggplot2", "knitr",
                  "xtable", "Zelig")

# Load packages
lapply(PackagesUsed, library,
       character.only = TRUE)

# Create package BibTeX file
knitr::write_bib(PackagesUsed,
                 file = "Packages.bib")
```

In the first executable line we just create our list of packages to load and cite. The next command is `lapply` (list apply). This applies the function `library` to all of the items in *PackagesUsed*. `character.only = TRUE` is a `library` argument that allows us to use character string versions of the package names as R sees them in the *PackagesUsed* vector, rather than as objects (how we have used `library` up until now). If you include these commands in a code chunk at the beginning of your knitted document, then you can be sure that you will have a BibTeX file with all of your packages.

The full LaTeX document example I showed you earlier uses the `LoadandCite` command from the *repmis* package. This simplifies the process of loading and citing R packages.[16]

11.3 Presentations with LaTeX Beamer

You can make slideshow presentations with LaTeX. Creating a presentation with a markup language can take a bit more effort than using a WYSIWYG program like Microsoft PowerPoint or Apple's Keynote. However, combining LaTeX and *knitr* can make fully reproducible presentations that dynamically create and present results. I have found this particularly useful in my teaching as dynamically produced presentations allow me to provide my students with fully replicable examples of how I created a figure on a slide, for example. *knitr* also makes it easy to beautifully present code examples.

One of the most popular LaTeX tools for slideshows is the beamer class. When you compile a beamer class document, a PDF will be created where every page is a different slide (see Figure 11.2). All major PDF viewer programs have some sort of "View Full Screen" option to view beamer PDFs as

[16]It can also install the packages if the option `install = TRUE`. You can have it install specific package versions by entering the version numbers with the `versions` argument. This is very useful for enabling the replication of analyses that rely on specific package versions.

full screen slideshows. Usually you can navigate through the slides with the forward and back arrows on the keyboard.

In this section we will take a brief look at the basics of creating slideshows with beamer, highlighting special considerations that need to be made when working with beamer and *knitr*. A full example of a knittable beamer presentation with illustrations of the many of the points discussed here is printed at the end of the chapter.

11.3.1 Beamer basics

knitr largely works the same way in LaTeX slideshows as it does in article or book class documents. There are a few differences to look out for.

The Beamer preamble

You use `documentclass` to set a LaTeX document as a `beamer` slideshow. You can also include global style information in the preamble by using the commands `usetheme`, `usecolortheme`, `useinnertheme`, `useoutertheme`. For a fairly comprehensive compilation of beamer themes see the Hartwork's Beamer theme matrix: `http://www.hartwork.org/beamer-theme-matrix/`.

Slide frames

After the preamble, you start your document as usual by beginning the `document` environment. Then you need to start creating slides. Individual beamer slides are created using the `frame` environments. Create a frame title using `frametitle`.

```
\frame{
        \frametitle{An example frame}


}
```

Note that you can also use the usual `\begin{frame} . . \end{frame}` syntax. Unlike in a WYSIWYG slide show program, you will not be able to tell if you have tried to put more information on one slide than it can handle until after you compile the document.[17]

[17]One way to deal with frames that span multiple slides is to use the `allowframebreaks` command, i.e. `\begin{frame}[allowframebreaks]`.

FIGURE 11.2
Knitted Beamer PDF Example

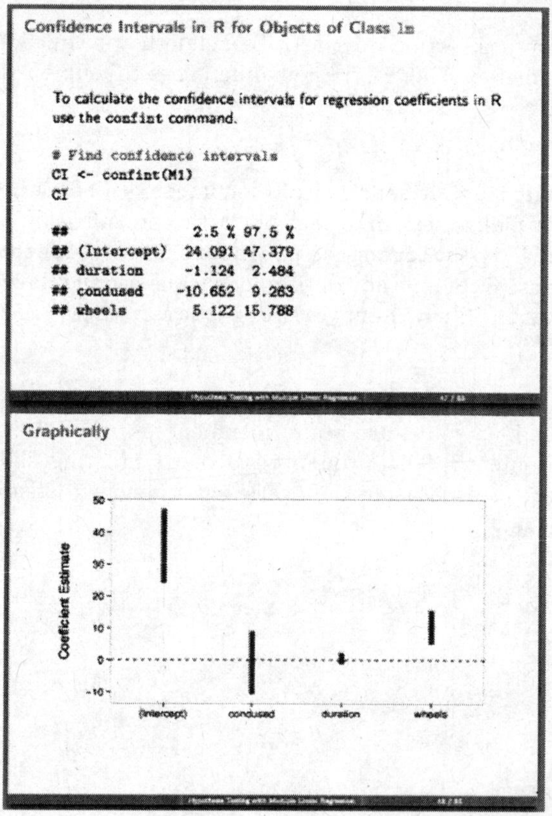

The presentation in this example was created using a custom beamer theme available at: `https://GitHub.com/christophergandrud/Make-Projects/tree/master/Rnw_Lecture`.

Title frames

One important difference from a regular LaTeX article is that instead of using `maketitle` to place your title information, in beamer you place the `titlepage` inside of a frame by itself.

Sections & outlines

We can use section commands in much the same way as we do in other types of LaTeX documents. Section commands do not need to be placed inside of frames. After the title slide, many slideshows have a presentation outline. You can automatically create one from your section headings using the `tableofcontents` command. Like the `titlepage` command, `tableofcontents` can go on its own frame, i.e.

```
%%% Title slide
\frame{
    \titlepage
}

%% Table of contents slide
\frame{
    \frametitle{Outline}
        \tableofcontents
}
```

Make list items appear

Lists work the same way in beamer as they do in other LaTeX document classes. They do have an added feature in that you can have each item appear as you progress through the slide show. After `\item`, place the number of the order in which the item should appear. Enclose the number in `< ->`. For example,

```
\begin{itemize}
    \item<1-> The first item.
    \item<2-> The second item.
    \item<2-> The third item.
\end{itemize}
```

In this example the first item will appear before the next two. These two will appear at the same time.

11.3.2 *knitr* with LaTeX slideshows

knitr code chunks have the same syntax in LaTeX slideshows as in other LaTeX documents. You do need to make one change to the `frame` options, however, to include highlighted *knitr* code chunks on your slides. You should add the `fragile` option to the `frame` command.[18] Here is an example:

```
\begin{frame}[fragile]
    \frametitle{An example fragile frame.}

\end{frame}
```

Here is a complete knittable beamer example:

```
\documentclass{beamer}

\begin{document}

%% Title page inforamtion
\title{Example Beamer/\emph{knitr} Slideshow}
\author{\href{mailto:gandrud@hertie-school.org}{Christopher Gandrud}}

%%% Title slide
\frame{
    \titlepage
}

%% Table of contents slide
\frame{
    \frametitle{Outline}
    \tableofcontents
}

%%% The code
\section{Access the code}
\begin{frame}[fragile]
    \frametitle{Access the code}
        The code to create the following figure is available online.

        To access it we can type:
<<eval=FALSE>>=
```

[18]For a detailed discussion of why you need to use the `fragile` option with the `verbatim` environment that *knitr* uses to display highlighted text in LaTeX documents see this blog post by Pieter Belmans: `http://pbelmans.wordpress.com/2011/02/20/why-latex-beamer-needs-fragile-when-using-verbatim/` (posted 20 February 2011).

```
# Access and run the code to create a caterpillar plot
devtools::source_url("http://bit.ly/VRKphr")
@
\end{frame}

%%% The figure
\section{The Figure}
\begin{frame}[fragile]
    \frametitle{The resulting figure}
<<echo=FALSE, message=FALSE, out.width='\\textwidth', out.height='0.8\\textheight'>>=
# Access and run the figure code
devtools::source_url("http://bit.ly/VRKphr")
@
\end{frame}

\end{document}
```

In Chapter 13 we will see how to use the *rmarkdown* package to create beamer presentations with the much simpler Markdown syntax.

Chapter summary

In this chapter we have learned the nitty-gritty of how to create simple LaTeX documents–articles and slideshows–that we can embed our reproducible research in using *knitr*. In the next chapter we look at how to create more complex LaTeX documents, including theses, books, and batch reports.

12

Large knitr/LaTeX Documents: Theses, Books, and Batch Reports

In the previous chapter we learned the basics of how to make LaTeX documents to create and present research findings. So far we have only learned how to create short documents, like articles and slideshows. For longer and more complex documents, such as theses and books, a single LaTeX markup file can become very unwieldy very quickly, especially when it includes *knitr* code chunks as well. Ideally we would segment the markup file into individual chapter files and then bring them all together when we compile the whole document. This would allow us to benefit from a modular file structure while producing one presentation document with continuous section and page numbering. To do this we can take advantage of LaTeX and *knitr* to separate markup files into manageable pieces. Like directories, these pieces are called **child** files, which are combined using a **parent** document.

Many of these tools can also be used to create batch reports: documents that present results for a selected part of a data set. For example, a researcher may want to create individual reports of answers to survey questions from interviewees with a specific age. In the latter part of this chapter we will rely on *knitr* and the *brew* package (Horner, 2011) to create batch reports.

In this chapter we will first briefly discuss how to plan a large document's file structure. We will then look at three methods for including child documents into parent documents. The first is very simple and uses the LaTeX command `input`. The second uses *knitr* to include knittable child documents. The final method is a special case of the *knitr* method that uses the command-line program Pandoc to convert child documents written in non-LaTeX markup languages and include them into a LaTeX parent. After this we will look at how to create batch reports.

12.1 Planning Large Documents

Before discussing the specifics of each of these methods, it's worth taking a moment to carefully plan the structure of our child and parent documents. Books and theses have a natural parent-child structure, i.e. they are single documents comprised of multiple chapters. They often include other child-like features such as title pages, bibliographies, figures, and appendices. You could include most of these features directly into one markup file. But this file would become very large and unwieldy. It would be difficult to find the one part or section that you want to edit. If your presentation markup files are difficult to navigate, they are difficult to reproduce.

Instead of one long markup file, you can break the document at natural division points, like chapters, into multiple child documents. These can then be combined with a parent document. The parent document acts like the skeleton that organizes the children in a specific order. The parent document can be compiled and all of the children will be in the right place. In LaTeX, a parent document will include the preamble where the document class (`book` for example) is set and all of the necessary LaTeX packages are loaded. It also includes *knitr* global options, the `maketitle`, `\begin{document}` and `\end{document}`, and the `bibliography`. When you compile the parent document you will compile the entire document. Notice that if the parent document contains the preamble and so on, that the children cannot contain this information as well. This can create some issues if you only want to compile one chapter rather than the whole document. We will see how to overcome this problem with *knitr* later in the chapter.

To make your many child and parent documents manageable, it is a good idea to store your child files in a subdirectory of the folder storing the parent file. This book was created using a knittable parent and child structure, so please see the markup files on GitHub for a complete example of how to use *knitr* with large documents.[1] When segmenting your presentation documents into parents and children, the remainder of your research project structure can stay largely the same as we have seen so far.

12.2 Large Documents with Traditional LaTeX

Imagine that we are writing a book with three chapters. No part of the document includes *knitr* code chunks. We can split the book into three child documents and place them in a subdirectory of the parent document's folder called *Children*. The child documents should not contain a preamble, `\begin{document}`, or `\end{document}`. Because they are chapters, we will begin the documents simply with the `chapter` heading. For example, the chapter in this book has:

```
\chapter{Large \emph{knitr}/LaTeX Documents: Theses, Books, \& Batch Reports}
\label{LargeDocs}
```

As we saw earlier, the `label` command is used for cross-referencing.

[1]See: `https://github.com/christophergandrud/Rep-Res-Book/tree/master/Source`.

12.2.1 Inputting/including children

Now in the parent document we can place the `input` command where we would like the child to show up in the final document. If we want there to be a clear page on either side of the included document we should use the `include` command instead. In the `input` or `include` command, we simply place the child document's file path. Here is an example parent document with three child documents (*Chapter1.tex*, *Chapter2.tex*, and *Chapter3.tex*) all located in a subdirectory of the parent document called *Children*:

```
%%%%%%%%%%%%%% Article Preamble %%%%%%%%%%%%%
\documentclass{book}

%%%% Load LaTeX packages
\usepackage{hyperref}
\usepackage{makeidx}
\usepackage[authoryear]{natbib}

%%%% Start document body
\begin{document}

%%%%%%%%%%%%% Create title %%%%%%%%%%%%%%%%%
\title{An Example LaTeX Book}
\author{Christopher Gandrud}

\maketitle

%%%%%%%%%%%%% Frontmatter %%%%%%%%%%%%%%%%%%%
\tableofcontents
\listoffigures
\listoftables

%%%% Start index
\makeindex

%%%%%%%%%%%% Input child documents %%%%%%%%%
%%%% Chapter 1
\input{Children/Chapter1.tex}

%%%% Chapter 2
\input{Children/Chapter2.tex}

%%%% Chapter 3
```

```
\input{Children/Chapter3.tex}

%%%%%%%%% Bibliography %%%%%%%%%%%%%%%%%%%%
\bibliographystyle{apa}
\bibliography{Main.bib,Packages.bib}

%%%%%%%%% Index %%%%%%%%%%%%%%%%%%%%%%%%%%
\clearpage
\printindex


\end{document}
```

12.2.2 Other common features of large documents

There are some other commands in this example parent document that we have not seen before. These commands create the book's front matter–tables of contents, lists of figures and tables–as well as blank pages and the book's index.

Table of contents

If you are using LaTeX's section headings (e.g. `chapter`, `section`) you can automatically generate a table of contents with the `tableofcontents` command. We saw an example earlier when we created a beamer slideshow. Simply place this command where you want the table of contents to appear. Usually this is after the `maketitle` command near the beginning of the document.

Lists of figures and tables

It is also common for large documents to include lists of its figures and tables. Usually these are placed after the table of contents. LaTeX will automatically create these lists from the `captions` you place in `table` and `figure` environments. To create these lists, use the `listoffigures` and `listoftables` commands.

Blank Pages

Sometimes we want to make sure that an index, a bibliography, or some other item begins on a new page. To do this, simply place the `clearpage` command directly before the item.

Index

You can automatically create an index with the *makeidx* (make index) LaTeX package. To set up this package, include it in your preamble. Then, near the beginning of your document, enable the index by placing `\makeindex`. You will probably want the actual index to be printed near the end of the document. To do this, place `\printindex` after the bibliography or somewhere else before `\end{document}`. Throughout the child documents, you can use `\index{INDEX_KEY}` at places that you would like the index to refer to. For example, if we wanted to create an index entry for this spot in this book with the `INDEX_KEY` "indices" we type: `\index{indices}`.

12.3 *knitr* and Large Documents

LaTeX's own parent-child functions are very useful if you are creating plain, non-knittable documents. For knittable documents we need to use *knitr*'s parent-child options. Not only do these allow us to include knittable children in parent documents, it also allows us to `knit` each child document separately. This can be very useful working on document drafts as we don't need to compile the whole document every time we want to look at changes made in one chapter.

12.3.1 The parent document

Like regular LaTeX parent documents, knittable parent documents include commands to create the preamble, front matter, bibliography, and so on. *knitr* global chunk options and package/data loading should also be set at the beginning of the parent document if you want them to apply to the entire thing.

Rather than using the `input` or `include` commands, we use the `child` code chunk option to include child documents with *knitr*. The `child` option simply takes as its value the child document's file path. For example:

```
<<SetChild, child='Children/Chapter1.Rnw', include=FALSE>>=
@
```

We can include the other child documents either in their own code chunks or all in one chunk as a character vector. You can also use `Sexpr` with the option `knit_child`.

```
\Sexpr{knit_child('Children/Chapter1.Rnw')}
```

This is the same thing as using the `child` option in a code chunk. Note also that you can continue to use `input`, `include`, and code chunks with the `child` option in the same document if you like.

When you have your child code chunks set up in your parent document, just `knit` the parent like you would any other knittable file. The knittable children will be knit and included every time you knit the parent document.

12.3.2 Knitting child documents

You can use *knitr* to compile individual child documents. To do this, place a code chunk at the beginning of the child document. In the code chunk (not as a option) use the `set_parent` command to specify where the parent file is. Here is an example child file with a parent located at */ExampleProject/Parent.Rnw*:

```
%%%%%%%% Set parent %%%%%%%%
<<SetParent, include=FALSE>>=
set_parent('/ExampleProject/Parent.Rnw')
@

%%%%%%%% Chapter heading %%%%
\chapter{The first chapter}

This chapter is very short
```

You can also use `set_parent` with `Sexpr`. When you have set the parent document you can `knit` the child document by itself. In addition to knitting the code chunks, *knitr* will include all of the preamble information from the parent document as well as `\begin{document}` and `\end{document}`.[2]

Other markup languages

We can use *knitr*'s parent-child functions in any of the markup languages it supports. For example, we can `knit` R Markdown children into R Markdown parent documents. We don't look at specific examples in this book. The *knitr*

[2]If you are using custom LaTeX style files (they have the file extension `.sty`) then *knitr* won't include these in the knitted document unless you include a copy of the style file in the child document's directory.

options syntax is the same, but as usual, syntax for opening and closing the code chunks is specific to the markup language.

12.4 Child Documents in a Different Markup Language

Because *knitr* is able to run not only R code but also command-line programs, you can use the Pandoc program to convert child documents written in a different markup language into the primary markup language you are using for your document. If you have Pandoc installed on your computer,[3] you can call it directly from your parent document by including the Pandoc commands in a code chunk with the `engine` option set to either `'bash'` or `'sh'`.[4]

For example, the Stylistic Conventions (page xvii) part of this book is written in Markdown. The source file is called *StylisticConventions.md* and is in a subdirectory of the parent's directory called: *Children/FrontMatter* It was faster to write the list of conventions using the simpler Markdown syntax than LaTeX, which as we saw has a more complicated way of creating lists. However, I wanted to include this file in the LaTeX-produced book. Pandoc can convert the Markdown document into a LaTeX file. This file can then be input into the main document with the LaTeX command `input`.

In the parent document I added a code chunk with the following command to convert the Markdown syntax in *StylisticConventions.md* to LaTeX and save it in a file called *StyleTemp.tex*.

```
<<StyleConventions, include=FALSE, engine='sh'>>=
# Use pandoc to convert MD to TEX
pandoc Children/FrontMattter/StylisticConventions.md -f markdown\
    -t latex -o StyleTemp.tex
@

% Input converted StyleTemp document
\input{StyleTemp.tex}
```

The options `-f markdown` and `-t latex` tell Pandoc to convert *Stylistic-Conventions.md* from Markdown to LaTeX syntax. `-o StyleTemp.tex` in-

[3]Pandoc installation instructions can be found at: `http://johnmacfarlane.net/pandoc/installing.html`.

[4]Alternatively, you can run Pandoc in an R code chunk using the `system` command. For example: `system("pandoc Children/FrontMattter/StylisticConventions.md -f markdown -t latex -o StyleTemp.tex")`. *knitr* also has a `pandoc` command that is a wrapper for converting Markdown documents to other formats with Pandoc.

FIGURE 12.1
The *brew* + *knitr* Process

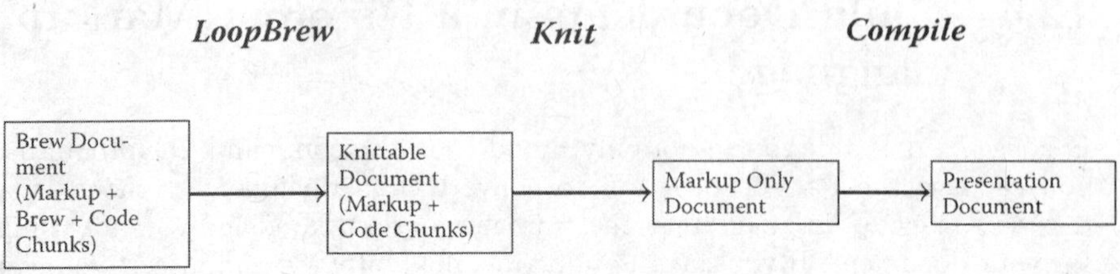

structs Pandoc to save the resulting LaTeX markup to a new file called *StyleTemp.tex*.

I only need to include a backslash (\) at the end of the first line because I wanted to split the code over two lines. The code wouldn't fit on this page otherwise. The backslash tells the shell not to treat the following line as a different line. Unlike in R, the shell only recognizes a command's arguments if they are on the same line as the command.

You'll notice that after the code chunk we use `input` to include the new *StyleTemp.tex* document. Note that using this method to include a child document that needs to be knit will require extra steps not covered in this book.

12.5 Creating Batch Reports

When we create batch reports we want to somehow subset a data set into multiple pieces and use these pieces as the input for *knitr* code chunks in different presentation documents for each subset of the data set. The *brew* package (Horner, 2011) is maybe the most popular tool for creating batch reports in R. Using *brew* with multiple subsets of a data set adds two steps to the process of creating *knitr* presentation documents (see Figure 12.1):

1. Create a *brew* template document.
2. Create a function to subset the data, brew, and knit each file.

knitr's `knit_expand` command can also be used to create batch reports. Because *brew* is the dominant way to create batch reports in R and currently has more capabilities than `knit_expand` we will cover *brew* rather than `knit_expand` in detail.

Imagine that we are using the *MainData* data set discussed in the previous chapters and we want to create a LaTeX document for each country displaying its average fertilizer consumption (*FertilizerConsumption*).[5]

[5]The files needed to create this example are available at: `http://bit.ly/XJbyCK`.

First, let's create a *brew* template document. This document will include all of our markup and the code chunks we want in our *knitr* document. There is one small difference from regular knittable documents: it will use *brew* syntax to include information from the subsetted data. Text in a *brew* template document is printed 'as is' when we `brew` it unless it is between *brew*'s delimiters. The delimiters are:[6]

- `<\# . . . %>`: Comment delimiter, i.e. contents are thrown away when brewed.
- `<% . . . %>`: R functions inside the delimiters are run, but the results aren't printed.
- `<%= . . . %>`: Contents are printed.

In the following example we use the latter two. Here is our *brew* template:

```
\documentclass{article}

\begin{document}

% Create numeric vector
<% NewFC <- FC %>

{\LARGE <%= Name %>}



The mean fertilizer consumption for <%= Name %> is
\Sexpr{round(mean(NewFC, na.rm = TRUE), digits = 1)} kilograms
per hectare of arable land.

\end{document}
```

There are a few things to note. The line `<% NewFC <- FC %>` will create a vector called *NewFC* from the object *FC*. As we will see when we create the *brew* function, *FC* contains the values of *FertilizerConsumption* for each country. We need to put *FC* into a new object because if we typed `<%= FC %>` *brew* would print the numbers literally, not in a numeric vector like we need

[6]Note that the spaces between the delimiter and its contents are important.

later for the `mean` command. `<%= Name %>` prints the country name in the subsetted data. We'll see how to create *Name* in the *brew* function below. We save this template in *BatchReports/Template*, i.e. in a subdirectory of *BatchReports* called *Template*. Let's give it the file name *BrewTemplate.Rnw*.

Now let's create the R code to subset the data, `brew`, and `knit` the reports:

```
# Set working directory
setwd("/BatchReports")

#### Download Data ####
# Load repmis
library(repmis)

# Download data
MainData <- source_data("http://bit.ly/V0ldsf")

# Create vector of country names
COUNTRY <- as.character(unique(MainData$country))

#### Create BatchReports Function ####
BatchReports <- function(Name){
  # Create file names for individual reports
  ## Remove white space in country names
  CountryNoWhite <- gsub(" ", "", x = Name)
  KnitFile <- paste(CountryNoWhite, ".Rnw", sep = "")

  # Subset data
  SubData <- subset(MainData, country == Name)

  # Create vector of the country's fertilizer consumption
  FC <- SubData$FertilizerConsumption

  # Brew and Knit
  brew::brew("Template/BrewTemplate.Rnw", KnitFile)
  knitr::knit2pdf(KnitFile)
}

#### Run function and cleanup ####
lapply(COUNTRY, BatchReports)

# Keep only pdf reports
unlink(c("*.aux", "*.log", "*.Rnw", "*.tex"))
```

Ok, this is a lot of new code. Let's go through it step by step:

1. Set the working directory to */BatchReports.*
2. Download *MainData.csv* using the `source_data` function, as we've done before.
3. Create a vector for the country names in the data. We will use this vector to subset the data.
4. Create a `function` called *BatchReports* for subsetting the data, brewing it, and knitting it.
    - The `function` command allows us create a new function.[7] Arguments are specified in parentheses (these are also called the formals) and R expressions are put in the curly brackets that denote the function's body. The expressions do things with the arguments. Our argument here is `Name` and the contents of the curly brackets subset, brew, and knit the data according to *Name*'s value.[8]
    - An important step in the `BatchReports` function is creating a new name to give our brewed and knit files. Some country names like "United Arab Emirates" have white spaces in them. We cannot run LaTeX on a file with a name containing white spaces. We remove the white spaces with the `gsub` command, i.e. we substitute a space with no white space. We then use the `paste` command to create a name that will be used for the brewed file. *knitr* will automatically create a name for the final PDFs.
5. `lapply` allows us to run our `BatchReports` function separately for every value of the *COUNTRY* vector. `BatchReport`'s *Name* argument takes the value *COUNTRY*. Note: it is important to end the *BrewTemplate.Rnw* with a blank line for `lapply` to work correctly.
6. Finally, we use the `unlink` command to delete all of the ancillary files used to create the final batch report PDFs. Always be careful with the `unlink` command as it permanently deletes files. Because we used the asterisk wildcard (see Section 6.1.2.1), `unlink` will delete all files in the working directory with the extensions `.aux`, `.log`, `.Rnw` and `.tex`.

Figure 12.2 shows you a sample of what the final PDF created by this *brew*/*knitr* process for Afghanistan looks like. This was a very simple example illustrating the basic process for combining *brew* and *knitr* to create batch

[7] User-created functions are just like most other R functions.

[8] For more information on functions see Hadley Wickham's page on the topic: `http://adv-r.had.co.nz/Functions.html`.

FIGURE 12.2
Snippet of an Example PDF Document Created with *brew* + *knitr*

Afghanistan

The mean fertilizer consumption for Afghanistan is **4.3** kilograms per hectare of arable land.

reports. The process can be used to create much more complex documents and with other markup languages.

Chapter summary

In this chapter we have learned how to create more complex LaTeX documents to present our reproducible research. In particular we learned how to take advantage of parent and child document structures using both basic LaTeX and *knitr* tools. These allow us to more easily work with very large presentation documents. We saw how Pandoc can be combined with these tools so that we can create our documents using multiple markup languages. We also learned how to create *brew* templates that can be used to create multiple documents presenting information from subsets of our data. In the next chapter we will learn how to create documents for presenting reproducible research on the web with Markdown. We will also see how to use *rmarkdown* to easily create documents in other formats as well.

13

Presenting on the Web and Other Formats with R Markdown

LaTeX is the standard markup language for creating academic-quality articles and books. If we want to present research findings via the internet, our best option is HTML. HTML syntax can be tedious to write, as we saw in Chapter 9. Luckily the Markdown language was created as a simplified way of writing HTML documents. As we have seen, Markdown can be fully integrated with *knitr*/*rmarkdown* for creating reproducible research HTML presentation documents. In addition, the *rmarkdown* package allows us to write documents in Markdown and render them to PDF and MS Word.

In this chapter we will learn about Markdown editors and the basic Markdown syntax for creating simple reproducible documents, including many of the things we covered for *knitr*/LaTeX documents such as headings and text formatting. Please refer back to previous chapters for syntax used to display code and code chunks (Chapter 8), tables (Chapter 9), and figures (Chapter 10) with R Markdown documents. In this chapter will also briefly look at some more advanced features for including math with MathJax, footnotes and bibliographies with Pandoc, and customizing styles with CSS. Then we will learn how to create HTML slideshows. We'll finish up the chapter by looking at options for publishing Markdown-created HTML documents, including locally on your computer, Dropbox, and GitHub Pages.

13.1 The Basics

Markdown was created specifically to make it easy to write HTML (or XHTML[1]) using a syntax that is human readable and possibly publishable without compiling. For example, compare the Markdown table syntax in Chapter 9 to the HTML syntax for virtually the same table.[2] That being said, to make Markdown simple, it does not have as many capabilities as HTML. To get around this problem you can still use HTML in Markdown, though note that Markdown syntax cannot be used between HTML element tags. Pandoc and *rmarkdown* have extended Markdown so that it can be used to create reproducible PDF and MS Word documents.

[1] Extensible HyperText Markup Language

[2] For more information see John Gruber's website: `http://daringfireball.net/projects/markdown/`.

Note: if you are using *rmarkdown* to compile a document to PDF or Word, using raw HTML syntax will often not work as intended, if at all. As a rule, syntax specific to LaTeX or HTML that is included in an R Markdown document can only be properly compiled to a PDF or HTML document, respectively. Similarly, you are only able to include graphics that are of types supported by the output format. You are not be able to include a JavaScript plot directly in a PDF.

13.1.1 Getting started with Markdown editors

Like for R LaTeX, RStudio functions as a very good editor for R Markdown documents and regular non-knittable Markdown documents as well. To create a new R Markdown document in RStudio, click `File` in the menu bar then `New` → `R Markdown`. You will then be able to select what output format you would like. RStudio has full syntax highlighting for code chunks and can compile `.Rmd` files into `.md`, then render them in *.html*, for example, with one click of the `Knit HTML` button (). As we saw in Chapter 3 (Figure 3.6), when you knit a Markdown document in RStudio, it will preview the HTML document for you. You can always view HTML documents by opening them with your web browser. You can do this directly from RStudio's **Preview HTML** window by clicking the `Open in Browser` button ().

FIGURE 13.1
R Markdown Compile Dropdown Menu

If you click on the downward arrow next to `Knit HTML` you will see the drop-down menu in Figure 13.1. This allows you to also compile the document to PDF or MS Word, regardless of which format you originally chose when you created the document. As with HTML you will be given a preview of the PDF or Word document when it is compiled.

In Figure 13.1 you'll also notice the question mark button. Click this for a quick guide to the Markdown syntax used in RStudio.

Being plain-text, you can also use any other text editor to modify Markdown documents, though they will lack the level of integration with *knitr*/*rmarkdown* that RStudio has.

13.1.2 Preamble and document structure

That was kind of a trick subsection title. Unlike LaTeX documents, plain Markdown documents do not have a preamble. *rmarkdown* documents can have a header, basically another name for a preamble, but we will get to that later. There is also no need to start a body environment or anything like that. HTML head elements (HTMLs preamble equivalent) are added automatically when you render Markdown documents into HTML. So with Markdown, you can just start typing.

Here is an example of an R Markdown document that creates the map we saw in Chapter 10:[3] We'll go through all of the code below.

```
# Example R Markdown File
## from "Reproducible Research with R and RStudio"
### Christopher Gandrud
### 15 January 2015

------------

```{r LoadPackages, include=FALSE}
# Load required packages
library(devtools)
```

We can use the
[googleVis](http://code.google.com/p/google-motion-charts-with-r/)
package to create interactive JavaScript tables, charts, and maps.
Here is an example of how to create a map with *googleVis*'s
`gvisGeoChart` function.

Let's first download some data from [GitHub](https://GitHub.com/).
See chapters 6 and 7 for details about this data as well as the
[variable description page](https://GitHub.com/christophergandrud/
Rep-Res-Examples/blob/master/DataGather_Merge/
MainData_VariableDescriptions.md).

Fertilizer Consumption (kilograms per hectare of arable land) in 2003

Data from [World Bank](http://data.worldbank.org/indicator/AG.CON.
FERT.ZS)

```{r CreategvisGeoChart, echo=FALSE, message=FALSE, results='asis'}
# Create geo map of global fertilizer consumption for 2003
# The data is loaded from GitHub (http://bit.ly/V0ldsf)
## The data gathering process used to create this data set
## is completely reproducible. For more information see:
## http://bit.ly/YnMKBG
```

[3]This code is available on GitHub at: `https://GitHub.com/christophergandrud/Rep-Res-Examples/blob/master/RMarkdownExamples/ExampleKnitrDocument/ExampleKnitrMarkdown.Rmd`.
```

FIGURE 13.2
Example Rendered R Markdown Document

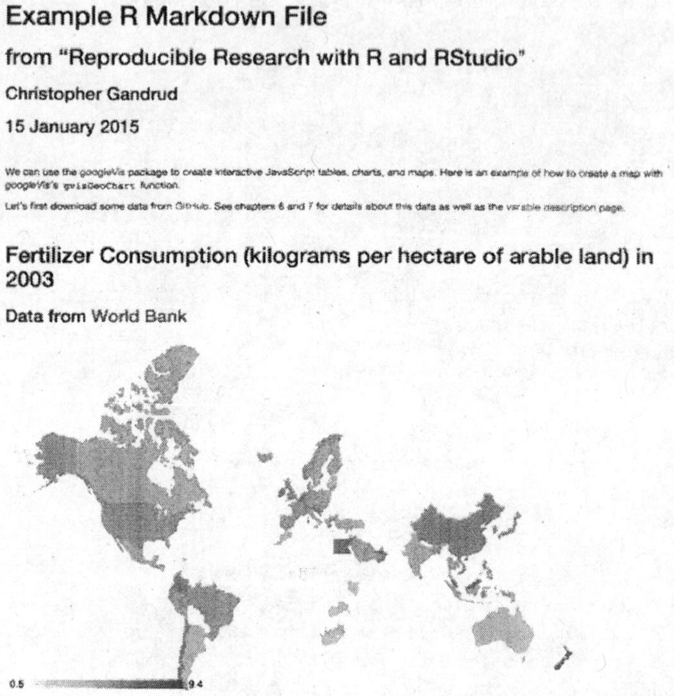


```
source_url("http://bit.ly/VNnZxS")
```

```
-----------
```

When knitted in RStudio and viewed in the Google Chrome web browser, the final presentation document looks like Figure 13.2.

13.1.3 Headings

Headings in Markdown are extremely simple. Note that Markdown headings and R Markdown headers are not the same thing. The latter gives instructions for how to render the document, the former are section titles in the text. To create a line in the topmost heading style–maybe a title–just place one hash mark (#) at the beginning of the line. The second-tier heading gets two hashes (##) and so on. You can also put the hash mark(s) at the end of the heading, but this is not necessary. Here is an example of the three headings:

```
# A level one heading
## A level two heading
### A level three heading
```

There are six heading levels in Markdown. You can also create a level-one heading by following a line of text with equal signs. Level-two headings can be created by following a line of text with dashes:

```
A level one heading
===================

A level two heading
-------------------
```

13.1.4 Horizontal lines

If you would like to create horizontal lines that run the width of the page in Markdown, simply place three or more equal signs or dashes separated by text from above by one blank line:

```
Create a horizontal line.

=========
```

13.1.5 Paragraphs and new lines

Just like in LaTeX, new paragraphs are created by putting text on a new line separated from previous text with a blank line. For example:

```
This is the first paragraph.

This is the second paragraph.
```

You might have noticed that in the headers example we did not need to separate the header with a blank line.

Separating lines with a blank line places a blank line in the final document. End a line with two or more white spaces ( ) to create a new line that is not separated by a blank line.

13.1.6 Italics and bold

To *italicize* a word in Markdown, simply place it between two asterisks, e.g. `*Italicize these words*`. To make words **bold**, place them between four asterisks, two on either side: `**Make these words bold**`.

13.1.7 Links

To create hyper-links in Markdown, use the `[LINK_TEXT](URL)` syntax.[4] `LINK_TEXT` is the text that you would like to show up as the hyper-link text. When you click on this text it will take you to the linked site specified by `URL`. If you want to show only a URL as the text, type it in both the square brackets and parentheses. This is a little tedious, so in RStudio you can just type the URL and it will be hyper-linked. In regular Markdown place the URL between less-than and greater-than signs (`<URL>`).

13.1.8 Special characters and font customization

Unlike LaTeX rendered with pdfLaTeX, Markdown can include almost any letters and characters included in your system. The main exceptions are characters used by Markdown syntax (e.g. `*`, `#`, `\` and so on). You will have to escape these (see below). Font sizes and typefaces cannot be set directly with Markdown syntax. You need to set these with HTML or CSS, which I don't cover here, though below we will look at how to use a custom CSS file.

13.1.9 Lists

To create itemized lists in Markdown, simply place the items after one dash:

[4] You can also include a `title` attribute after the URL, though this is generally not very useful. See Section 10.1.2 for a discussion.

```
- Item 1
- Another item
- Item 3
```

To create a numbered list, use numbers and periods rather than dashes.

```
1. Item 1
2. Another item
3. Item 3
```

13.1.10 Escape characters

Markdown, like LaTeX and R, uses a backslash (\) as an escape character. For example, if you want to have an asterisk in the text of your document (rather than start to italicize your text, e.g. `*some italicized text*`), type: `\*`. Two characters–ampersand (&) and the less-than sign (<)–have special meanings in HTML.[5] So, to have them printed literally in your text you have to use the HTML code for the characters. Ampersands are created with `&amp`. Less-than signs are created with `&lt`.

13.1.11 Math with MathJax

Markdown by itself can't format mathematical equations. We can create LaTeX-style equations by adding on the MathJax JavaScript engine. MathJax syntax is the same as LaTeX syntax (see Section 11.1.8), especially when used from RStudio or when rendered with *rmarkdown*. Markdown documents rendered in RStudio automatically link to the MathJax engine online.[6] If you want to use another program to render Markdown documents with MathJax equations, you may need to take extra steps to link to MathJax. For more details see: `http://docs.mathjax.org/en/latest/start.html#mathjax-cdn`.

Because backslashes are Markdown escape characters, in many Markdown editors you will have to use two backslashes to create math environments with MathJax. For example, in LaTeX and RStudio's Markdown you can create a display equation like this:

$$s^2 = \frac{\sum(x - \bar{x})^2}{n - 1}$$

[5] Ampersands declare the beginning of a special HTML character. Less-than signs begin HTML tags.

[6] You will not be able to render equations when you are not online.

by typing:[7]

```
\[
s^{2} = \frac{\sum(x - \bar{x})^2}{n - 1}
\]
```

But, in other Markdown programs you may have to use:

```
\\[
s^{2} = \frac{\sum(x - \bar{x})^2}{n - 1}
\\]
```

To make inline equations, use parentheses instead of square brackets as in LaTeX, e.g. `\( s^{2} = \frac{\sum(x - \bar{x})^2}{n - 1} \)`.

13.2 Further Customizability with *rmarkdown*

Markdown is simple and easy to use. But being simple means that it lacks important functionality for presenting research results, such as footnotes and bibliographies, and custom formatting. In this section we will learn how to overcome these limitations with Pandoc and CSS via *rmarkdown*.

13.2.1 More on *rmarkdown* Headers

In Chapter 3 (page 48) we first saw an *rmarkdown* header written in YAML. Just as a refresher, here is the basic header we looked at:

```
---
title: "A Basic PDF Presentation Document"
author: "Christopher Gandrud"
date: "30 November 2015"
output: pdf_document:
    toc: true
```

[7]In RStudio you can also use dollar signs to delimit MathJax equations as in LaTeX. See the footnotes in Section 11.1.8 for more information.

```
---
```

This header provides instructions for what to do when the document is rendered, gives instructions to render the document as a PDF (via LaTeX), and inserts a title, author, date, and table of contents at the beginning.

We also have the option to include other formatting options, many of which we would include in a *knitr* LaTeX document's preamble. You include these at the top level, i.e. without being tabbed. *rmarkdown* refers to these options as "metadata". For example, to change the font size to 11-point we could use:

```
---
title: "A Basic PDF Presentation Document"
author: "Christopher Gandrud"
date: "30 November 2015"
output: pdf_document:
    toc: true
fontsize: 11pt
---
```

We could double-space the PDF document with a similar top-level entry: `linestretch: 2`.[8] To find more options for PDF documents, type `?pdf_document` into your R console. Note that these options will only affect your PDF document, not a rendered HTML file.

Remember from Chapter 3 (page 61) that we can specify rendering instructions for multiple output formats in the same header. Here is a longer header, building on what we just saw. We'll go through it in detail:

```
---
title: "An Example rmarkdown Article"
author: "Christopher Gandrud"
date: "15 January 2015"
output:
    pdf_document:
        latex_engine: xelatex
        number_sections: yes
```

[8]1 would be for single space and 1.5 would be for one and a half spacing.

```
        toc: yes
    html_document:
        toc: no
        theme: "flatly"
linestretch: 2
fontsize: 11pt
bibliography:
    - Main.bib
    - Packages.bib
---
```

Ok, let's go through this in detail. We have already seen the `title`, `author`, `date`, `linestretch`, and `fontsize` options. Notice that we used `latex_engine` to set the LaTeX engine to XeLaTeX, which is useful for documents that include non-standard English characters. We also specified with `number_sections` that the PDF document should have numbered section headings.

For the HTML version of the document we do not want a table of contents as we set `toc: no`. We specified a CSS theme called Flatly for our HTML document using `theme: "flatly"`. As of this writing, *rmarkdown* has a built-in ability to use a range of themes from Bootswatch (`http://bootswatch.com/`). Alternatively, you can link to a custom CSS file with the `css` option. Use `html_document` to see other options. Notice that we can use `no` and `yes` instead of `false` and `true`, respectively.

We linked to two BibTeX files with the `bibliography` option. Using Pandoc syntax, the references will apply to both the PDF and HTML documents.

If you want to also enable the creation of a Microsoft Word document, include `output: word_document` in the header.

Bibliographies with Pandoc

Pandoc via *rmarkdown* allows us to insert citations from normal BibTeX files (see Chapter 11) specified in the header with `bibliography`. The main difference is that Pandoc has a different syntax from LaTeX for making in-text citations. Basic Pandoc citations begin with `@` followed by the BibTeX citation key. Square brackets (`[]`) create parentheses around the citation. Here is an example:

```
This is a citation [@Donoho2009].
```

TABLE 13.1
A Selection of Pandoc In-text Citations

Markup	Result
`[@Donoho2009]`	(Donoho 2009)
`[-@Donoho2009]`	(2009)
`[see @Donoho2009]`	(see Donoho 2009)
`[see @Donoho2009, 10-11]`	(see Donoho 2009, 10–11)
`[@Donoho2009; @Box1973]`	(Donoho 2009; Box 1973)
`@Donoho2009 [10-11]`	Donoho (2009, 10–11)

Pandoc uses *natbib* by default, so the citation `[@Donoho2009]` will appear as (Donoho et al., 2009). To add text before and after the citation inside of the parentheses, use something like this: `[see @Donoho2009, 10]`; which creates: (see Donoho et al. 2009, 10). If you do not want the parentheses around the entire citation (only the year) then omit the square brackets. To include only the year and not the authors' surnames, add a minus sign, e.g. `[-@Donoho2009]`. See Table 13.1 for more options.

Full bibliographic information for each item that is cited in the text will be produced at the end of the output document. I suggest placing a heading like `# References` at the very end of your document so that the bibliography will be differentiated from the document's text.

Footnotes with Pandoc

You can also include footnotes in documents rendered with *rmarkdown* by using Pandoc's footnote syntax. In the text where you would like a footnote to be located use: `[^NOTE_KEY]`. Then at the end of your document, place `[^NOTE_KEY]: The footnote text.`[9] `NOTE_KEY`s generally follow the same rules as BibTeX citation keys, so no spaces. The footnotes will be numbered sequentially when rendered.

To sum up, here is an example of document that can be rendered in HTML or PDF using *rmarkdown*. It includes footnotes and a bibliography.

[9] You can actually put this almost anywhere and it will be placed and numbered correctly in the output document, but I find it easier to organize the footnotes when they are placed at the end.

```
---
title: "Minimal rmarkdown Example"
output:
    pdf_document:
        toc: true
    html_document:
        toc: false
bibliography: Main.bib
---

This is some text.[^FirstNote]

This is a *knitr* code chunk:

```{r}
plot(cars$speed, cars$dist)
```

This is a citation [see @Donoho2009, 10].

[^FirstNote]: This is a footnote.

References
```

We have only covered a small proportion of Pandoc's capabilities that you can take advantage of with *rmarkdown*. For full range of Pandoc's abilities see: `http://johnmacfarlane.net/pandoc/README.html`.

13.2.2 CSS style files and Markdown

You can customize the formatting of HTML documents created with Markdown files using custom CSS style sheets. CSS files allow you to specify the way a rendered Markdown file looks in a web browser including fonts, margins, background color, and so on. We don't have space to cover CSS syntax here. There are numerous online resources for learning CSS. One of the best ways may be to just copy a CSS style sheet into a new file and play around with it to see how things change. A really good resource for this is Google Chrome's Developer Tools. The Developer Tools allows you to edit your webpages, including their CSS, and see a live preview. It is a really nice way to experiment with CSS (and HTML and JavaScript).[10] There are also numerous pre-made style sheets available online.[11]

Rendering R Markdown files to HTML using custom CSS

The simplest way to use a custom CSS style sheet is to include the file path to the CSS file in an *rmarkdown* header. As mentioned earlier, *rmarkdown* has a number of built-in CSS file options that you can access with `style`. If you want to use another custom CSS file, use the `css` option. If our custom CSS file is called *Markdown.css* in the same directory as the R Markdown document, then a basic header would be:

```
---
output:
    html_document:
        css: Markdown.css
---
```

If you are using the *knitr* package to render an R Markdown document to HTML you can also include a custom CSS file. First use `knit` to knit the document to a plain Markdown file. Then use the `markdownToHTML` function from the *markdown* package (Allaire et al., 2015b) to render the plain Markdown document in HTML, including the `stylesheet` argument with the path to the CSS file.

13.3 Slideshows with Markdown, *rmarkdown*, and HTML

Because R Markdown documents can be compiled into HTML files it is possible to use them to create HTML5 slideshows.[12] There are a number of advantages to creating HTML presentations with Markdown:

- You can use the relatively simple Markdown syntax.
- HTML presentations are a nice native way to show content on the web.

[10]For more information on how to access and use Developer Tools in Chrome see: `https://developers.google.com/chrome-developer-tools/`.

[11]One small note: when you create a new style sheet or copy an old one, make sure the final line is blank. Otherwise you may get an "incomplete final line" error when you render the document.

[12]The slideshows created by the tools in this section use features introduced in the 5th version of HTML, i.e. HTML5. In this section I often refer to HTML5 as just HTML for simplicity.

- HTML presentations can incorporate virtually any content that can be included in a webpage. This includes interactive content, like motion charts created by *googleVis* (see Chapter 10).

Let's look at how to create HTML slideshows from Markdown documents using (a) the *rmarkdown* package and (b) RStudio's built-in slideshow files, called R Presentations. You can also use *rmarkdown* to create beamer presentations.

HTML5 frameworks

Before getting into the details of how to use *rmarkdown* for presentations and R Presentations, let's briefly look more into what an HTML5 slideshow is and the frameworks that make them possible. HTML5 slideshows rely on a number of web technologies in addition to HTML5, including CSS, and JavaScript to create a website that behaves like a LaTeX beamer or PowerPoint presentation. They run in your web browser and you may need to be connected to the internet for them to work properly as key components are often located remotely. Most browsers have a `Full Screen` mode you can use to view presentations.

There are a number of different HTML5 slideshow frameworks that let you create and style your slideshows. In all of the frameworks you view the slideshow in your web browser and advance through slides with the forward arrow key on your keyboard. You can go back with the back arrow. Despite these similarities, the frameworks have different looks and capabilities.

13.3.1 HTML Slideshows with *rmarkdown*

It is very easy to create an HTML presentation using *rmarkdown* and the IO Slides[13] or Slidy[14] HTML5 frameworks. The syntax for IO Slides and Slidy presentations with *rmarkdown* presentations is almost exactly the same as the syntax we have seen throughout this chapter. There are two main differences from the syntax we have seen so far. First, `ioslides_presentation` for IO Slides or `slidy_presentation` for Slidy presentations is the output type to set in the header. Second, two hashes (`##`) set a frame's header.[15] For example,

```
---
title: "Simple rmarkdown Presentation Example"
author: "Christopher Gandrud"
date: "26 December 2015"
```

[13]`https://code.google.com/p/io-2012-slides/`

[14]`http://www.w3.org/Talks/Tools/Slidy2/#(1)`

[15]You can create sections with one hash.

FIGURE 13.3
rmarkdown/IO Slides Example Title Slide

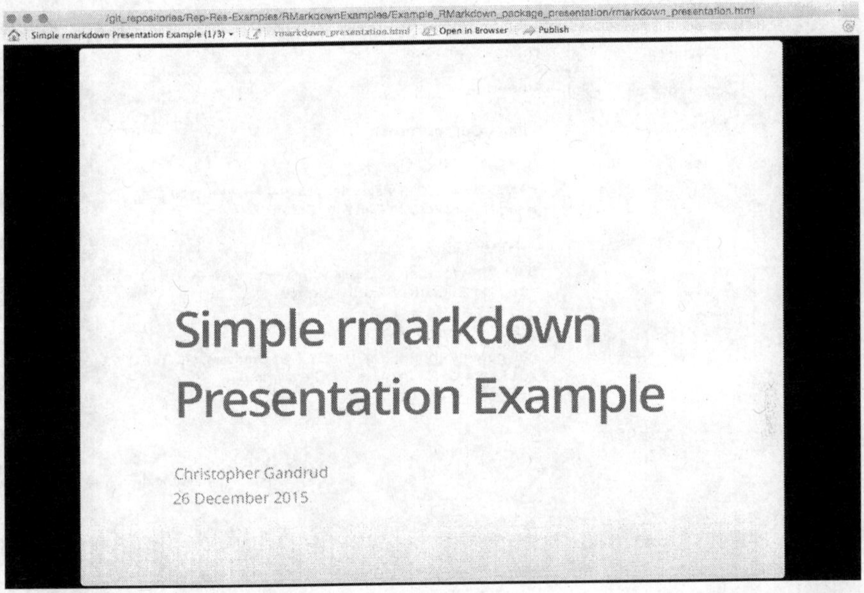


```
output:
    ioslides_presentation:
        incremental: true
---

## Access the code

The code to create the following figure is available online.
```

This code creates a slide show that begins with the slide in Figure 13.3. Bullet points will be brought in incrementally because we used `incremental: true` under `output: ioslides_presentation`. Bullets are created using Markdown list syntax.

Use three dashes (`---`) to delineate a new slide without a header. You can style the presentation further using the `css` option in the header to link to a custom CSS file.

You can create a new IO Slides or Slidy *rmarkdown* presentation in RStudio by selecting `File` → `R Markdown...` then `Presentation` in the menu on

FIGURE 13.4
Create New *rmarkdown* Presentation in RStudio

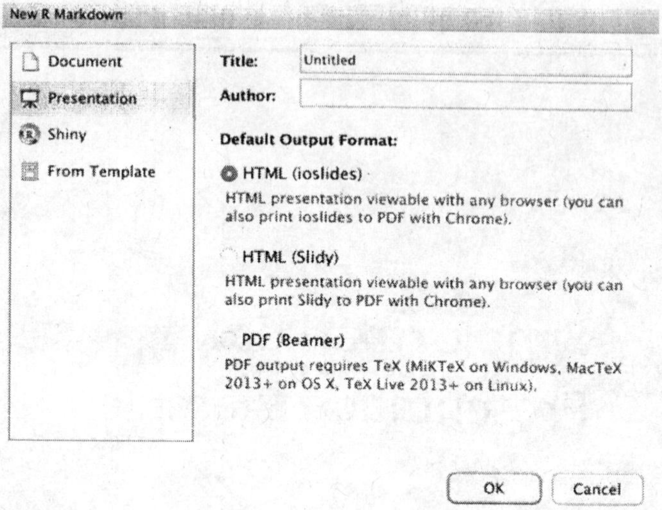

the left of the window (shown in Figure 13.4). Finally, click `HTML (ioslides)` or `HTML (Slidy)`.

13.3.2 LaTeX Beamer Slideshows with *rmarkdown*

As we saw in Chapter 11, creating a presentation with LaTeX beamer involves rather convoluted syntax. Luckily, we can use *rmarkdown* to create beamer presentations using much cleaner Markdown syntax.

An *rmarkdown* beamer presentation uses the same syntax that we just saw with HTML presentations. The main difference is in the header where we use `output: beamer_presentation`. You create a new R Markdown beamer document in RStudio in a similar way as IO Slides or Slidy. The only difference is that we select `PDF (Beamer)` in the window shown in Figure 13.4. As before, frame titles are delineated with two hashes (`##`). You can mark sections in much the same way with one hash. In the header you can switch the beamer theme, font theme, and color theme with `theme`, `colortheme`, and `fonttheme`, respectively. For example, to create the slide show that begins with the slide in Figure 13.5:

FIGURE 13.5
rmarkdown/Beamer Example Title Slide

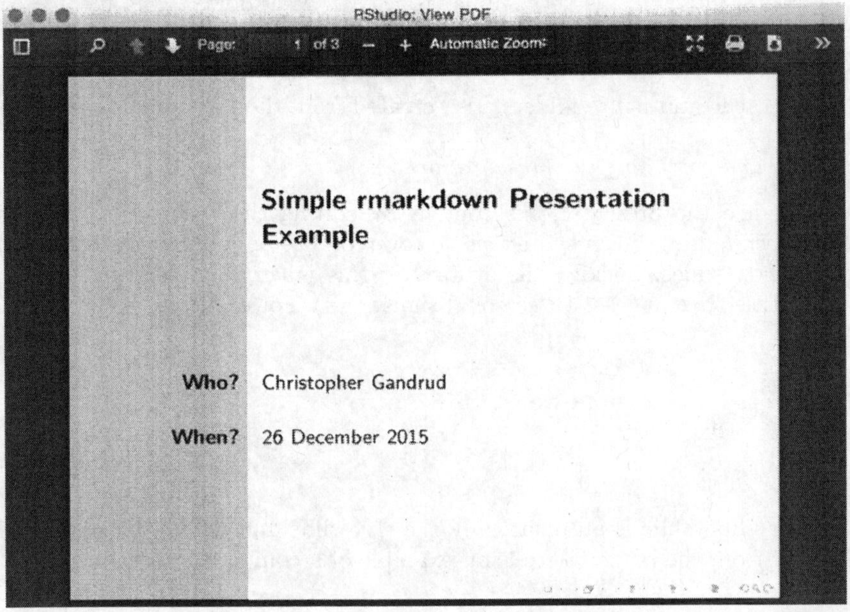


```
output:
    beamer_presentation:
        incremental: true
        theme: "Bergen"
        colortheme: "crane"
        fonttheme: "structurebold"
```

Note that themes are placed in quotation marks. You can also include a custom template with the `template` option followed by the path to the custom template file.

13.3.3 Slideshows with Markdown and RStudio's R Presentations

Another easy, but less customizable way to create HTML slideshows is with RStudio's R Presentation documents. To get started, open RStudio and click `File` → `New` → `R Presentation`. RStudio will then ask you to give the presentation a name and save it in a particular file. The reason RStudio does this is because an R Presentation is not just one file. Instead it includes:

- A *.Rpres* file, which is very similar to a *knitr* Markdown *.Rmd* file.
- A *.md* Markdown file created from the *.Rpres* file.
- *knitr* cache and figure folders, also created from the *.Rpres* file.

Editing and compiling the presentation

You change the presentation's content by editing the *.Rpres* file using the normal *knitr* Markdown syntax we've covered. The only difference is how you create new slides. Luckily, the syntax for this is very simple. Just type the slide's title then at least three equal signs (===). For example,

```
This is an Example .Rpres Slide Title
===
```

The very first slide is automatically the title slide and will be formatted differently from the rest.[16] Here is an example of a complete *.Rpres* file:

````
Example R Presentation
===

## Christopher Gandrud

## 1 July 2015

Access the Code
===

The code to create the following figure is available online.

To access it we type:

```{r, eval=FALSE}
# Access and run the code to create a caterpillar plot

devtools::source_url("http://bit.ly/VRKphr")
````

[16] As of this writing it is a blue slide with white letters.
````

~~~~
```

Caterpillar Plot
===

```{r, echo=FALSE, message=FALSE}
# Access and run the code to create a caterpillar plot

devtools::source_url("http://bit.ly/VRKphr")
```

Fertilizer Consumption Map (2003)
===

```{r CreategvisGeoMap, echo=FALSE, message=FALSE, results='asis'}
# Create geo map of global fertilizer consumption for 2003
devtools::source_url("http://bit.ly/VNnZxS")
```
~~~~

This example includes four slides and three code chunks. The last code chunk uses the *googleVis* package to create the global map of fertilizer consumption we saw earlier in Figure 10.6. Because the slideshow we are creating is in HTML, the map will be fully dynamic. Note that like before you will not be able to see the map in the RStudio preview, only in a web browser.

To compile the slideshow, either click the `Preview` button (Preview) or save the *.Rpres* document. When you do this, you can view your updated slideshow in the *Presentation* pane. For example, see Figure 13.6. You can navigate through the slideshow using the arrow buttons at the bottom right of the *Presentation* pane. If you click the magnifying glass icon ( ) at the top of the *Presentation* pane you will get a much larger view of the slideshow. You can also view the slideshow in your web browser by clicking on the `More` icon (More), then `View in Browser`.

Publishing slideshows

You can of course, view your slideshows locally. To share your presentation with others, you probably want to either publish the presentation to a standalone HTML file and host it, for example, on a Dropbox *Public* folder or publish it directly to RPubs. For R Presentations, create a standalone HTML file by simply clicking the `More` button in the *Presentation* pane, then `Save as Webpage...`. Under the `More` button you can also choose the option `Publish to RPubs...`.

FIGURE 13.6
RStudio R Presentation Pane

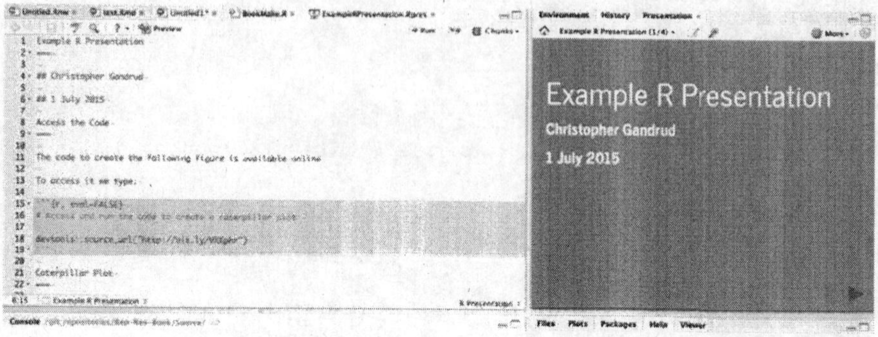

13.4 Publishing HTML Documents Created by R Markdown

In Chapter 3 (Section 3.3.8) we saw how to publish other R Markdown documents compiled with RStudio to RPubs. The *knitr* function `knit2wp` can be used to post a knitted Markdown file to WordPress[17] sites, which are often used for blogging. In this section we will look at two other ways to publish R Markdown documents using Dropbox and GitHub.

13.4.1 Standalone HTML files

Of course, you can simply open the HTML file rendered from any R Markdown document in your web browser. If the HTML file contains the full information for the page as they generally do when created by *rmarkdown*, e.g. the file does not depend on any auxiliary files, you can simply share this file via email or whatnot and anyone with a web browser can open it. We can Of course, also send auxiliary files if need be, but this can get unwieldy.

13.4.2 Hosting webpages with Dropbox

Probably one of the easiest ways to host an HTML file created with R Markdown is on your Dropbox *Public* folder.[18] Any HTML file Slideshows in the *Public* folder will be rendered and widely accessible simply by entering the public link into a web browser.

[17] `http://wordpress.com`

[18] See Section 5.2.2 for instructions on how to enable this folder if you created your Dropbox account after 4 October 2012.

13.4.3 GitHub Pages

GitHub also offers a free hosting service for webpages. These can be much more complex than a single HTML file. The simplest way to create one of these pages is to create a repository with a file called *README.Rmd*. You can `knit` this file and then create your GitHub Page with it. To do this, go to the `Settings` → `GitHub Pages` on your repository's main GitHub website. Then click `Automatic Page Generator`. This places the contents of your *README.md* file in the page and provides you with formatting options. Click `Publish` and you will have a new website.

Clicking `Publish` creates a new orphan branch[19] called *gh-pages*. When these branches are pushed to GitHub it will create a website based on a file called *index.html* that you include in the branch. This will be the website's main page.

If you want to create more customized and larger websites with GitHub Pages, you can manually create a GitHub Pages orphan branch and push it to GitHub. This is essentially what *slidify* did for us with its `publish` command. Imagine we have our working directory set as a repository containing an R Markdown file that we have rendered into an HTML file called *index.html*. Let's create a new orphan branch:

```
# Create orphan gh-pages branch
git checkout --orphan gh-pages
```

Now `add` the files, `commit` the changes and `push` it to GitHub. Push it to the *gh-pages* branch like this:

```
# Add files
git add .

# Commit changes
git commit -am "First gh-pages commit"

# Push branch to GitHub Pages
git push origin gh-pages
```

A new webpage will be created at: *USERNAME.GitHub.io/REPO_NAME* You can also add custom domain names. For details see: `https://help.GitHub.com/articles/setting-up-a-custom-domain-with-GitHub-pages/`.

[19]An orphan branch is a branch with a different root from other repository branches. Another way of thinking about this is that they have their own history.

13.4.4 Further information on R Markdown

We have covered many of the core capabilities of *rmarkdown* for creating reproducible research documents. Please see RStudio's R Markdown documentation (`http://rmarkdown.rstudio.com/`) for even more information. Another tool to look into for interactive results presentation is the *shiny* package (Chang et al., 2015). It gives R the capability to create interactive web applications, not just the static websites that we have covered in this chapter. This package is well integrated with RStudio. For more information please see: `http://shiny.rstudio.com/`.

Chapter summary

In this chapter we learned a number of tools for dynamically presenting our reproducible research on the web as well as how to create PDFs with the simple R Markdown syntax. Though LaTeX and PDFs will likely remain the main tools for presenting research in published journals and books for some time to come, choosing to also make your research available in online native formats can make it more accessible to general readers. It also allows you to take advantage of interactive tools for presenting your research. *rmarkdown* also makes it easy to create documents in a variety of formats using the simple R Markdown format. For relatively simple documents this can be a very useful tool.

14

Conclusion

Well, we have completed our journey. The only thing left to do now is practice, practice, practice. (Shotts Jr., 2012, 432)

In this book we learned a workflow for highly reproducible computational research and many of the tools needed to actually do it. Hopefully, if you haven't already, you will begin using and benefiting from these tools in your own work. Though we've covered enough material in this book to get you well on your way, there is still a lot more to learn. With most things computational (possibly most things in general), one of the best ways to continue learning is to practice and try new things. Inevitably you will hit walls, but there are almost always solutions that can be found with curiosity and patience. The R and reproducible research community is extremely helpful when it comes to finding and sharing solutions. I highly recommend getting involved in and eventually contributing to this community to get the most out of reproducible research.[1]

Before ending the book, I want to briefly address five issues we have not covered so far that are important for reproducible research: citing reproducible research, licensing this research, sharing your code with R packages, whether or not to make your research files public before publishing the results, and whether or not it is possible to completely future-proof your research.

14.1 Citing Reproducible Research

There are a number of well-established methods for citing presentation documents, especially published articles and books. However, as we discussed in the beginning, these documents are just the advertising for research findings rather than the actual research (Buckheit and Donoho, 1995; Donoho, 2010, 385). If other researchers are going to use the data and source code used to create the findings in their own work, they need a way of actually citing

[1]A good point of entry into the R reproducible research community is R-bloggers (`http://www.r-bloggers.com/`). The site aggregates many different blogs on R-related topics from both advanced and relatively new R users. I have found that beyond just consuming other peoplės' insights, contributing to R-bloggers–having to clearly write down my steps–has sharpened my understanding of the reproducible research process and enabled me to get great feedback. Other really useful resources are the R Stack Overflow (`http://stackoverflow.com/questions/tagged/r`) and Cross Validated (`http://stats.stackexchange.com/questions/tagged/r`) sites.

the particular data and source code they used. Citing data and source code presents unique problems. Data and source code can change and be updated over time in a way that published articles and books generally are not. As such we have a much less developed, or at least less commonly used set of standards for citing these types of materials.

One possibility is a standard for citing quantitative data sets laid out by Altman and King (2007) (see also King, 2007). They argue that quantitative data set citations should:

- allow a reader to quickly understand the nature of the cited data set,
- unambiguously identify a particular version of the data set, and
- enable reliable location, retrieval, and verification of the data set.

The first issue can be solved by having a citation that includes the author, the date the data set was made public, and its title. However, these things do not unambiguously identify the data set as it may be updated or changed and it does not enable its location and retrieval. To solve this problem, Altman and King suggest that these citations also include:

- a unique global identifier (UGI),
- a universal numeric fingerprint (UNF), and
- a bridge service.

A UGI uniquely identifies the data set. Examples include Document Object Identifiers (DOI) and the Handel System.[2] UGIs by themselves do not uniquely identify a particular version of a data set. This is where UNFs come in. They uniquely identify each version of a data set. Finally, a bridge service links the UGI and UNF to an actual document, usually posted online, so that it can be retrieved.

There are many ways to register DOIs and Handel UGIs. Most of these also include means for creating UNFs and a bridge service. Examples of services that store your work and assign it DOIs are figshare[3] and Zenodo.[4] Zenodo can be integrated with GitHub so that it will store and create citations for a specific commit of a GitHub repository whenever you create a tag. For more information about integrating GitHub and Zenodo see: `https://guides.GitHub.com/activities/citable-code/`. Please see Altman and King (2007) for details of other services.[5]

Though Altman and King are interested in data sets, their system could

[2]See: `http://www.handle.net/`.

[3]`http://figshare.com/`

[4]`https://zenodo.org/`

[5]The Dataverse Project (`http://thedata.org/`) offers a free service to host files that also uses the Handel System to assign UGIs, UNFs, and provides a bridge service. See Gandrud (2013a) for a comparison of Dataverse with GitHub and Dropbox for data storage.

easily be applied to source code as well. UGIs could identify a source code file or collection of files. The UNF could identify a particular version and a bridge service would create a link to the actual files.

14.2 Licensing Your Reproducible Research

In the United States and many other countries, research, including computer code made available via the internet, is automatically given copyright protection. However, copyright protection works against the scientific goals of reproducible research, because work derived from the research falls under the original copyright protections (Stodden, 2009b, 36). To solve this problem, some authors have suggested placing code under an open source software license like the GNU General Public License (GPL) (Vandewalle et al., 2007). Stodden (2009b) argues that this type of license is not really adequate for making available the data, code, and other material needed to reproduce research findings in a way that enables scientific validation and knowledge growth. I don't want to explore the intricacies of these issues here. Nonetheless, they are important for computational researchers to think about, especially if their data and source code is publicly available. Two good places to go for more information are Stodden (2009b) and Creative Commons (2012).

14.3 Sharing Your Code in Packages

Developing R functions and putting them into packages is a good way to enable cumulative knowledge development. Many researchers spend a considerable amount of time writing code to solve problems that no one has addressed yet, or haven't addressed in a way that they believe is adequate. It is very useful if they make this code publicly accessible so that others can perhaps adopt and use it in their own work without having to duplicate the effort used to create the original functions. Abstracting your code into functions so that they can be applied to many problems and distributing them in easily installed packages makes it much easier for other researchers to adopt and use your code to help solve their research problems. The active community of researcher/package developers is one of the main reasons that R has become such a widely used and useful statistical language.

Many of the tools we have covered in this book provide a good basis to start making and distributing functions. We have discussed many of the R commands and concepts that are important for creating functions. We have also looked at Git and GitHub, which are very helpful for developing and distributing packages. Learning about Hadley Wickham's *devtools* package is probably the best next step for you to take to be able to develop and distribute functions in packages. He has an excellent introduction to *devtools* and R package development in general at `http://adv-r.had.co.nz/Philosophy.html#introduction-to-devtools`.

RStudio Projects have excellent *devtools* integration and are certainly worth using. To begin creating a new package in RStudio, start a new project, preferably with Git version control (see Section 5.4.1). In the **New Project** window select `Package`. Now you will have a new Project with all of the files and directories you need to get started making packages that will hopefully be directly useful for the computational research community.

14.4 Project Development: Public or Private?

Hopefully I have made a convincing case in this book that research results, especially in academia, should almost always be highly reproducible. The files used to create the results need to be publicly available for the research to be really reproducible.[6] During the development of a research project, however, should files be public or private?

On the one hand, openness encourages transparency and feedback. Other researchers may alert you to mistakes before a result is published. On the other hand, there are worries that you may be "scooped". Another researcher might see your files, take your idea, and publish it before you have a chance to. In general, this worry may be a bit overblown. Especially if you use a version control system that clearly dates all of your file versions, it would be very easy to make the case that someone has stolen your work. Hopefully this possibility would discourage any malfeasance. That being said, unlike the clear need to make research files available after publication, during research development there are good reasons for both making files public and keeping them private.

Researchers should probably make this decision on a case-by-case basis. In general, I choose to make my research repositories public to increase transparency and encourage feedback. The community of researchers in my field is relatively small and close knit. It would be hard for someone to take my work and pass it off as their own. This is especially true if many people already know that they are my ideas, because I have made by research files publicly available. However, during the development of this book, which has a more general appeal, I kept the repository private to avoid being "scooped". Regardless, cloud storage systems like GitHub make it easy to choose whether or not to make your files public or private. You can easily keep a repository private while you create a piece of research and then make it public once the results are published.

---

[6] There are obvious exceptions, such as when a study's participants' identities need to remain confidential.

14.5 Is it Possible to Completely Future-Proof Your Research?

In this book we've looked at a number of ways to help future-proof your research so that future researchers (and you) are able to actually reproduce it. These included storing your research in text files, clearly commenting on your code, and recording information about the software environment you used by, for example, recording your session info. Are these steps enough to completely ensure that your research will always be reproducible? The simple answer is probably no. Software changes, but it is difficult to foresee what these changes will be. Nonetheless, beyond what we have discussed so far there are other steps we can take to make our reproducible research as future-proof as possible.

One of the main obstacles to completely future-proofing your research is that no (or at least very few) pieces of software are complete. R packages are updated. R is updated. Your operating system is updated. These and other software programs discussed in this book may not only be updated, but also discontinued. Changes to the software you used to find your results may change the results someone reproducing your research gets. This problem becomes larger as you use more pieces of software in your research

That being said, many of the software tools we have learned about in this book have future-proofing at their heart. TeX, the typesetting system that underlies LaTeX, is probably the best example. TeX was created in 1978 and has since been maintained with future-proofing in mind (Knuth, 1990). Though changes and new versions continue to be made, we are still able to use TeX to recreate documents in their original intended form even if they were written over thirty years ago. We also saw that, though R and especially R packages change rapidly, the Comprehensive R Archive Network stores and makes accessible old versions (as the name suggests). Old versions can be downloaded by anyone wishing to reproduce a piece of research, provided the original researcher has recorded which versions they used. This is very easy using *repmis*'s `LoadandCite` command. This command lets you specify particular package versions to install and load from the CRAN package archive.[7] Another approach is to use the *packrat* R package (Ushey et al., 2015) for managing the packages your project depends on. Some of the other technologies discussed in this book may be less reliable over time, so some caution should be taken if you intend to use them to create fully reproducible research.

In addition to documenting what software you used and using software that archives old versions, some have suggested another step to future-proof reproducible research: encapsulate it in a virtual machine that is available on a cloud storage system. See in particular Howe (2012). A virtual reproducible research machine would store a "snapshot [of] a researcher's entire working environment, including data, software, dependencies, notes, logs, scripts, and

[7]Do this by entering specific package version numbers in the `versions` argument.

more". If the virtual machine is stored on a cloud server, then anyone wanting to reproduce the research could access the full computing environment used to create a piece of research (Howe, 2012, 36). As long as others could run the virtual machine and access the cloud storage system, you would not have to worry about changing software, because the exact versions of the software you used would be available in one place.

We don't have space to cover the specifics of how to create a virtual machine in this book. However, using a virtual machine is a tool that can be added to the workflow discussed in this book, rather than being a replacement for it. Carefully documenting your steps, clearly organizing your files, and dynamically tying together your data gathering, analysis, and presentation files helps you and others understand how you created a result after a research project's results have been published. Being able to understand your research will give it higher research impact as others can more easily build on it. The steps covered in this book will still encourage you to have better work habits from the beginning of your research projects even if you will be using a virtual machine. The tools and workflow will also continue to facilitate collaboration and make it easier to dynamically update your research documents when you make changes.

Now, get started with reproducible research!

Bibliography

Allaire, J., Cheng, J., Xie, Y., McPherson, J., Chang, W., Allen, J., Wickham, H., and Hyndman, R. (2015a). *rmarkdown: Dynamic Documents for R*. R package version 0.5.1.

Allaire, J., Horner, J., Marti, V., and Porte, N. (2015b). *markdown: 'Markdown' Rendering for R*. R package version 0.7.7.

Altman, M. and King, G. (2007). A proposed standard for the scholarly citation of quantitative data. *D-Lib Magazine*, 13(3/4).

Arel-Bundock, V. (2013). *WDI: World Development Indicators (World Bank)*. R package version 2.4.

Arel-Bundock, V. (2014). *countrycode: Convert Country Names and Country Codes*. R package version 0.18.

Bååth, R. (2012). The state of naming conventions in R. *The R Journal*, 4(2):74–75.

Bache, S. M. and Wickham, H. (2014). *magrittr: A Forward-Pipe Operator for R*. R package version 1.5.

Bacon, F. R. (1267/1859). *Opera quaedam hactenus inedita. Vol. I. containing I.–Opus tertium. II.–Opus minus. III.–Compendium philosophiae.* Google eBook. Retrieved from `http://books.google.com/books?id=wMUKAAAAYAAJ`.

Ball, R. and Medeiros, N. (2011). Teaching integrity in empirical research: A protcol for documenting data management and analysis. *The Journal of Economic Education*, 43(2):182–189.

Barr, C. D. (2012). Establishing a culture of reproducibility and openness in medical research with an emphasis on the training years. *Chance*, 25(3):8–10.

Boettiger, C. and Temple Lang, D. (2012). Treebase: An R package for discovery, access and manipulation of online phylogenies. *Methods in Ecology and Evolution*, 3(6):1060–1066.

Bowers, J. (2011). Six steps to a better relationship with your future self. *The Political Methodologist*, 18(2):2–8.

Box, G. E. and Cox, D. R. (1964). An analysis of transformations. *Journal of the Royal Statistical Society. Series B (Methodological)*, 26:211–252.

Braude, S. (1979). *ESP and Psychokinesis. A Philosophical Examination.* Temple University Press, Philadelphia, PA.

Buckheit, J. B. and Donoho, D. L. (1995). Wavelab and reproducible research. In Antoniadis, A., editor, *Wavelets and Statistics*, pages 55–81. Springer, New York.

Burbidge, J. B. and Robb, L. (1988). Alternative transformations to handle extreme values of the dependent variable. *Journal of the American Statistical Association*, 83(401):123–127.

Carslaw, D. and Ropkins, K. (2015). *openair: Tools for the Analysis of Air Pollution Data.* R package version 1.5.

Chang, W. (2012). *R Graphics Cookbook: Practical Recipes for Visualizing Data.* O'Reilly Media, Inc., Sebastopol, CA.

Chang, W., Cheng, J., Allaire, J., Xie, Y., and McPherson, J. (2015). *shiny: Web Application Framework for R.* R package version 0.11.1.

Couture-Beil, A. (2014). *rjson: JSON for R.* R package version 0.2.15.

Crawley, M. J. (2005). *Statistics: An Introduction Using R.* John Wiley and Sons Ltd., Chichester.

Crawley, M. J. (2013). *The R Book.* John Wiley and Sons Ltd., Chichester, 2nd edition.

Creative Commons (2012). Data. `http://wiki.creativecommons.org/Data`.

Donoho, D. L. (2002). How to be a highly cited author in mathematical sciences. *in-cites.* `http://www.in-cites.com/scientists/DrDavidDonoho.html`.

Donoho, D. L. (2010). An invitation to reproducible computational research. *Biostatistics*, 11(3):385–388.

Donoho, D. L., Maleki, A., Shahram, M., Rahman, I. U., and Stodden, V. (2009). Reproducible research in computational harmonic analysis. *Computing in Science & Engineering*, 11(1):8–18.

Dowle, M., Short, T., Lianoglou, S., with contributions from R Saporta, A. S., and Antonyan, E. (2014). *data.table: Extension of data.frame.* R package version 1.9.4.

Ehrenberg, A. S. C. (1977). Rudiments of numeracy. *Journal of the Royal Statistical Society. Series A General*, 140(3):277–297.

Fomel, S. and Claerbout, J. F. (2009). Reproducible Research. *Computing in Science & Engineering*, 11(1):5–7.

Frazier, M. (2008). Bash parameter expansion. *The Linux Journal*. Available at: `http://www.linuxjournal.com/content/bash-parameter-expansion`.

Gandrud, C. (2013a). Github: A tool for social data set development and verification in the cloud. *The Political Methodologist*, 20(2):2–7.

Gandrud, C. (2013b). The diffusion of financial supervisory governance ideas. *Review of International Political Economy*, 20(4):881–916.

Gandrud, C. (2015). *repmis: Miscellaneous Tools for Reproducible Research*. R package version 0.4.2.

Gandrud, C. and Grafström, C. (2015). Inflated expectations: How government partisanship shapes bureaucrats' inflation forecasts. *Political Science Research and Methods*. Available at: `http://dx.doi.org/10.1017/psrm.2014.34`.

Gelman, A. (2011). Tables as graphs: The Ramanujan principle. *Significance*, 8(4):183.

Gentry, J. (2015). *twitteR: R Based Twitter Client*. R package version 1.1.8.

Gesmann, M. and de Castillo, D. (2015). *googleVis: R Interface to Google Charts*. R package version 0.5.8.

Goodrich, B. and Lu, Y. (2007). normal.bayes: Bayesian normal linear regression. *Zelig Everyone's Statistical Software*. Available at: `http://gking.harvard.edu/zelig`.

Herndon, T., Ash, M., and Pollin, R. (2014). Does high public debt consistently stifle economic growth? a critique of reinhart and rogoff. *Cambridge Journal of Economics*, 38(2):257–279.

Hlavac, M. (2014). *stargazer: LaTeX/HTML code and ASCII text for well-formatted regression and summary statistics tables*. R package version 5.1.

Horner, J. (2011). *brew: Templating Framework for Report Generation*. R package version 1.0-6.

Howe, B. (2012). Virtual appliances, cloud computing, and reproducible research. *Computing in Science & Engineering*, 14(4):36–41.

Hyndman, R. J. (2010). Transforming data with zeros. Available at: `http://robjhyndman.com/hyndsight/transformations/`. Accessed March 2015.

Kelly, C. D. (2006). Replicating empirical research in behavioral ecology: How and why it should be done but rarely ever is. *The Quarterly Review of Biology*, 81(3):221–236.

King, G. (1995). Replication, replication. *PS: Political Science and Politics*, 28(3):444–452.

King, G. (2007). An introduction to the dataverse network as an infrastructure for data sharing. *Sociological Methods & Research*, 36(2):173–199.

King, G., Keohane, R., and Verba, S. (1994). *Designing Social Inquiry*. Princeton University Press, Princeton.

Knuth, D. E. (1990). The future of tex and metafont. *NTG: Maps*, 5:145.

Knuth, D. E. (1992). *Literate Programming*. CSLI Lecture Notes. Center for the Study of Language and Information, Stanford, CA.

Leifeld, P. (2015). *texreg: Conversion of R Regression Output to LaTeX or HTML Tables*. R package version 1.35.

Leisch, F. (2002). Sweave: Dynamic generation of statistical reports using literate data analysis. In Härdle, W. and Rönz, B., editors, *Compstat 2002: Proceedings in Computational Statistics*, pages 575–580. Physica Verlag, Heidelberg. `http://www.stat.uni-muenchen.de/~leisch/Sweave`.

Lykken, D. T. (1968). Statistical significance in psychological research. *Psychologial Bulletin*, 70:151–159.

MacFarlane, J. (2014). *Pandoc: A Universal Document Converter*. Version 1.13.0.1.

Makel, M. C. and Plucker, J. A. (2014). Facts are more important than novelty: Replication in the education sciences. *Educational Researcher*, 43(6):304–316.

Matloff, N. (2011). *The Art of Programming in R: A Tour of Statistical Programming Design*. No Starch Press, San Francisco.

Mesirov, J. P. (2010). Accessible reproducible research. *Science*, 327(5964):415–416.

Meyer, A. (2006). Repeating patterns of mimicry. *PLoS Biol*, 4(10).

Munzert, S., Rubba, C., Meißner, P., and Nyhuis, D. (2015). *Automated Data Collection with R: A Practical Guide to Web Scraping and Text Mining*. Wiley, Chichester.

Murrell, P. (2011). *R Graphics*. Chapman and Hall/CRC Press, Boca Raton, FL, 2nd edition.

Nagler, J. (1995). Coding style and good computing practices. *PS: Political Science and Politics*, 28(3):488–492.

Nosek, B. A., Spies, J. R., and Motyl, M. (2012). Scientific utopia: II. Restructring incentives and practices to promote truth over publishability. *Perspectives on Psychological Science*, 7(6):615–631.

O'Neal, C. and Schutt, R. (2013). *Doing Data Science: Straight Talk from the Frontline*. O'Reilly Media Inc., Sebastopol, CA.

Owen, M. (2011). *ZeligBayesian: A Zelig Model*. R package version 0.1.

Owen, M., Imai, K., King, G., and Lau, O. (2013). *Zelig: Everyone's Statistical Software*. R package version 4.2-1.

Pemstein, D., Meserve, S. A., and Melton, J. (2010). Democratic compromise: A latent variable analysis of ten measures of regime type. *Political Analysis*, 18(4):426–449.

Peng, R. D. (2009). Reproducible research and biostatistics. *Biostatistics*, 10(3):405–408.

Peng, R. D. (2011). Reproducible research in computational science. *Science*, 334:1226–1227.

Peng, R. D. (2014). The real reason reproducible research is important. *Simply Statistics*. `http://simplystatistics.org/2014/06/06/the-real-reason-reproducible-research-is-important/`.

Piwowar, H. A., Day, R. S., and Fridsma, D. B. (2007). Sharing detailed research data is associated with increased citation rate. *PLoS ONE*, 2(3):1–5.

R Core Team (2014). *R: A Language and Environment for Statistical Computing*. R Foundation for Statistical Computing, Vienna, Austria. `http://www.R-project.org/`.

Ramsey, N. (2011). Noweb: A simple, extensible tool for literate programming. `http://www.cs.tufts.edu/~nr/noweb/`.

Reinhart, C. and Rogoff, K. (2010). Growth in a time of debt. *American Economic Review: Papers & Proceedings*, 100.

Ripley, B. and Murdoch, D. (2012). *Rtools: Building R for Windows*. `http://cran.r-project.org/bin/windows/Rtools/`.

RStudio, Inc. (2015). *RStudio: Integrated development environment for R*. Boston, MA. Version 0.99.

Ryan, J. A. (2015). *quantmod: Quantitative Financial Modelling Framework*. R package version 0.4-4.

Shotts Jr., W. E. (2012). *The Linux Command-line: A Complete Introduction.* No Starch Press, San Francisco.

Stodden, V. (2009a). The reproducible research standard: Reducing legal barriers to scientific knowledge and innovation. In *Communia: Global Science & Economics of Knowledge-Sharing Institutions Torino, Italy June 30.* `http://www.stanford.edu/~vcs/talks/VictoriaStoddenCommuniaJune2009-2.pdf`.

Stodden, V. (2009b). The legal framework for reproducible scientific research. *Computing in Science & Engineering*, 11(1):35–40.

Temple Lang, D. (2013). *XML: Tools for parsing and generating XML within R and S-Plus.* R package version 3.98-1.1.

Temple Lang, D. (2014). *RJSONIO: Serialize R objects to JSON, JavaScript Object Notation.* R package version 1.3-0.

Temple Lang, D. (2015). *RCurl: General network (HTTP/FTP/...) client interface for R.* R package version 1.95-4.6.

Therneau, T. M. (2015). *survival: Survival Analysis.* R package version 2.38-1.

Tufte, E. R. (2001). *The Visual Display of Quantitative Information.* Graphics Press, Cheshire, CT, 2nd edition.

Ushey, K., McPherson, J., Cheng, J., and Allaire, J. (2015). *packrat: A Dependency Management System for Projects and their R Package Dependencies.* R package version 0.4.3.

Vaidyanathan, R., Cheng, J., Allaire, J., Xie, Y., , and Russell, K. (2014). *htmlwidgets: HTML Widgets for R.* R package version 0.3.2.

van Belle, G. (2008). *Statistical Rules of Thumb.* John Wiley and Sons, Hoboken, NJ, 2nd edition.

Vandewalle, P. (2012). Code sharing is associated with research impact in image processing. *Computing in Science & Engineering*, 14(4):42–47.

Vandewalle, P., Barrenetxea, G., Jovanovic, I., Ridolfi, A., and Vetterli, M. (2007). Experiences with reproducible research in various facets of signal processing research. *Acoustics, Speech and Signal Processing*, 4:1253–1256.

Wickham, H. (2009). *ggplot2: Elegant Graphics for Data Analysis.* Springer, New York, 2nd edition.

Wickham, H. (2010). A layered grammar of graphics. *Journal of Computational and Graphical Statistics*, 19(1):3–28.

Wickham, H. (2014a). *Advanced R.* Chapman and Hall/CRC Press, Boca Raton, FL.

Wickham, H. (2014b). Tidy Data. *Journal of Statistical Software*, 59(10):1–23.

Wickham, H. (2014c). *tidyr: Easily Tidy Data with spread() and gather() Functions.* R package version 0.2.0.

Wickham, H. (2015a). *httr: Tools for Working with URLs and HTTP.* R package version 0.6.1.

Wickham, H. (2015b). *rvest: Easily Harvest (Scrape) Web Pages.* R package version 0.2.0.

Wickham, H. and Chang, W. (2015a). *devtools: Tools to Make Developing R Packages Easier.* R package version 1.7.0.

Wickham, H. and Chang, W. (2015b). *ggplot2: An Implementation of the Grammar of Graphics.* R package version 1.0.1.

Wickham, H. and Francois, R. (2015). *dplyr: A Grammar of Data Manipulation.* R package version 0.4.1.

Wilson, G., Aruliah, D. A., Brown, C. T., Hong, N. P. C., Davis, M., Guy, R. T., Haddock, S. H. D., Huff, K., Mitchell, I. M., Plumbley, M. D., Waugh, B., White, E. P., and Wilson, P. (2012). Best practices for scientific computing. *arXiv*, 29 November 2012:1–6. Available at: `http://arxiv.org/pdf/1210.0530v3`.

World Bank (2015). World development indicators. `http://data.worldbank.org/data-catalog/world-development-indicators`.

Xie, Y. (2013). *Dynamic Documents with R and knitr.* Chapman and Hall/CRC Press, Boca Raton, FL.

Xie, Y. (2014). *animation: A gallery of animations in statistics and utilities to create animations.* R package version 2.3.

Xie, Y. (2015a). *formatR: Format R Code Automatically.* R package version 1.2.

Xie, Y. (2015b). *knitr: A General-Purpose Package for Dynamic Report Generation in R.* R package version 1.10.

Index